I Wish to Thank
and to
Dedicate This Book to

my long time friend and mentor talk show host Herman Bailey for his help and unwavering commitment to me and his listeners in providing exceptional programing. Herman taught me the fundamentals of broadcast quality in the beginning of my career. These principles have been the underlying component which have allowed me to help the millions of listeners who have benefited from my books, tapes, seminars and media appearances.

Thank you Herman

FOREWORD

We are "fearfully and wonderfully made" (Psalm 139:14). It seems that every year, scientists discover another layer of complexity with which God has "knit"us together. A prime example is the human brain...the most complex organ in the human body, containing some 100 billion neurons (nerve cells). Our brains are far more intricate than the most sophisticated computer on the planet, and although they make up only 2 percent of our body weight, our brains consume 20-30 percent of our energy. It certainly warrants us using some of that energy in taking good care of it!

We do not often give much "thought to our thoughts" or consider the amazing sequence of coordinated activities taking place right now in our brains as we read and comprehend the words on this page. When we talk about health, it is usually in reference to the rest of our body, and what happens "up top" is simply ignored and taken for granted. But now a scientist and internationally recognized health expert is saying it's time to think more deeply about the health of our brains.

In this book by Dr. Ted Broer, he introduces us to the idea that our diet can actually have a profound effect on our thinking and memory. When I met Dr. Broer and learned what studies have proven in this area, I felt it was vital information for everyone. I propose that it is especially relevant for those who want to follow Jesus in what He considered the greatest commandment... and that is to "love the Lord your God with all your heart, with all your soul, and with all your MIND" (Matthew 22:37).

As you read Dr. Broer's well-researched recommendations, I encourage you to be "open-minded" and try it for yourself.

Ron Mainse
President
Crossroads Christian Communications Inc.
Host of *100 Huntley Street*

MAXIMUM MEMORY

TED BROER

MAXIMUM MEMORY by Ted Broer
Published by B & A Publications
100 Ariana Blvd
Auburndale, Florida 33823

Library of Congress Catalog Card Number:
ISBN 0-9716215-0-0

This book is not intended to provide medical advice or to take the place of medical advice and treatment from your personal physician. Readers are advised to consult their own doctors or other qualified health professional regarding the treatment of their medical problems. Neither the publisher nor the author takes any responsibility for any possible consequences from any treatment, action or application of medicine, supplement, herb or preparation to any person reading or following the information in this book. If readers are taking prescription medications, they should consult with their physicians and not take themselves off medicines to start supplementation without the proper supervision of a physician.

Printed in the United States of America
Crossroads Partner Edition printed in Canada

CONTENTS

THERE'S NOTHING COOL ABOUT DEMENTIA

A number of years ago when I was a student at Florida State University, I had a friend and roommate named Don who was 6 feet 6 inches tall. If that wasn't tall enough, he wore three-inch platform shoes. And if that still wasn't tall enough, he styled his hair into an "Afro" that added another two to three inches to his height. His hair was red—so believe me, he could *not* be missed in a crowd!

What most people didn't know about Don was that the Afro was a toupee. Don was so tall that hardly anybody could get close enough to his "Fro" to tell if it was real or not. Don had lost his hair when he was in his late teens. At that age, and especially in that era, there was nothing "cool" about baldness.

There's also nothing "cool" about dementia. Unlike Don's baldness, however, dementia cannot be hidden. There is no mask for declining brain function—it's there for the world to see *even if you don't*. Dementia calls attention to itself—very much like a mop of red hair bobbing nearly seven feet in the air—and in many cases, dementia evokes pity and rejection from those who see it, as well as depression and anxiety in those who are experiencing it.

According to a recent Canadian study on health and aging, the loss of cognitive function is the major concern of most individuals as they age. Many of today's "baby boomers" have watched or are watching their parents lose mental acuity, even though they have not been diagnosed with Alzheimer's or other neurological disease.[1] And they don't like what they see.

Memory failing.

Decision-making faltering.

Less and less ability to care for one's own financial, legal, and practical responsibilities.

Dementia for most people means a long, slow good-bye to everything that was once cherished as "quality" of life.

The good news for you today is that you do *not* have to experience dementia. Senility is *not* inevitable. There's much that can be done to retain a healthy mind and a good memory *all your life.*

Part of what needs to be done, is *physical*. No matter how old you are at present, it's time to feed both your body and brain the right nutrients for strong mental functioning. It's time to exercise your body for better blood flow to the brain and a release of stress. It's time to stop taking in brain poisons. Senility and dementia are not signs of old age nearly as much as they are signs of poisoning, nutrient deficiency, disease, injury, or neglect.

Part of what needs to be done is *environmental*. You need to rid your life, as well as your body and brain, of the common toxins that pollute brain function. In addition, you need to feed your brain the nutrients that it needs to give you a lifetime of top performance and to heal the damage that environmental poisons may have caused.

Part of what needs to be done is *mental*. You need to do what you can through mental exercises to strengthen your memory and general brain function.

This book takes a comprehensive look at brain function with a special focus on memory, which is essential to all other intellectual faculties. There are, however, no quick fixes.

My role is not only to give you solid, scientifically-based information, but also to do what I can to motivate you to make changes in your life that will keep your mind strong and healthy as you age.

When I was in graduate school at Florida State University, which is located in Tallahassee, I went for a motorcycle ride one evening with my girlfriend at the time. We headed out to the Lighthouse at St. Mark's. As we rode, suddenly, a deer leaped out into the roadway right into the path of my motorcycle. The deer twisted his body at just the last second and missed the windshield of the cycle—and us—by just inches. We had barely recovered our composure when we came across an alligator that was about fourteen feet long. He was stretched from one side to the other of the narrow two-lane road. He was *not* moving—he was enjoying the warmth that remained in the pavement. I had to stop my motorcycle completely. After repeated and prolonged honking, the alligator finally became so annoyed that it moved on.

Part of my goal in this book is to scare you a little.

Part of my goal is also to do the same thing I did to that alligator and that is to "annoy" you enough to get you to take action to improve your health.

I make no apologies for either. The facts are scary enough. The annoyance that the facts may prompt—if it moves you to action —is worth it.

Let me assure you of two things at the outset:

First, it's never too early to make a commitment to improving your memory.

Second, it takes time to develop a better memory and to improve brain function. It takes intentional effort to know as much as you can about the way memory works. It takes discipline to make sure you are taking in all of the nutrients necessary for good brain health. It also takes discipline to exercise both body and mind.

I believe you can do what is required. I believe you *can* make the commitment to improve your memory. And if what I believe is correct, then I *know* the material in this book will be of great benefit to you!

---

1. Graham, H.J.E., Rockwood, K., Beattie B.L., et al. Prevalence and severity of cognitive impairment with and without dementia in an elderly population. *Lancet* 349 (1997): 1793–96.

MEMORY 101

A man once said to me, "Memory? Oh yeah, that's what I use to forget with."

He wasn't smiling.

Most of us are not concerned with what we don't want to remember...we're concerned about what we *can't* remember.

Few of us, however, really understand one of our greatest assets—our memory.

Intelligence is a very broad term that encompasses many brain functions, including memory, the ability to learn new tasks, the ability to understand complex information, and the ability to generate new ideas from existing information (commonly called creativity). Many genetic, social, family, environmental, and other factors influence intelligence as a whole. Scientists and medical researchers are increasingly coming to the conclusion that dietary practices can and do impact intelligence. Intelligence is *not* fixed at birth. It fluctuates throughout life to a certain degree and virtually any person can engage in activities and nutritional programs to *enhance* intelligence. The same is true for the sharpness of our memory.

Memory is a key factor in intelligence and thinking. A person must be able to recall ideas and words to be able to think about things, much less reason to a logical conclusion. A person must be able to remember how to do basic life functions in order to have control of their personal life. Memory is ultimately what gives our life "quality."

What exactly is memory?

Memory is not simply a matter of passively storing information and recalling it later. Memory is an *active* process—it is a mental function that requires new and stimulating information. The old axiom, "Use it or lose it" is true of brain function as much as for the function of any muscle in the body. When the brain stops processing new information, it begins to stagnate. In other words, when nothing interesting or challenging happens, brain function changes.

Memory tends to be the first mental capacity to go. It is a precursor of other types of diminishing brain functions. Keep the memory strong and you are likely to keep all brain functions strong. Certainly memory loss is one of the first things we and others notice when it comes to brain capacity. We tend not to notice the gradual loss of smell or a decrease in reasoning power. We do notice, however, if we suddenly can't remember a joke that we've told a hundred times.

For all we know about memory, a great deal is still unknown. Far more is known about how the brain acquires and stores information than about how information is retrieved for later use. Given that disclaimer, let's explore several facets of memory that are important to building a *stronger* recall ability.

Four Types Of Memory

We each have four general types of memory, each of which can be impacted by certain chemicals:

1. Short-Term Memory. Short-term memory is in operation when you remember something for a matter of seconds or minutes.

Short-term memory has also been called *immediate* memory, although some distinguish these two types of memory. Immediate memory tends to be concerned with recall of information within seconds of receiving information, whereas short-term memory relates to information held for recall within minutes or hours.

Research through the years has shown that most of us can only contain seven "chunks" or bunches of information—plus or minus two. This axiom about short-term memory was first determined by psychologist George A. Miller in 1956.[1]

The key to developing and maintaining good immediate and short-term memory is *concentration*. When we attend to information and focus on it, we are able to imprint it with enough weight to hold that information in our memory bank temporarily. In most cases, we *intend* at the time we perceive and concentrate on the information only to store it temporarily.

The good news is that short-term memory is the type of memory that tends to respond best to "mental exercises" aimed at improving memory.

2. Long-Term Memory. Long-term memory, by contrast, occurs when we experience or think about something long enough that we can recall it at will. Short-term memories tend to become long-term memories through repeated recall of the initial information. For example, you may remember a person's name and telephone number just long enough to write it down before you leave the party. If you recall that person's face and dial that telephone number often enough, the information becomes "long-term" in the memory.

The time parameters for long-term memory vary, and often vary according to the importance we give to the information at the time we first receive it. A student, for example, may commit something to memory knowing that he needs to remember the information in order to score a good grade on a final exam several months away. He may very well remember that information for a year or so, especially if he thinks it is likely to relate to future courses or an ultimate knowledge exam down the line. He may not, however, remember the information for five years. Even so, the memory is considered long-term.

Much of the information that relates to our jobs, the facts we know about our friends, and our ability to get around a specific geographic environment, is committed to long-term memory.

We may be able to store up to a quadrillion—that's 10 to the power of 15—bits of information in long-term memory in different regions of the brain. Amazing!

The brain is highly selective about which information is stored in long-term memory. Some estimates are that only about one percent of all information entering the brain is stored for long-term retrieval.

An unexplained feature of memory is that even when details of an experience are lost, the main concept may be retained.

The key to developing and maintaining good immediate and short-term memory is *concentration*. When we attend to information and focus on it, we are able to imprint it with enough weight to hold that information in our memory bank temporarily. In most cases, we *intend* at the time we perceive and concentrate on the information only to store it temporarily.

3. Working Memory. This type of memory was identified in the 1950's. It falls someplace between short-term and long-term memory. In this type of memory, we store important information for the period in which we use it. Then, after a period of no use, we forget.

I once had a woman tell me about her experience studying overseas for two years. She knew all of the names of her professors, the other students in her study program, and the names of many of the women who lived in her housing unit. She remembered these names for the full duration of her study abroad, and for a few years after, she remembered the names of those with whom she went to special events or had a special bond of friendship. Twenty years later, however, she could recall only the name of her major professor, whom she called her tutor, and the name of two of her closest friends. She had maintained contact, of course, with these two friends through the years and periodically saw them or corresponded with them. This type of memory is a fairly typical example of "working memory."

A teacher who has a "working memory" of all the children in her classroom—and perhaps even their parents' names, may find that she cannot remember most of these names several years after the students leave her classroom.

The same for a physician and his clients, a cook who tends to make the same recipes over and over for a period of time, or a security guard who has to remember certain codes and phone numbers during a period of employment.

4. Vital Memory. Vital memory is the core of memory. In fact, this type of memory is also called "core" or "remote" memory. It is essential to our unique functioning in the world. Vital memory includes those memories laid down very early in life—such as how to dress, rules for good manners, rules of safety, and such things as when and how to use a toilet or brush one's teeth. To a great extent, our vital memories define who we are—they are deeply connected to our personality and our emotions. This type of memory is essentially "unforgettable knowledge"—much of it we have had all our lives and we rarely remember when we first encountered the information.

One woman told me about visiting her grandmother who was placed in a nursing home after a stroke. Her grandmother tended to greet her family members and other visitors in German, the language of her childhood. When this woman pointed out to her grandmother that she was someone her grandmother had met after she emigrated to the "new country," her grandmother would switch immediately to English. This woman said to me, "I didn't even know my grandmother remembered any German. I was eighteen at the time my grandmother had her stroke, and I had never heard her speak German at any time during my lifetime. I was surprised that she still could speak the language fluently. A few German-speaking people who visited this elderly woman noted her German was flawless in both vocabulary and accent. For this woman, speaking German was a "remote" memory that had not been impacted by a stroke.

Remote memory is not only what we access routinely and unconsciously as we go through most of the behavioral habits of a day, but it is the memory that is most closely linked to our feelings and preferences. Often it is something that has been stored in remote memory that triggers an "unexpected" response in us—perhaps a sudden feeling of revulsion, fear, or exuberance.

The degree to which information is repeated and transmitted in the brain, and the degree to which information is "connected" to other information seem to be what leads to short-term memory becoming a working memory, long-term memory, or vital memory.

This is one reason that elderly people often seem to have no short-term memory, yet they can remember things that happened in their early childhood. The ability for them to create new short-term and working memory memories is reduced because the *neurons and neurotransmitters no longer are healthy enough to encode information to memory or make sufficient "connections."* Stop! Read the italicized portion of the preceding sentence again. It's one of the key points of this book!

Remote memory seems to decline very little with age.

What Are You Thinking About?

Another way of looking at memory is to look at the kinds of information that are being encountered.

Facts tend to be stored in short-term memory, and occasionally in long-term memory.

Concepts tend to be stored in long-term memory. Concepts may be considered to be clusters of facts to which a layer of meaning has been attached. We may very well remember what happened as the *result* of an event, without remember the date of the event. We may very well remember the broad knowledge or the general conclusion about something, without remembering the specific bits of fact.

Procedures, principles, and "absolute rules" for behavior tend to be stored in core or remote memory. Procedures and rules are related to how we act, speak, and behave in routine day-to-day settings. They include such things as how to ride a bicycle, how to fill a glass and pick it up and drink from it, how to walk, when to say "please" and "thank you," and how to wait for the light to change before crossing a street.

There's an old saying that "Little" people—people who do not seek personal greatness—think and talk about people...often the "facts" are woven into gossip. "Great" people think and talk about events. But "Truly Great" people talk about lasting concepts and absolutes.

Something to think about....

We Tend to Remember
What Is Pleasant to Remember

There is always an emotional aspect to our remembering. To a great extent, this aspect of memory is unconscious. We tend to forget those experiences that are painful for us to remember, and to remember those things that we believe would hurt or harm us to forget. Many women, for example, tend to forget the trauma and pain of childbirth, yet they remember the rush of joy they felt as they held their baby for the first time.

One of the theories underlying depression is that a person has experienced a malfunction in this process—the depressed person tends to remember things that are bad or hurtful to remember, and tends to forget those things that are pleasant.

There's great wisdom in what the apostle Paul wrote to the early Christian church:

> Whatever things are true, whatever things are noble, whatever things are just, whatever things are pure, whatever things are lovely, whatever things are of good report, if there is any virtue and if there is anything praiseworthy—meditate on these things. (Phil. 4:8)

Good thoughts produce good memories, and good memories tend to last.

Memory Begins with Paying Attention

Memory involves a number of mental processes, and in particular, these three functions: "attending," "focusing," and "concentrating."

Attention. The single most important aspect of gathering new information and storing it in memory is "paying attention." You simply can't remember something you never fully perceive in the first place.

Attention is related to alertness. You first must perceive information (intellectual or sensory). The mind must be alert and ready to receive information that is encountered in the surrounding environment.

We've all told our children, "Pay attention" or, "Wake up and focus!" At times we need to tell ourselves the same thing because we will not remember something unless we first attend to it.

We tend to remember the unusual aspects of an event, encounter, or visual image. Something "catches our eye." If you are attempting to commit something to memory, you are well advised to remove as many potential distractions as you can from your involvement with the event, person, or information you desire to recall later.

Attention is both a matter of physical perception—we must be able to perceive an object with accurate sensory input. For example, the more clearly a person sees an object, the more accurate his visual memory of it is going to be.

Attention can be impacted by a number of factors. Preconceptions or prejudices, for example, can cause us to weight new information so it is skewed. A number of studies on racial prejudice have shown that people tend to remember people of their own race in visual recall tests.

Too much emotion surrounding an experience can also influence attention. For example, studies have shown that the greater the amount of emotion experienced at a crime scene, the less completely a witness will remember all the events of the crime—the memory of the central event is likely to be strong, but the peripheral details are likely to be weaker.

Focus. Attention leads to focus, which is the process of filtering out some information in order to be able to concentrate on a particular fact, concept, or principle. The plain fact of life is that not all stimuli in the environment is worthy of examination, concentration, or committing to memory. A person must be selective about what is going to be mentally processed. We must "choose" what we will perceive and recall, labeling all other bits of information encountered at that time as extraneous or unimportant.

This filtering of information is done at something of a risk. There is always a chance that we will filter out a key piece of information or an important fact that we *should* put into the memory bank. If we *mis-think* or misperceive initially, we cannot help but *mis-remember*. Our memory is never more accurate than our first initial encoding of an idea.

Over time, a person may accumulate a number of false memories. This sometimes occurs not only because the information may have been miscoded initially, but because with subsequent recalls of the information, new bits of information were added or old bits of information were altered. The result can be general confusion about a past event or experience. This occurs at all ages and is not only a fault of memory, but also a fault in thinking, reasoning, or selecting information to place into memory.

And then there's the factor of "disuse." If a particular memory is not accessed often enough, the neuronal pathways between the neurons weakens and the memory is eventually lost through lack of regular use. Maintenance of a memory requires periodic review of the information. *What we no longer think about, we no longer remember.* (Read that last sentence again, please!)

Finally, IQ and educational level seem to make a difference in our ability to remember. Perhaps those who have a greater ability to think, and those who have had more cause to think, tend to have a greater ability to remember and more cause to remember. The reasons are unclear but research consistently has shown that level of education and baseline intelligence are good predictors of memory in old age.[2]

Concentration. Concentration may be defined as "sustained focus." It means attending to and focusing on information with an intent to understand it. Concentration is the phase in which *meaning* is ascribed to information. There is nearly always an attempt in the concentration phase to "apply" the information in some way, or to give a "cause" for the information to be remembered.

The less time you spend concentrating on something, the less likely that information is going to be stored for long-term retrieval. The more distractions, the less likely new information is going to be learned or old information recalled.

All of these various facets of the memory process lead us to a rather simple conclusion: memory is only one aspect of *mental functioning.* It is virtually impossible to separate memory from other processes in the mind. And since all mental processes are linked to a physical organ we call the brain, we can refer to memory and a host of other mental processes as "mind functions" or "mental functions."

What you choose to think about is as important as the brain involved in the thinking process. Pay attention to what captures your attention...what you focus upon...and what you spend time concentrating upon.

---

1. Miller, G.A. The magical number seven: Plus or minus two. Some limits on our capacity for processing information. *Psych Rev* 9 (1956): 81–97.

2. Ritchie, K., Touchon, J., Ledesert, B, Liebovici, D., and Gorce, A.M. Establishing the limits and characteristics of normal age-related cognitive decline. *Revue d'Epidemilogie et de Sante Publique* 45 (1997;5): 373–381.

   Perlmutter, M., Metzger, R., Nezworski, T., and Miller, K. Spatial and temporal memory in 20 to 60 year olds. *Jour Gerontology* 36 (1981;1): 59–65.

   Small, G.W., La Rue, A., Komo, S., Kaplan, A., and Mandelkern, M.A. Predictors of cognitive change in middle-aged and older adults with memory loss. *Am Jour of Psych* 152 (1995;12): 1757–1764

   West, R.L., Crook, T.H., and Barron, K.L. Everyday memory performance across the life span: Effects of age and noncognitive individual differences. *Psych and Aging* 7 (1992;1): 72-82.

TAKING ACTION FOR HEALTHY MENTAL FUNCTION

1. Develop your ability to attend to, focus upon, and concentrate upon stimuli.

2. Choose to think about concepts, rules, and principles more than transient facts.

3. Choose to think about what is good, noble, positive, pleasant, and pure.

4. Choose to think about what you want to remember.

CHAPTER 2

WHEN SHOULD YOU BE CONCERNED THAT YOU CAN'T REMEMBER?

A friend who knew that I was working on a book about memory sent me this little poem that he had received in his e-mail:

My Rememberer

My forgetter's getting better
But my rememberer is broke.
To you that may seem funny,
But, to me, that is no joke.

For when I'm "here" I'm wondering
If I really should be "there,"
And, when I try to think it through,
I haven't got a prayer!

Oft times I walk into a room,
Say "what am I here for?"
I wrack my brain, but all in vain—
A zero is my score.

At times I put something away
Where it is safe, but, Gee!
The person it is safest from
Is, generally, me!

When shopping I may see someone,
Say "Hi" and have a chat,
Then, when the person walks away
I ask myself, "who's that?"

Yes, my forgetter's getting better
While my rememberer is broke,
And it's driving me plumb crazy
And that isn't any joke.

A failing memory is not something that most of us can or feel we should ignore. To the contrary, memory is vital. For most people, a loss of memory and general brain function is one of the most frightening aspects of old age.

When should a person be concerned about memory loss? In general, you do not need to be concerned if you

- forget names of people you meet casually
- aren't able to find your car in a parking lot
- misplace your keys or eyeglasses
- aren't able to remember items to purchase at the store
- don't immediately recognize someone in an unfamiliar ("out of normal context") environment

These are problems more likely associating with "paying attention," "focusing," or "concentrating" than recall.

Memory loss typically is gradual. It is usually a fairly slow process, unless a person experiences a brain injury, stroke, or undergoes extensive chemotherapy.

Benign Memory Loss

One form of memory loss is called "benign memory loss." Most people experience this from time to time in their lives, especially those over age forty. It may be a temporary forgetting of a name or telephone number. This type of memory loss seems to occur more often when people are under a lot of stress. The memory loss, however, does not usually alter general mental performance.

Depression and panic are often related to this type of memory loss. Depression erodes a person's ability to concentrate, which keeps a person from fully "attending" to information; It is the same for fear. Unfortunately, fear can often fuel depression, which in turn leaves a person feeling more vulnerable and fearful—it's a vicious cycle to avoid!

Depression, sadly, seems to impact a great many elderly people. Their lives tend to be more sedentary. Others, thinking them incapable of certain responsibilities "at their age" tend to jump in and do certain tasks for them, which removes the need for the person to be "mentally engaged" in an activity. Also, many elderly people are taking medications—often a wrong prescription, a bad combination of drugs, or excessive medication—and this can lead to a "deadening" effect of the mind.

In many cases, depression is triggered when a person becomes incapacitated owing to an injury or illness, or when a person loses a beloved spouse or other close family member. Sadness can lead to depression, which in turn can lead to agitation, which in turn can lead to the prescribing of antidepressants, which can lead to bewilderment. At that point, children often intervene and perhaps even more medication is prescribed. If you put such a person in a drab, sterile nursing home environment, dementia usually isn't long in coming! We need to do a better job of helping those who are grieving or ill, rather than *allow* them to slip into depression that isolates them from other people.

By the way, those who suffer memory loss because they are depressed or over-medicated generally do well on routine tests of intellectual ability—for example, the ability to match pairs of like items, put items into sequence, write, and do simple math problems. However, those with genuine Alzheimer's disease have a consistently reduced ability to perform these "reasoning" exercises.

Memory Loss
Owing to Amnesia

Short-term memory loss is sometimes reversible, for reasons that often cannot be explained. A phenomenon called transient global amnesia may cause a person to lose all memory for several hours. It may reoccur but rarely occurs more than a few times in a person who experiences this form of amnesia. The condition seems to be caused by a temporary chemical or electrical imbalance in the brain, or perhaps a very small stroke. When such episodes are accompanied by a loss of consciousness, the problem is far more serious.

Concussions, especially those against the bony base of the skull, can cause a mild form of amnesia. Actually, any strong blow to the head can cause this type of amnesia. Memory may return in several minutes, or days, or weeks, or months. The return of memory is difficult to predict.

Memory Loss that
Should Signal Concern

One you have eliminated benign memory loss and amnesia as being the root of a memory problem, take a look at these symptoms. If any of these symptoms exist, you should be concerned:

- having periods of confusion over what time it is or where one is
- telling the same stories over and over to the same people in a short period of time
- getting lost while driving a familiar route (a route traveled frequently)

- completely forgetting important appointments (with some consistency in forgetting)
- being unable to take care of simple financial transactions or manage a checkbook
- difficulty in naming objects
- having a sudden change in personality
- experiencing a sudden change in musical or artistic ability

These problems should be addressed sooner than later if the memory loss keeps a person from his daily activity level or from performing work functions.

Five Basic Memory Tests

There are five basic tests that physicians and others use in determining mental function, usually with those who have been injured or who are elderly. They can be used by any person, of course, at any age.

Memory Test #1:
Personal Orientation

The first basic memory test is one related to a person's orientation.

"Can you tell me who you are?" This question should not be limited to a person's name, but also *relationships*. Everybody is somebody's son or daughter, and usually somebody's brother or sister, mother or father, aunt or uncle, neighbor or friend. Ask questions about a person's relationships.

"Where are you?" Does the person know where he presently is sitting, walking, or lying down? Look for answers beyond "hospital bed" or "my home." What's the address? What city and state? What's in the area—in the immediate neighborhood and nearby?

"What year is this?" Many people know the *day* of the week, but are not sure the year!

Other questions that are very basic include:

"When did you wake up?" Follow up by asking what the person has done through the day.

"What was the last meal you ate?" Ask specifically what foods the person ate.

"Where did you last go shopping?" Ask what the person purchased.

"Who did you talk to last before talking to me?" Ask what subjects were covered in the conversation.

Those who can quickly and accurately and *expansively* answer these questions have a good sense of their own orientation in the world. Those who don't know who they are, where they are, or what year they are living are likely to have serious mental impairment.

Memory Test #2:
Basic Language Skills

Many neurologists ask patients to repeat a well-known and very basic phrase: "No ifs, ands, or buts." If you are testing yourself, shut your eyes and repeat the phrase. You probably will have no difficulty recalling it. The person who has mental impairment or memory loss, however, is likely to hesitate, slur the words, leave out a portion of the phrase, or invert words.

You can also ask a person to read a short sentence from a newspaper or magazine and then, from memory, write down the sentence word for word.

If both of these tests are passed easily, try pointing to familiar objects within easy sight—such as ring, bracelet, watch, eye glasses. The person should be able to name these common items quickly, without pause. Progress to items that may be a little more difficult to name—perhaps the *parts* of a chair, door, or wristwatch.

These are all very simple tests. Two tests that are a little more advanced are these:

First, ask the person to spell a common word *backwards*. Choose a word that has one or two syllables—such as people, market, flower, or even *brain*!

Second, ask the person to name as many animals as he or she can in a minute. A person should be able to come up with at least fifteen to twenty animals in that time.

A person with even minimal or temporary impairment—for example, someone who has had too much alcohol to drink—will have difficulty with these last two tests.

Memory Test #3:
Cross-Over Skills

Ask the person to comb his hair or tie his shoelaces. These skills usually require what are called "cross-over functions." A person with severe damage to the language center of the brain, or a person with deep brain lesions, generally cannot do crossover tasks. Asking a person to cross his right hand over his left ear, and vice versa, is another type of crossover command you can give to determine this level of mental functioning. If the person cannot remember which is his left or right hand, he likely has significant memory loss. A complete failure to do cross-over tasks means that mental functioning is seriously impaired.

Memory Test #4:
Completion Skills

There are two tests that are good for determining higher intellectual abilities and memory. Both involve "completion" —either of an equation or a sentence.

The first is a simple math test. Ask the person to subtract 26 (or some other number) from 100. Then ask the person to multiply 12 times 13. This latter question takes a person beyond the rote memorization of the "twelves," which usually ends with twelve times twelve. It requires a simple means of multiplication or a combination of simple addition and multiplication. Make sure in doing math tests, however, that you are not testing a person beyond their schooling. Some people never learned their multiplication tables!

The second high-cognitive test that is helpful is to ask a person to complete a well-known proverb. Again, make sure that the person is native to the culture in which the proverb is common. For example,

"A stitch in times..." (saves nine)

"Those who live in glass houses..." (should not throw stones)

"An apple a day..." (keeps the doctor away)

Sometimes this exercise can be done with well-known songs—asking a person to give the next few words in the lyrics. Again, make certain the song is one the person is likely to have sung many times. For example,

"Oh, say can you see by the..." (dawn's early light)

"Amazing grace, how..." (sweet the sound)

Or, you may choose a saying that is well-known to the person, such as "I pledge allegiance to..." (the flag)

Those with serious mental impairments or memory problems have difficulty with these types of completion exercises.

Memory Test #5:
Word and Concept Sequence

Try giving the person a sequence of three words, which are not related, such as "desk, shoes, and baseball" or "window, bathtub, and book." A person with a normal memory will get three out of three each time. Some impairment of memory is involved if the person only gets two of the three. If the person is only able to recall one of the three words or concepts, serious mental impairment should be suspected.

You may also ask the person the name of the current president of the United States. Then ask the person to name the previous three presidents.

I know one man who was asked shortly after surgery, "Can you tell me who the president of the United States is?" He smiled slightly and said, "I don't like him. I didn't vote for him. And I'm trying to forget him." The nurse asked, "But do you know his name?" The man answered correctly. There was nothing wrong with his memory!

If you conduct these tests in an average nursing home, you are likely to find that ninety percent of the residents have trouble with these very simple tests. The more complex the material, the greater the inability to recall it accurately.

Are you feeling off the hook when it comes to memory loss?

Recall quickly and without looking back over the previous few pages the five basic memory tests? If not . . . there's some improvement you, too, might seek for your memory!

Discerning a Profile of Memory Loss

If a person scores low on these basic memory tests, the problem may be one that involves the thalamus, the hippocampus, or the fornix (areas of the brain). People with problems in these areas of the brain usually have other medical symptoms, such as blackouts or disorientation. If no other signs or symptoms of brain loss are present, however, it's less likely that deep brain structures are involved.

The kind, severity, and duration of memory loss is dependent on the location of the brain that has been damaged, as well as the cause and extent of the damage.

Diagnosing Memory Impairment in the Elderly

In diagnosing age-related memory impairment, physicians often use the following more formal "inclusion-exclusion" criteria below:

Inclusion Criteria

1. Males and females at least fifty years of age.

2. Complaints of memory loss in every day life—such as difficulty remembering names of persons after being introduced, misplacing objects, difficulty remembering telephone numbers or mailing codes, and difficulty recalling information quickly or following a distraction. Onset of memory loss must be described as gradual, without sudden worsening in recent months.

3. Memory test performances that are at least one standard deviation below the mean established for young adults on a standardized test of secondary memory (recent memory) with adequate normative data. The following are examples of specific tests and cut-off scores:

   - Benton Visual Retention Test (Benton, 1963) (number correct, Administration A) 7 or less
   - Logical memory subtest of the Wechsler Memory Scale (WMS) (Weschler and Stone, 1983) 6 or less
   - Associate learning subtest of the WMB (score on "hard" associates) 6 or less

4. Evidence of adequate intellectual function as determined by a scaled score of at least 9 (raw score of at least 32) on the Vocabulary Subtest of the Wechsler Adult intelligence Scale (Wechsler, 1955)

5. Absence of dementia as determined by a score of 24 or higher on the Mini-Mental State Examination (Folstein et al, 1974). Many investigators have chosen a score of 27 rather than 24 to exclude questionable cases of dementia.

Exclusion Criteria

1. Evidence of delirium, confusion, or other disturbances of consciousness.

2. Any neurologic disorder that could produce cognitive deterioration as determined by history, clinical neurologic examination, and, if indicated, neuroradiologic examination. Such disorders include AD, Parkinson's disease, stroke, intracranial hemorrhage, local brain lesions, including tumors, and normal pressure hydrocephalus.

3. History of any infective or inflammatory brain disease, including viral, fungal, and syphilitic.

4. Evidence of significant cerebral vascular disease as determined by a Hachinski Ischaemia Score (modified version; Rosen et al, 1980) of 4 or more or by neuroradiologic examination.

5. History of repeated minor head injury (as in boxing) or single injury resulting in a period of unconsciousness for one hour or more.

6. Current psychiatric diagnosis according to DSM-IIIR (American Psychological Association, 1980) criteria of depression, mania, or any major psychiatric disorder.

7. Current diagnosis or history of alcoholism or drug dependence.

8. Evidence of depression as determined by a Hamilton Depression Rating Scale (Hamilton, 1967) score of 13 or more.

9. Any medical disorder that could produce cognitive deterioration, including renal, respiratory, cardiac, and hepatic disease; diabetes melitis unless well controlled by diet or oral hypoglycemic agents; endocrine, metabolic, or hematologic disturbances; and malignancy not in remission for more than two years. Determination should be based on complete medical history, clinical examination (including electrocardiogram), and appropriate laboratory tests.

10. Use of any psychotropic drug or any other drug that may significantly affect cognitive function during the month before psychometric testing.[1]

---

1. Crook, T.H. and Adderly, B. *The Memory Cure*, New York: Pocket Books, 1998:193–4.

TAKING ACTION FOR HEALTHY MENTAL FUNCTION

1. Don't be overly concerned about minor lapses of memory.

2. If you are concerned about your ability to remember, test yourself.

3. If you see major warning signs related to memory, seek professional help.

CHAPTER 3

BOOSTING
YOUR BRAIN POWER

In 1993, Dominic O'Brien of Great Britain was given one look at a random sequence of 40 decks of cards that had been shuffled together—a total of 2,080 cards. He then recited back the entire sequence, making only one mistake.

Hideaki Tomoyori of Yokohama, Japan, recited the number of pi to 40,000 places on March 9–10 in 1987. The feat took him 17 hours and 21 minutes (including breaks that totaled four hours and fifteen minutes. (*The Guinness Book of Records* does not say how long it took him to memorize the information in the first place!)

The famous orchestra conductor Arturo Toscanini actively developed his memory in part to compensate for his poor eyesight. He ultimately memorized every note played by every instrument for 100 operas and 250 symphonies. When Toscanini was only nineteen years old, a bassoonist came to him and informed him that his instrument was broken and he would not be able to play the lowest note a bassoon can play. Toscanini searched his memory for a few moments and then informed the bassoonist that he was in luck because that note did not appear in any of the music the orchestra was performing that evening.

You may not be able to develop your memory to such heights...but isn't it nice to know that somebody has?

What each of us can strive for are not the ultimate memory feats, but rather, to *increase* both brain function and mental functions. Actually, many of the same techniques used to help people recover from strokes and brain injuries are the same techniques that are helpful in *improving* mental functions.

The Link Between Brain and Mind

Let me give you two broad generalizations about brain function. **First**, the functions of the brain that are in the "inner" part of the brain are those most directly linked to memory. People who suffer injuries or have tumors or strokes in the interior of the brain tend to experience the greatest loss of memory, and their recovery time from these "brain insults" is much longer than that of people who have injuries to the outer part of the brain.

Second, the extent of recovery from brain injury and stroke has been shown to be related to an individual's educational and intellectual level. Those with more schooling and higher intellectual activity tend to recover from brain-related injuries faster than those who have been less mentally active. The reason for this seems to be that we tend to "over learn" certain functions. Those functions that we practice routinely—such as reading, writing, and puzzle solving—are more widely represented throughout the brain. In other words, many more connections have been made among brain cells. Thus, if one area of cells is damaged, other cells may pick up the slack in function.

This is perhaps one of the strongest arguments for life-long learning. Insist that your children stay in school and that they learn to *value* learning. Keep your brain active and engaged. This is one of the reasons I continually take courses and read on a regular basis.

As an aside, you may find it interesting that left-handed people tend to recover from brain injuries more rapidly than right-handed people. Why? Right-handed people tend to have their speech functions localized in their left cerebral hemisphere, whereas many left-handed people have speech function more evenly distributed between the two hemispheres of the brain. After a stroke, for example, a left-handed person may have some speech loss, but that loss is more rapidly compensated by the other half of the brain that retains speech function.

Functions related to music and poetry of speech (prosody) tend to be in the right side of the brain. People who are right-handed, and who develop their abilities in music and prosody prior to a stroke, tend to recover from strokes in the left hemisphere of the brain more quickly than those who have not developed skills that are located in the left side of the brain.

What can we draw practically from this information? Two main conclusions:

1. Stay Alert Mentally. The first implication we can draw from these generalizations is that we are wise to "use it or lose it" when it comes to the brain. Just as we need to eat good nutritious food and exercise our bodies for physical health, so we need to take in good-quality information and exercise our brains for mental health.

Don't stop reading and writing. Take on new mental challenges. Work mental and word puzzles. Keep the nerve connections in your brain "alive and producing."

Television is *not* mental exercise. The vast majority of studies in educational research have shown that television is largely a passive activity. It requires very little brain power to process the visual and auditory information provided by TV.

Radio provides more mental exercise than television because radio messages force a person to process two "bands" of information—the auditory messages being received and the visual images present around the listener (or evoked through imagination).

Reading—both fiction and nonfiction in the form of books, magazines, web site information—requires a high quality mental exercise. So does writing. Keep a journal. Write notes and letters. Keep up an e-mail correspondence with family and friends. Work on that screenplay or novel that almost every American thinks he has lurking in his soul!

The more challenging the information you are reading, and the more detailed or complex the thoughts you are writing, the greater the mental exercise. We all know the phrase, "Garbage in, garbage out" when it comes to viewing or consuming "junk information." Take this to heart when it comes to brain health and memory function. Is what you are learning and reading today going to be *worth* remembering tomorrow or twenty years from now? If not, choose higher-quality "input" for your mind!

I strongly recommend that you read the materials that are the most beneficial and inspirational to your *spirit*. These materials are the ones to which you are likely to give greater weight and to which you are likely to return most often (not only in consumption but in memory). The result is that the connections drawn among these materials in the nerve cells of the brain are likely to be more extensive.

2. Pursue a Balance of Mental Activities. A well-known principle when it comes to physical health and exercise is that a "balance" of exercises works better than just one form of exercise—in other words, a person tends to have better physical function if he engages in strength-training (weights), aerobics, and flexibility exercises. A varied exercise routine tends to be more fun, more motivating, and also better for the muscles of the body—in other words, walk some, cycle some, swim some, and so forth. When it comes to the mind, a variety of "exercise" is also helpful.

Don't ignore the musical side of your brain. If you play an instrument—or once played an instrument—keep practicing or resume practicing. Make up songs. Memorize the lyrics to favorite songs—all the verses! Join a singing group or choir or orchestra, or perhaps form your own vocal group or band.

If you aren't musical, you can certainly read poetry. Read it aloud and memorize lines from favorite poems. Not all poetry is sentimental or romantic—find poems you find amusing. Memorize poetic passages from books you read.

A variety in the information you take in can serve you well in the long run of your life.

Learning Style Becomes Memory Style

Every person tends to rely mainly upon one sensory system for processing stimuli. This dominant sensory system becomes the way a person learns, and thus, remembers.

Visual Learners. About sixty-five percent of all people are visual learners. They remember best what they see written down. They enjoy making diagrams, outlines, and sketches related to the information they want to remember. They tend to remember lists in their "mind's eye."

If you are a visual learner, you are probably going to find writing notes very helpful in assisting your memory.

Kinesthetic Learners. About fifteen percent of all people learn best if they can associate a situation or idea with movement of some type. Dancers, for example, have no difficulty remembering a long sequence of sometimes very complex steps and upper body movements. Many athletes find that their best rehearsal is to mentally picture themselves going through all the movements of their particular sport. PET (positron emission tomography) scans have shown, by the way, that imagined activity stimulates the same parts of the brain as real activity.

If you are a kinesthetic learner, you may want to assign key facts or concepts you want to recall to a form of movement. One child I know memorized the capitals of the states by assigning each state to a body part and developing something of a rap-dance to go with the information.

Auditory Learners. About twenty percent of all people learn most effectively by hearing. They often find they study best if they can read their texts or notes aloud.

If you are an auditory learner, don't be afraid to talk to yourself. Don't mumble—speak with authority those things you want to remember as if you are *commanding* yourself to remember them. One woman could never seem to remember if she had unplugged her curling iron before she left for work. She developed the habit of saying to herself, "I am unplugging my curling iron right now and I won't have to think about it later."

Cross-Training. Even if you are a visual learner, you are likely to find that saying something aloud repeatedly will help you remember the information you "see" in your mind. Auditory learners—try to "visual" what you are talking about.

Mind-Building Exercises that Fold Easily into Daily Life

There are a number of things you can do to develop your mind and memory in the course of pursuing your normal, everyday life. Some of these are things that can directly help you "cross-train" your mind.

Develop the Artist in You. Take a sketch pad with you to a park. It doesn't matter whether you are an artist—draw what you see.

Actually, most artists will tell you that the key to becoming a good illustrator is to develop the ability to "see" details, angles, shadows, and proportions.

Read poetry. Read it aloud, which is the way most poetry is meant to be read. Then, illustrate the poem. You can even do this in our mind's eye. Imagine an environment that is suggested by the poem, even if the poem is not about a landscape.

Build Your Vocabulary. Continue to build your vocabulary. If you encounter a word you don't know, look it up. Begin to use the word.

Work Puzzles. There are a number of logic, crossword, and word puzzle books on the market. Choose one or more and spend a few minutes a day—or perhaps spend part of a Saturday morning or Sunday afternoon—doing one or more puzzles. Or, you may want to do the puzzles found in most daily newspapers.

Puzzle books are often great to take along to a doctor's appointment (or any appointment in which some waiting is likely to be required) or on an airline flight. You might want to find age-appropriate puzzle books for your children to do, or you may want to tackle a crossword puzzle together with your spouse or child.

You can make any puzzle-book exercise more challenging by giving yourself a time limit for the puzzle's completion.

Memorize Literature. Choose to commit certain passage of literature to memory. These may be quotes from famous people, lines of poetry, or verses from the Bible. Write out the passage you are intending to memorize. Say aloud the passage slowly. Repeat reading it aloud several times—if the passage is lengthy, you may need to break down this process into phrases or increments of just a few words each. Memorize phrase by phrase until you have memorized the whole.

Keep the card or piece of paper on which you have written the material you are memorizing with you in your purse, wallet, or perhaps tack it to the edge of a mirror in the bathroom or the visor of your car. Periodically throughout the day take a look at your "memory card." As you sit in traffic waiting for lights to change, try to recall the passage. Check your accuracy at the next light.

Memorize Song Lyrics. Most of us can sing the first verse of "Jingle Bells" but do you know the second verse? Can you sing more than one verse or a key "phrase" of other famous songs or hymns? Why not learn ALL the lyrics?

Again, memorize the lyrics—along with the tune—phrase by phrase or line by line. You may recall from the discussion at the beginning of this chapter that you are exercising the left side of the brain when you are doing this. You are actually engaging in *both* music and prosody.

Practice Writing with the "Wrong Hand." Develop your ability to write with the hand you don't normally use. In addition to learning to write letters, try drawing symbols or figures with the hand that is not the one you usually use for writing or drawing. (A small chalkboard is actually one of the best tools to use when learning to write with your "other hand.") Don't put too much pressure on the chalk, pen, or pencil you are using. Relax—you are likely to have some difficulty forming letters and you'll only find this more difficult if you tense the muscles in your hand. Start slowly, perhaps working only a couple of minutes a day on the letters of the alphabet. Work your way up to writing the entire alphabet in 15 seconds—upper case in fifteen seconds, and then lower case in fifteen seconds.

Next, try copying some phrases out of books. You might want to begin with children's books, which tend to have a predominance of one-syllable words. Work your way up to words that are longer in length.

To give yourself an added challenge, set a time limit on each passage you choose to copy and try to beat it.

Learn to Play the Piano or Another Musical Instrument. Even if you have never taken music lessons, *now* is a good time to start! Keyboards are relatively inexpensive—some are only about a hundred dollars. Learning to play the piano accomplishes several brain-function goals at the same time: you are forced to pay attention, concentrate, use both hands, and coordinate eye-hand movements. Over time, begin to memorize some simple pieces. At that point, you are not only exercising your brain, you are actively exercising your memory!

You may have learned to read music and play "by the book." You might want to consider setting a goal of playing "by ear." A different set of learning skills are required, which only leads to even more "connections" among nerve cells in the brain. In playing by ear, you will be exercising the memory both in recalling the original tune and remembering the notes and chords required to recreate that tune!

Play Memory Games on Your Computer. A number of memory games and exercises are available on the internet. Here is a good site to access:

http://www.search.com/?ctb.search

Under the heading "computing," choose "gaming" and then on the next screen, choose "games download" and then when you have an opportunity to type in the type of game you are seeking, type in memory. Games are available for both Mac and PC users.)

Turn TV Watching to Good Advantage. Challenge your children to a memory quiz after watching their favorite television show. Ask them

- to name all the characters that were on the program.

- how many different locations were shown.
- to identify as many pieces of furniture or props in one of the main "rooms" in which the program takes place.
- to identify all the models of cars that were shown—not only in the show but during the commercials.

Organize "Memories in the Making." In times past, memory boxes were common. People kept various mementos and souvenirs in special boxes—and periodically revisited the items in those boxes to talk about past events and experiences with friends old and new.

Scrapbooks and photo albums served much the same purpose.

I suggest you annotate any scrapbook or photo album you make—not only identify the people, place, and date, but also make a few notes about other things that happened in association with that trip, party, or event. Keep these items out and available to look at them periodically—don't stash them away in an attic.

Keeping a daily diary or journal is another good way to keep track of "memories in the making." Don't just list things you did, but describe people, places and events in as much detail as possible, including your feelings, reactions, and bits of dialog.

Choose to Live in a Stimulating, Enriching, Playful Environment

Recent research has shown that brain size, and presumably the connections, spaces, and cells in the brain, can be increased by an enriched physical environment—an environment rich in color, texture, variation, stimuli. People respond very positively to environments that evoke their creativity and their sense of play.

The "fun" factor is rarely addressed when it comes to mental function, but it is an important factor nonetheless. When we do things that are fun to us—which generally means the activities are interesting, pleasurable, rewarding, and challenging—we attend to the event with greater focus and we tend to remember the event longer. If one is focused and excited about something, one tends to put in a better performance. One researcher concluded, "The more the brain is stimulated, even in advanced age, the more tissue there is to keep stimulating."[1]

As you look back through the activities suggested in this chapter, choose the ones that sound the most interesting and fun to you. Those are the activities that you are likely to stick with and therefore, they are the activities that are likely to produce the greatest benefits for you.

Your memory should not be a burden to you. "Learning"should not be a bore. Remembering should not be painful.

---

1. Rosenfeld, A. *Pro-Longevity II: An Updated Report on the Scientific Aspects of Adding Good Years to Life.* New York: Henry Holt, 1985.

TAKING ACTION FOR HEALTHY MENTAL FUNCTION

1. Keep learning, exploring, creating, growing.

2. Keep learning. exploring, creating, growing.

3. Keep learning, exploring, creating, growing.

4. Cross-train your mind.

CHAPTER 4

MEMORY EXERCISES AND TIPS

How many times have you heard yourself or someone else say, "Wow, I was into that. Time really flew by." It might have been a book you were reading, a movie you were watching, or an event in which you were participating. That's focus and concentration at work!

For most people, focus and concentration do not come easy. Concentration is a skill that needs to be developed.

Here are five general suggestions for developing better focus and concentration abilities:

1. During a break from work, perhaps a lunch break, go to a window or out into a park and "stare" at a particular object. It may be a statue, a garden plot, a grove of trees, a pond, a fountain, a section of pavement, or a vendor cart. Observe everything you can about the object of your focus. Pay attention to details. Note similarities and differences. Then, back at your desk or work station, close your eyes for a few moments and try to visually recreate the object or scene in your mind.

2. When someone is speaking to you, block out everything else. You may find looking into the person's eyes distracting. If so, look down at some neutral object and blot out all other sounds.

3. Turn off all competing sounds and stimuli. Don't try to read a book, magazine, or scientific journal article—at least if you want to remember the information it conveys—with the radio or television at full blast in the background.

4. Build up your mental stamina. Start by concentrating intently for a few minutes. Then seek to increase the time you concentrate on material. Practice your concentration routinely until you can focus on a project, music practice session, or book for forty-five minutes to an hour without feeling restless or feeling "the need for a break." Perhaps it is not surprising, but the attention span of most people in the United States born after 1955 tends to be the average length of time between commercial breaks! It's sad how television has conditioned our society. Work to extend attention span, not only in yourself but your children!

5. Take time to organize information in a way that makes sense to you before you concentrate on it with the intent of holding it in memory. Various outlining techniques may be useful to you as you organize "thoughts" and "facts," even if those outlines were not used as part of the way the thoughts or facts were presented to you. Cluster key ideas together. "Mind mapping"—which clusters ideas visually—is a device that many people use and claim to be extremely helpful in recalling large and sometimes complex bodies of thought. Facts and ideas are clustered together as key concepts, then linked to other key concepts, in one visual "spread" so that all of the pertinent information can be seen as a whole.

Six Attention and Concentration Exercises

Six exercises are provided here that are aimed at helping improve your mental ability to attend to information, focus on it, or concentrate on it. It's best to work with another person in doing these. Your partner can be your time-keeper and scorer, and then you, in turn, can keep time and score for your partner.

Parents, scout leaders, trip chaperones, and other "adults in charge"—these are good exercises to keep children busy on a road trip or as a rainy day activity. First, assign the children to "develop" or "write" the tests. Then have them do the tests in pairs, timing and scoring each other. Keep track of scores for each exercise during the duration of the day or the entire trip. Hold out a special reward for the "brain power" champion of your family or group.

1. Dutch Air Force Exercise. This exercise was developed to help Dutch Air Force personnel to increase their attention and concentration span. The test is very simple. Within a strict time limit—such as ten seconds or fifteen seconds—circle every number "3" and every letter "n" in a block of random letters and numbers such as the following:

> 8 v f g 4 k j 2 e o d 2 h w r 9 s 3 5 e 8 f s g f 6 n 7 c
> 6 o I a u f g f e 7 f g g f t d c l 6 f t d c l 6 f 3 l c d t
> s d u g 5 d c s x 6 e r n h 6 f x d s b y 4 g d 8 4 t 4 d
> y s 3 t o 2 c p g d 8 2 r x s e x n 4 f 1 d 5 x 3 w l k s
> r g 4 g c 2 f m k n f j b v 4 3 l 7 n 6 e 3 t b 8 n 6 e v
> d t 1 w q 3 x n t g

If keeping score: Give one point each for every 3 or "n" circled in the given time frame. Repeat the exercise several times, using different grids of letters.

You can get more mileage out of any random block of letters and numbers by asking the person to pick out two other letters or numbers, such as "8" and "f", or "2" and "d."

The less time you give the person to find the selected numbers, the more difficult the challenge.

2. Timing Test. Have one person pick an increment of time at random—such as 23 seconds or 123 seconds. The person should say the time increment and write it down. Then ask the subject to start the stopwatch and stop it at *exactly* the time increment designated.

If keeping score: Take away one point from a total score for each second the person stops the watch before or after the designated time increment. Play the game repeated times. Rather than deal in negative numbers, you may want to have each person start with a total score of 100 and subtract seconds from that total. (Note: This is more difficult than it sounds. To make the test a little more difficult, don't start the watch at the 60-second mark. Start it, perhaps at the 7 second mark. That way, there's both attending and math involved.)

3. Time Estimate Test. This is the same exercise as the one above except that the person who holds the stopwatch is the person who picks the increment of time. The other person must pace himself in counting silently the seconds as they tick—giving the instruction to start and stop.

If keeping score: Take away one point from a total score for each second the person asks the stopwatch to be stopped before of after the designated time increment.

4. Torn Paper Exercise. Have one person tear a piece of paper into twelve small pieces. Insist that each piece have at least two "jagged" edges—do not fold the paper first and tear it in straight lines. The point is to have *jagged* edges that only "fit" with the neighboring pieces of paper in one way. Hand the pieces of paper to the other person, who then proceeds to put back together the pieces into a unified whole. (In other words, this is something of a make-your-own jigsaw puzzle.) The more uniform the pieces are in general size and shape, the more difficult this puzzle will be to do. Again, this is more difficult than it sounds, especially if the paper pieces are on plain paper and are jumbled so the person cannot tell one side of the paper from the other.

If keeping score: Give the person an overall time limit for completing the puzzle—perhaps three minutes. Give the person the total points in seconds that are left in the three-minute time frame.

5. Number and Letter Match. Have one person tear up a piece of paper into *ten* pieces. One each piece, he should write a letter of the alphabet (at random). Then, on a separate sheet of paper, list the ten letters and assign each letter a numerical value from one to one hundred. (For example, A=19, S=91, N=28, D=14, and so forth.)

Then the "examiner" holds up each piece of paper with a letter on it and *tells* the person the number value assigned to that letter. Give the subject a few seconds to commit the visual and auditory information to memory.

After one pass through, ask the subject if he wants to see any of the letters again, and correspondingly, hear the numerical value again. Allow the subject to go through the set of ten letters no more than two complete times.

Then, the examiner should then hold up a letter *at random* and ask the subject to recall the numerical value associated with it.

If keeping score: For each combination that is correct, award the number of points associated with the letter. The numbers can get quite high with this game. That's good for giving a person an exercise in long addition. If you are keeping score over multiple games, or in association with other games, you may want to divide the final scores by 10—or even 100—at the end of play.

There are two good variations on this game:

- **Stopwatch and Letter.** Rather than ask the subject to recall the number value associated with a letter, ask the person to run the stopwatch for that length of time. (If keeping score: you can subtract one point for each second before or after the exact time increment assigned to the letter. Or, you may want to total all of the subject's stop-watch times—in other words, have the subject maintain a running time from one letter to the next—and compare it to the total time allotted to the ten letters.)

• Shapes, Letters, and Values. Rather than limit the ten pieces to letters, you may want to intersperse some shapes or use all shapes (square=10, triangle=23, rectangle=54, and so forth).

6. Basic Math. Doing math exercises can help with concentration. Make up a set of ten addition, subtraction, multiplication, and division equations. Designate how many digits may be used. (For example: Two-digit problems would include 76 - 43, 56 + 62, 90 ÷ 15, 14 x 71, and so forth.) Then trade your set of "problems" with those of another person. Take turns timing each other on completion of the problems.

This exercise can become easier or more difficult depending on how many digits are allowed.

If keeping score: Give each correct answer a point.

Four Memory-Building Exercises

Here are four exercises directly aimed at developing your ability to remember. I recently heard about a man who used a variation on the first of these exercises to keep his mind and memory intact while he was isolated for several days of procedures related to a bone marrow transplant. He was determined to keep his mind sharp and his memory alive. Months later, he won a national memory competition!

1. Deck of Cards. Shuffle a deck of playing cards and then go through them one by one and attempt to commit the cards to memory. After you have viewed a card, place it face down, placing each subsequent card face down on top of the new deck. Then attempt to recall the cards in sequence. "Two of spades, six of hearts, ten of diamonds," and so forth.

Start with just four cards. Then go to five cards, then six, and so forth, until you have worked your way up to 20 cards. (If you master 20 cards several times in a row, move on—you have a great memory and you can make it even greater!)

If keeping score: Give the subject one point for each card named correctly.

This is a game you can play by yourself. Be sure to score yourself honestly.

2. Photos into the Shopping Cart. Cut two dozen photos of items from an old ready-to-be-discarded magazine. The photos should be simple items, such as a flower, a baseball mitt, a car, and so forth. Then on a plain sheet of paper make a list of twenty-four items you are likely to find in a grocery store. Write the name of one of these items on the back of each photo. Spend a few minutes committing to memory the combinations you have selected (for example: flower and bath soap, baseball mitt and cantaloupe, a car and hamburger meat).

Lay out the photos in random order, photo side up.

Have the scorer call out six items for you to put into an imaginary grocery cart. These names should be selected at random from the list you have made. The subject's challenge is to recall which photo he had associated with the grocery item and pull that photo from the selection before him.

If keeping score: Give one point for each correct match.

The difficulty of this game can be adjusted by reducing or expanding the number of photos and grocery items.

There are several variations you can play on this game using sports:

- **Basketball Game.** Assign the names of items related to a basketball game, players, court, or team names to each photo. Then have the scorer pick out a "starting line-up" of five items and ask the subject to put them on the court.

- **Baseball Game.** Assign the names of items related to baseball to each photo. Then have the scorer pick out a "team" of nine players, plus a batter, and ask the subject to put them on a baseball field diagram in the correct position.

- **Football Game.** Assign the names of items related to football to each photo. Then have the scorer pick out a "team" of eleven players, and ask the subject to put them on a football field in correct "line up" position.

You need to know something about each of these games, of course, including the positioning of players, in order to place the photos correctly. If you are keeping score, you may want to give one point for each correct match, and one point for each correct position on the respective playing court, diamond, or field.

A variation on this game can be useful in helping you develop your ability to associate names with people:

- **Faces and Names.** Cut out only the faces of people from a magazine you are about to discard. Ideally, choose faces of people who are strangers—in other words, people for whom you do not already have a name association. Then, write a fictitious name on the back of each photo. Keep a list of these names and description of photo for the person (for example: Greg = short blond male with glasses). The scorer can then ask you to invite five people over for a dinner party, using the list of names as a referent.

- **New Names for Famous Person.** Cut out the faces of people who are FAMOUS—people for whom you already have a name. Then, using the same technique as the "Faces and Names" activity above, give each person a new name—not a nickname. Make a list of the real names and fictitious names. The scorer can then ask you to invite five "fictitious" people to a mystery-solving party.

3. Shopping List Acronyms. Many people learned the names of the letters on a musical staff with acronyms: the "space" notations form the acronym "face"—f, a, c, e. The "line" notations form a phrase: "every good boy does fine" for the notes e, g, b, d, f. Most of us know the letters ASAP stand for "as soon as possible." It can also be an acronym for asparagus, squash, artichoke, and pears. And many of us learned the Great Lakes by using the acronym HOMES: Huron, Ontario, Michigan, Erie, and Superior.

In this activity, a subject selects five items of a type. They may be five fruits, five animals, five vegetables, five countries, five pieces of sports equipment, and so forth. These items should be listed on a piece of paper. Then a phrase should be created with each word in the phrase beginning with the same letter as the first letter in each of the five items chosen. Or, items should be arranged so the five letters form another word or fictitious "word" that can be remembered. The order of items may be rearranged. Do not, however, change the names of items to fit an "idea" you have for an acronym or phrase. For example:

FIVE THINGS IN A LIVING ROOM:

television, radio, lamp, sofa, and table may be rearranged and assigned this acronym:

Lamp	L	Let's
Television	T	Take
Table	T	Things
Radio	R	Real
Sofa	S	Slow

Or the person may choose to remember it as LETTERS, sans the vowels.

FIVE THINGS RELATED TO AUTOMOBILES:

Horn	H	Harry
Antenna	A	and
Cell phone	C	Cecelia
Keys	K	Kept
Sunroof	S	Some

The result is also an acronym: HACKS

Make ten or more such lists of five things, putting each list on a separate sheet of paper. Create a phrase or acronym for each one. Spend a little time memorizing the lists and their respective acronyms.

Then give the sheets to the scorer. Have the scorer call out a CATEGORY of five things (for example: Five things related to automobiles.) It is up to the subject to list the five items.

If keeping score: Assign one point for each correct item.

4. Copying Visual Designs. Have each person draw ten visual "designs" using straight lines that intersect at different angles. Begin with only two lines and move up to the point where you have eleven lines. Here are some examples, from simple to complex:

3 lines

7 lines

10 lines

Put each design on a separate sheet of paper. Then trade sets of paper. The scorer should show the person a design for five seconds, and then remove it. It is up to the subject to draw the design on a plain sheet of paper, coming as close as possible to the original design.

If keeping score: This exercise obviously cannot be scored objectively. Scorer and subject should cooperate in assigning points to each drawing on a scale such as the following: 1, not much similarity; 5, some similarity but not complete likeness; 10 exact likeness or pretty close to it.

Valuable Memory "Crutches"

There's no reason *not* to use certain "crutches" to help your own memory. There's no law that says you can't do whatever is helpful to you to compensate for a memory decline or "lapses" in your memory. Do what works for you! You are likely to find that if you use some of these crutches regularly, you will be improving your memory.

1. Write it down. What you write down—at least, what you write down in a place you can readily access—you won't forget. One elderly man used to write down the time he was supposed to meet his girlfriend at the retirement center dining room. He tended to talk to his girlfriend in the early afternoon, and too many times, he found that he couldn't recall by late afternoon the exact time they had agreed to meet for dinner. He would write the agreed-upon time in bold, large numbers on a small note card with a hole punched at the top center. Then he hung the note card on a small nail next to his front door. His system worked! He didn't miss a dinner date in more than three years of using this system.

Take notes. Keep a journal. Write a "memo to file." What you write down immediately upon attending to new information is likely to be more accurate than what you write down a few hours or days later. Go over your notes, journal entry, or file memo to make certain you have included all of the pertinent information you believe should be available for recall later.

This method worked very well for one college student who opted to type his lecture notes in quite afternoon hours in his dorm within 48 hours of hearing a lecture. Typing the notes—doing a little organizing or them and adding to them along the way—helped commit the information to memory. Not only did he have a very clear set of notes from which to study later, but he found that he had to spend much less time in studying for major exams because the information had already been recalled once.

This method also works well for a friend of mine who is a teacher. She writes down ideas to incorporate into her lesson plans *as those ideas come to her.* She has a pen and a little tablet of paper next to every chair or sofa in her home, as well as by her bedside and her bathtub. She also has a pen and tablet attached to a clipboard she keeps in her car. As she reads books or articles, hears television or radio programs, or just spends time thinking about a subject, she writes down new ideas that come to her. Some of those ideas are directly related to subject matter she is teaching—other ideas relate to articles she would like to write, parties she might plan to hold, or people she may want to contact. She tears her ideas off the tablets and pierces them on a spindle nail. Then once a week, she goes through the slips of paper and types her ideas into categories in her computer or puts them on her list of things to do. She believes her system has not only helped her to be a better teacher, but a more creative and more organized person.

2. Use an appointment book or calendar to keep track of special events and appointments. Don't dry to hold all of your appointments, birthdays, anniversaries, or evens in memory. Keep track of them on a calendar and free up that memory space.

3. Don't try to hold a memory overnight. If you want to take your suit to the cleaners the next morning, put your suit by your wallet or money clip the night before, or take your suit out to the car.

4. Use automatic timers. Don't waste time and energy wondering if you turned off the coffee maker as you sit in freeway traffic several miles from home. Put appliances on turn-off timers.

5. Use a compartmentalized container for sorting your daily medications or supplements. A quick check of that day's "slot" or "section" can reassure you that you have taken all of that day's medications or supplements. If you are taking medications or supplements in the morning and evening, you may want to have two containers—perhaps one next to your bed for the items you take in the evening, and one next to your toothbrush for the items you take in the morning. If you take a number of medications or supplements at various times through the day, you may want to make up a master chart and duplicate it, and then cross-through or check items as you take them each day.

Visual Mnemonic Techniques. In Greek mythology, Mnemosyne (nee-MOS-en-nee) is the goddess of memory. She was the mother of the Muses. She herself knew everything past, present, and future. Her name is the basis for the word "mnemonics" (nee-MON-icks, with the first "m" silent). The word refers to strategies that help a person organize and remember information by linking items together. These techniques were considered to be so powerful that people in medieval times classified them as "magic."

One of the most popular mnemonic techniques is to imagine a house or building you know well—it may be your own home or place of business. Put information of like kinds in one room. One fact may be linked to the bed, another to the nightstand, one fact may be linked to each pillow on the bed, another fact to the lamp on the nightstand, and so forth. If the information is complex, put other related items of like kind in other rooms of the house. Visually "walk through" the house in your mind and recall as many of the individual associations you can.

This particular technique, which is called the Loci (LOW-kigh) Technique, is very old. It is based on the word "loci," which is the plural of the Greek word locus, meaning "place or location." The technique is attributed to Simonides, who lived in Greece about 500 BC. According to legend, a nobleman named Scopas gave a banquet to celebrate a wrestling victory. During the banquet, the roof of the hall fell in and crushed all the guests. Simonides was in the hall moments before its collapse. (He had been chanting a lyric poem in Scopas's honor,) He helped relatives of the deceased locate and identify their dead in the rubble by imagining the banquet hall room and the location of where each guest was sitting.

You don't need to imagine a room or rooms to use this technique. You can also imagine a golf course with which you are familiar—assigning various bits of information to water hazards, sand traps, and other aspects of each hole on the course.

If you are an auditory learner, you can enhance this technique by associating sounds with various items—the clicking on of a lamp, a cat purring on the bed, and so forth.

Rhymes and Songs. Most of us know this old familiar rhyme: "i before e except after c." And then there's...

> Thirty days hath September,
> April, June, and November.
> All the rest have 31,
> Save February which has 28
> (except in leap year, 29).

How many of us know the names of the notes on the musical scale (do-re-me-fa-so-la-ti-do) because we learned the famous song from *The Sound of Music*:"Doe, a deer, a female deer..."?

Chunking. A technique that especially seems to help visual learners is chunking. Break down long sequences of letters or numbers into smaller units, usually no more than three letters or numbers each.

> 175387652 becomes 175 - 387 - 652
> QYRXAJKSLAPW becomes QYR - XAJ - KSL - APW

Memorizing Numbers, Dates, and Phone Numbers. When trying to remember a number longer than three digits, try converting it to dollars and cents. For example 1,689 would become $16.89. The year 1492 might become $14.92. The number 78,653 would become $786.53.

If you are trying to memorize a phone number, you may want to break it down into two dollar amounts: 747-6413 would become $7.47 and $64.13.

People with a better special/visual memory than auditory/verbal memory may do better in memorizing phone numbers by noting the sequence of numbers punched on a digital phone: "Seeing"the number dialed is often easier for them to remember than recalling the number itself.

Testing Your
Own
Memory Improvement

How can you tell if you are making progress in improving your memory? Here is a very simple procedure.

First, make up your own "test." Personalize it to information that is important to you or information that you routinely encounter.

For example, one person made this her list of"important things to know":

1. Names of people at my church.
2. Names of the students in the classes I teach at the junior college.
3. News article topics on the front page of the newspaper. You may make this test as long or as short as you like, but write down the items. In this example, the woman used a church directory to list a hundred people at her church for whom she could associate a name and face. She had a class roster for the two classes she taught at a local community college. Every morning she listed the subjects of the news items on the front page of the paper.

Then, spend a minute or two focusing on one or more items on your list in the morning.

Finally, spend a few minutes in the afternoon—or perhaps the following morning—attempting to recall the information on your lists. Give yourself a"score"and compare it to your score a week later.

This woman used her afternoon walk—about thirty to forty minutes—to recall as many names of church people as she could, recall as many names of students as she could, and as many news topics as she could. She gave herself a"memory score"at the end of each walk, noting this information on the same log she kept for her exercise.

Be Encouraged

Don't allow yourself to become discouraged if you do not score high on these exercises, or if you find that you are making slow progress in improving your memory. Stay the course! Nobody ever became physically fit overnight after years of no exercise—it isn't likely you are going to find a quick fix for years of mental laxness.

Nearly everybody can do something to improve mental function, including memory. Do what you can. Refuse to give in to the temptation to become mentally lazy.

TAKING ACTION FOR HEALTHY MENTAL FUNCTION

1. Be intentional about improving your memory. Engage in mental exercises.

2. Use memory crutches as you need them.

3. Continue to work at improving your memory all your life.

CHAPTER 5

How Healthy Is Your Brain?

Can the brain be healthier than the body?

In a few cases this is possible—the brain *can* seem to function better than the body when it comes to some of the muscle-deteriorating diseases. As a general rule, however, the health of the body greatly impacts the functioning of the brain. In fact, in the vast majority of cases, the brain cannot be healthier than the body.

Your being functions as a whole. The brain and body share the same bloodstream and the same flow of nutrients. They function *together* in intricate ways we are just now beginning to understand more fully. If the heart isn't pumping efficiently, or if the lungs aren't working properly, the flow of blood and oxygen to the brain may be compromised. If electrolytes, minerals, nutrients, and metabolites are not kept at optimal levels, brain function can be diminished.

The hormones secreted by the endocrine glands—pituitary, adrenals, thyroid, parathyroid, and pancreas—all play a vital role in brain function. One of the most frequent alterations in brain function is the result of a hormone imbalance causing blood sugar imbalances (produced by variations in the insulin secretion of the pancreas).

To accurately address brain health, therefore, we need to address general health. The healthier the body as a whole, the healthier the brain tends to be.

For this reason, I want to lay a foundation of general health principles that are *vital* to strong brain functioning.

10 Strategies for General Health and Well-Being

In all of my books and writings for the past twenty years, I have emphasized a balanced, scientifically based, as well as Biblically based, approach to health. My top ten strategies for improved general health are summarized below:

1. Drink Lots of Pure Water. Water is the greatest of all "health potions." Be sure to place the emphasis on *pure*, which is generally distilled or water purified by a reverse osmosis process. You must have a pure source of water, not only for drinking but for cooking and bathing.

Most people do not begin to drink enough pure water. You need to be drinking one half the number of *ounces* of pure water based upon your body weight in pounds. In other words, if your body weight is 160 pounds, you need to be drinking 80 ounces of water a day. (That's ten cups—or two and a half quarts of water.) It may sound like a lot, but it's what your body needs to rid itself of toxins, keep the bloodstream and tissues hydrated, and keep the digestive tract and excretory systems functioning to their maximum levels.

Make sure to eliminate all chlorine and fluoride from your life. Find out if your community water system uses these substances—if so, find another source of water or invest in purification systems that directly target these chemicals. You may call our office for more information about water purification systems 1-800-726-1834. (There's more on fluoride later in this book.)

2. Take in Sufficient Fiber. Most of your fiber intake should be in the form of raw, fresh fruit and raw, fresh, or lightly steamed vegetables. Whole grains (if you are not attempting to lose weight) and bran are good sources of fiber.

I recommend a balance of fruits and vegetables, with a concentration on the leafy green vegetables (spinach, lettuce, other greens), as well as broccoli, cauliflower, and squash. Steam your vegetables or eat them fresh in a "salad" form for maximum nutrients.

Dried fruits, such as dates or figs, add substantial amounts of potassium, calcium, and phosphorus to the diet, as well as magnesium, iron, and zinc, but they contain very little vitamin C and are often high in sugar. Cantaloupe has a high amount of vitamins A, C, and folic acid. Oranges and other citrus fruits have adequate amounts of A, C, folic acid, as well as potassium, calcium, phosphorus, and magnesium. In general, fresh fruits are high in vitamins and low in minerals—dried fruits tend to be a rich source of minerals but are low in vitamins.

Canned vegetables, as well as soups, can be very high in sodium. Choose fresh instead.

3. Take a Daily Dose of Essential Fat. It is critically important that you cut out the *negative* fats from your diet—which are the trans fats, hydrogenated and partially hydrogenated oils, vegetable shortening, vegetable fat, and margarine products that are an ingredient in so many processed foods. By all means, do not eat Olestra(r) or other "fake fat" products. Read my book *Maximum Energy* for more details.

At the same time, you need to make certain that you are taking in the right kinds and amounts of essential fats to fuel both body and brain functions. There's much more about these *essential* fats later in this book.

4. Exercise Regularly. Develop a balance of aerobic exercise (walking, cycling, swimming), strength-building exercise (weights), and flexibility exercises (stretches). Exercise at least four times a week for forty-five minutes, and if you are trying to lose fat from your body, exercise daily until you are at your ideal weight. For more information on exercise or to obtain a copy of my exercise videos, call my office: 1-800-726-1834.

5. Don't Eat High-Fat Luncheon Meats. These are primarily pork products—bacon, ham, bologna, salami, hot dogs, pepperoni, and so forth. These foods not only are high in fat but high in nitrites, extremely dangerous substance for the body. One study from the University of Southern California has shown that if a child eats only twelve hot dogs a month, he can develop seven times the risk of leukemia!

Also trim fat from all beef and poultry (including removal of chicken skin). Limit your intake of beef and make sure your beef products are "extra lean" with less than ten percent fat.

Here's my general advice about protein: Consume about 30 percent of your calories in high-quality protein that is low in fat. Salmon, cod, and trout are perhaps the best animal proteins because they include essential omega-3 fatty acids.

If you are eating poultry, go for organic turkey breast or organic skinless chicken. Chickens raised on an algae-based chicken feed called "DHA Gold" have five to seven times the DHA (an essential omega-3 fatty acid) of normal chickens—look for this in stores that sell organic, range-fed chicken; it should appear on the label. Eggs from chickens fed this mix are also higher in DHA.

Limit your intake of eggs, but do not necessarily eliminate eggs. Eggs are a rich source of lecithin (an important phospholipid) as well as cholesterol—one fourth of the fat in brain cell myelin (the sheath around brain cells) is cholesterol.

Incorporate more legumes and soy products into your diet to reduce your dependence upon meat and dairy products for protein.

Keep in mind that the building blocks of proteins are amino acids. Not all amino acids have equal effects on the brain. Tryptophan and tyrosine are the most important amino acids that relate to our ability to concentrate and remain alert.

6. Don't Eat Shellfish. Shellfish tends to be loaded with toxins-after all, these creatures were intended to "clean" the earth's waterways. What *they* eat from the bottom of oceans and rivers should *not* be what you eat! Shellfish can be high in arsenic, lead, and mercury.

7. Don't Eat High-Sugar Junk Foods. Your pancreas will thank you. An over-stimulated insulin-producing system results, ultimately, in an overall exhaustion of the body, which in turn makes healing very difficult and degenerative diseases much more likely.

Drink fruit juice in every limited quantities. It is very high in sugar. And avoid sugar-laden soft drinks. They can cause an insulin secretion problem that can impact brain function.

When it comes to carbohydrate intake, keep in mind always that complex carbohydrates break down slower in the body than simple sugars. The slower breakdown results in a more even release of insulin, which keeps a person from experiencing "sugar highs" and the "bottoming out" feeling that often produces general feelings of anxiety. Starches present in whole-grain cereal products, root vegetables, and beans are also slower to metabolize for a more even release of insulin.

8. Don't Eat High-Fat Dairy Products. Choose nonfat milk, yogurt, cottage cheese, cheese, and other milk-related products as a good source of protein.

Milk products provide substantial amounts of protein, vitamin A, some B vitamins, and a substantial amount of electrolytes and minerals, especially calcium.

Be aware that cheese is not only high in fat content, but it also has a lot of sodium. A diet rich in cheese can elevate blood pressure. Many cheeses, as well as red wine, are high in "amines," which have been linked to severe headaches and construction of blood vessels in the brain.

The exception to my no-fat dairy rule is for children under the age of two. For that age group, I recommend raw certified goats milk, which is an excellent nutrient source.

9. Don't Drink or Take "Mood-Altering Substances"—Including Alcohol, Sugar-Free Sodas, and Caffeine. Substances that hype you up or mellow you out are nearly always addictive. Certainly the ones cited later in this book—alcohol, sugar-free sodas, and caffeine—are all highly addictive substances. (Yes, diet sodas are addictive—ask any person who has consumed a great many of them and then tries to quit drinking them.) A number of other drugs, herbs, and medications also have an addictive quality—for example, cigarettes, cocaine, and ephedrine. *None* of these substances promotes health! When it comes to their use, I can sum up my advice in one word: "never."

In the long run, these products not only produce no *positive* net effect for the body, but rather, they can produce great harm. I am especially concerned about the vast quantity of sugar-free sodas that are consumed by the American public. These sodas and other sugar-free products are nearly always made with aspartame (NutraSweet® or Equal®) which has been linked to some of the most vile and deadly diseases a person can experience, including brain cancer. (There's more on this later.)

10. Find a Way to Deal with Stress. We all experience stress —which means, we all must find a way of dealing with stress.

Exercise, as noted above, is an excellent means of de-stressing the *body*. Meditation, prayer, and other mental and spiritual activities can help a person de-stress the *mind*.

In many cases, dealing with stress involves the establishment of new priorities and the development of new habits. Only you can decide to make the changes that will result in greater health and an improved quality of life. I encourage you—make those changes!

A Foundation for Healthy Memory. These general health principles—along with proper supplementation—lay the foundation for healthy mental functioning, including a healthy memory and a sound ability to think rationally and make wise decisions. Any person who has ever built a house knows that a house cannot be structurally sound if the foundation is cracked or flawed in some other way. The same is true for brain health.

It is equally true, however, that a house can have a good foundation and still have other structural problems depending upon how the house has been built upon the foundation. So, too, with the brain. A general foundation of good health is not enough. We also need to address specifically those issues that are important for good brain function.

Are You Truly the Master of Your Life?

Are you truly the master of your own fate?

Not unless you have adequate brain power.

Many people in nursing homes are not there because they have abused their bodies, been drug addicts or alcoholics, or have failed to exercise. Many in nursing homes have physically survived heart attacks and cancer—some have survived strokes. A few have had major surgeries, broken hips, or even missing limbs.

Nearly all of them, however, have impairment in cognitive functioning and memory.

It is only when we have a fully functioning brain that we have an opportunity to control and influence the environment around us. In fact, the degree of control we have over our lives is directly proportional to the talents, skills, and abilities that are developed in the brain over a lifetime.

A healthy mind is one that is able to process, use, and remember information. It is a mind that is able to reason and relate new information to previously acquired information.

Consider the general health of your body to be a *general* goal. Once the general health of the body has been established, the health of your brain becomes a *targeted* goal.

Our Amazing Brains

Most of us spend too much time thinking *with* our brains to think much *about* them. Even so, our brains are one of the most awesome, complex, challenging, and interesting things any of us can think about!

Every day, the brain orchestrates trillions of activities, all beneath our level of consciousness. It is the brain that allows us to organize, catalog, and recall vast amounts of information and to contemplate the *meaning* of that information. It is our brains that allow our bodies to function with full power, endurance, and agility. It is our brains that coordinate all biochemical, neurological, muscular, cardiovascular, and digestive systems of our body so we can experience energy, vitality, and strength. It is our brains that give us the ability to love, laugh, cry, and then talk about how we feel.

The basic functions of a healthy brain are determined by four factors

- the physical structure of the brain and its chemistry
- the information received by the brain from the outside world and the rest of the body

- information stored from past experience
- associations made between the present and past information

This is certainly not a brain anatomy book, but I believe it may be helpful for you to understand in very simple terms several structures in the brain. Please bear with me—I need to cover this material in the beginning of our discussion on brain health so the rest of the book will be easier to follow.

Neurons. Neurons are the real work horses of nerve communication in the brain. These cells are specialized to send information through a vast network to control bodily functions. Some of these nerves are extremely long—in fact, they reach from the brain to the foot. Others are a small fraction of an inch in length.

Each neuron is surrounded by a membrane that is made of fatty material. This material is actually two layers of fatty molecules (phospholipids) that almost seem to "float" around the nerve cell.

Myelin. Many nerve fibers are surrounded by a shiny-white substance called myelin. Myelin functions to speed the transmission of nerve impulses. It is made of various fats, fatty acids, phospholipids, cholesterol, and protein. Seventy-five percent of myelin comes from fat. The formation of myelin is highly dependent upon dietary fatty acids.

Nodes are located along the myelinated nerves in regular patterns. These nodes aid the speed of transmission of an electrical impulse along the nerve. When myelin is damaged, the speed of nerve conduction slows. (MS is perhaps the best-known disease that impacts the myelin sheath surrounding nerves.)

There are certain critical windows of time during a child's development when nerve fibers must be "myelinated." If the body is missing the right nutrients and does not have the right stimulation at these key periods, overall intelligence tends to be lowered.

A Branching Network. One of the most amazing features of the brain is that it has the ability to make "new connections" based upon new experience or information. The brain forms new "branches" of nerve cells with each encounter in life. As the brain cells branch, they also form interconnections from cell to cell, which enhances the brain's ability to interpret more complex and diverse information. Over time, and given a rich source of nutrients and stimulation, the brain becomes increasingly "integrated." Neurons connect and interconnect with one another to form a vast network of connections. In its lifetime, just one neuron may make between 6,000 and 20,000 connections.

Synapses. There is a minute space where one nerve cell "connects" with another. This junction "gap" is called a synapse. Chemicals are released from one neuron, diffused through this space, and reform on the surface of the second neuron. The synapse is the real place where communication takes place. The number of synapses made by a nerve has a far greater bearing on intelligence and brain function than the number of nerve cells in the brain. And here again, fatty acids play a critical role. The delicate membrane covering the synapse space has an extremely high concentration of long-chain fatty acids. The concentration of the fatty acid DHA is higher here than almost any tissue in the body. If this environment for the synapse is low in DHA, the synapse does not "fire" with normal efficiency. Over time, the neuron may function poorly, or even die.

A single neuron can have as many as 100,000 synapses connecting it with its neighboring neurons. There may be as many as 100 billion neurons in the brain—researchers aren't exactly sure. If you multiply the number of neurons by the number of synapses, the possible connections go into the trillions. No computer comes even close to handling that many "transactions" in moments of time.

Like most cells, neurons are electrically charged. A neuron normally exists in a resting state, called "resting potential," with a slightly negative charge inside pushing against the positively charged atoms that are outside the cell. When the neuron is stimulated, the electrical charge inside the cell increases. This active charge is called the "action potential" of the neuron and the charge spreads along the cell wall until it reaches out to other cells.

Neurotransmitters. What causes neurons to begin to "fire" messages to other neurons and to build connections from one nerve cell to another? Substances called neurotransmitters are released. Neurotransmitters are usually proteins or amino acids that are released by one nerve, drift cross the synapse to interact with the next nerve, and proceed on their way—forming what might accurately be called the true "information highway."

Various neurotransmitters have been linked to specific functions. For example, we know that the neurotransmitter serotonin is crucial to normal behavior and mood. Insulin and dopamine are two other common neurotransmitters.

While neurotransmitters are *not* fats, their ability to land in the right place and trigger the right reaction is dependant upon fatty acids.

All along a nerve cell are places called "receptors." A neurotransmitter may be likened to a ship seeking the right "receptor" as a place to dock. The receptors are held in place along the nerve by phospholipds and fatty acids. If the receptor is not positioned properly, the transmitter cannot effectively unload its cargo of "the message." Communication is altered along the nerve.

There are six major neurotransmitters that help keep the brain "connected:"

- **Acetylcholine.** This neurotransmitter plays a crucial role in memory. It acts to trigger the "firing" of nerve cells for transmitting information from one cell to the next and making connections.

- **Gamma-Aminobutyric Acid (GABA).** This neurotransmitter inhibits message transmission, which is as important as transmission because it keeps nerve cells from firing too fast and thus, overloading or exhausting the brain cells. GABA and acetylcholine need to work in harmony.

- **Serotonin.** This neurotransmitter also slows down the system and is related to the brain's general state of alertness. It also helps regulate pain and mood, and helps the body to sleep, which is important for rejuvenation of cells. (Foods rich in serotonin are bananas, turkey, and potatoes. That's one of the reasons that most people who eat a big Thanksgiving dinner of turkey and mashed potatoes feel the need for a nap afterwards!)

- **Dopamine.** This chemical helps control physical movement. Parkinson's disease, which its characteristic tremors and repetitive movements, is linked to very low dopamine levels. Too much dopamine in certain areas of the brain may result in schizophrenia. (Note: Caffeine seems to derive part of its stimulating effect from interacting with the brain's dopamine levels.)

- **Norepinephrine.** This neurohormone stimulates the capillaries in the brain so more blood can flow through brain tissues. It speeds up brain activity and alertness and is found in high concentrations in the lower brain and brain stem. Very high levels of norepinephrine have been linked to mania, which is characterized by a state of extreme overstimulation.

- **Endorphins.** These neurohormones are the "feel-good" chemicals of the brain. They motivate us to *continue* acting or thinking and in this way, they facilitate mental processing.

Blood cells and blood vessels. Not only are nerves made of fatty acid molecules, but also the blood cells and blood vessels of the body. The fate of the blood supply and the fate of the brain are so closely intertwined that they develop simultaneously. If blood supply is interrupted during a critical fetal period, the corresponding portion of the brain may be negatively impacted. In an adult, the gradual loss of blood supply to the brain is one of the major causes of mental impairment.

Fatty acids impact the "spasm" mechanism of blood vessels. This spasm mechanism is vital for blood flow to remain even, and as a consequence, oxygen flow to the brain to remain even. Fatty acids also affect the viscosity, or thickness, of the blood. When blood becomes deficient in fatty acids, it may become too thick, or sludge-like. It then can form platelets that clump to help create plaque on the sides of vessel walls, a major factor in atherosclerosis or hardening of the arteries, which in turn is a major factor in strokes. When blood becomes too thick, mental functions are also impaired. [1]

How many times have you heard me say on audio tapes, or read in my printed material or books, "Take cod liver oil and flaxseed oil for essential fatty acids"? I hope you are doing so!

In more than one research study, children who had uncommonly narrow blood vessels for their age were found to have vessels very low in omega-3 fatty acids (EPA) and too high in omega-6 fatty acids (linoleic acid).[1] From very early in life, the balance between omega-3 and omega-6 oils must be achieved.

In general, we must not only be concerned with the fatty acids in the blood, but also triglyceride and cholesterol levels. Both triglycerides and cholesterol are involved in making blood more "sludge-like."

The Brain's Immune System. In addition to neurons (nerve cells), the brain has another family of cells called glial cells. One type of cell in this family is the microglia, which is part of the brain's immune system. The signals that activate the microglia are sent by chemicals called cytokines—these chemicals are strongly influenced by essential fatty acids.

The Basic Causes of Brain Decline

There are three basic causes for a diminishing of overall brain power with age.

1. The Death of Brain Cells. The first cause of brain decline is a loss that occurs because brain cells (neurons) have died. *Some* loss of neurons is inevitable. Over time, there is some shrinkage in overall brain mass. For many years, however, the medical community assumed that a loss of mental function was an automatic result of aging owing to a *vast* loss of neurons. We now know that simply *is not true.*

The death of brain cells is actually fairly minimal in *healthy* aging, and it is not likely to account for age-related impairment in memory and cognitive function.[2] Rather, factors related to *lifestyle, diet, and environment* tend to increase a person's susceptibility to developing inflammation-inducing and oxidizing conditions. These conditions, in turn, result in decreased brain function. We will address these conditions specifically in this book so you can help minimize them.

We also know that the brain has two main compensatory processes to accommodate for the loss of cells. One, the sheath around the fibers that carry nerve impulses away from the nerve cells becomes thicker with a fatty substance called myelin. This thickening begins in infancy and continues throughout life as long as brain tissue is healthy. The thickening of the myelin sheath is correlated with *increased* brain function. The myelin acts like the insulation on an electrical wire. It keeps the signal from the brain from being lost.

Two, the older a person grows, the more the fibers of the brain develop "branches." These fibers produce greater communication among the cells of the brain. Autopsies performed by a University of Rochester researcher on people sixty to ninety years old who died of causes other than brain problems showed that the neuron's "dendritic trees" kept growing longer and continued to make new connections even in old age. The better brain cells communicate with one another, the better a person is able to think and remember.

The conclusion being drawn by many scientists is that brain cells can certainly be *regenerated and renewed,* even if new brain cells cannot be created or old cells completely kept from dying. Our goal, therefore, should be to do all we can to nurture the health of myelin sheaths and the branching of brain neurons. Great nutritional support is possible for both of these processes.

2. A Shrinking of Synapses. The second cause for the decline in brain function is a shrinking of the synapses, the spaces between the neurons. This leads to a loss of conductivity among neurons. The healthier the neurons, the healthier the synapses between them. If we succeed in nurturing brain cells so they remain as healthy as possible, we automatically address this synapse shrinking problem.

3. Lower Level of Neurotransmitters. The third cause for the decline in brain function is a lower level of neurotransmitters and other important chemicals in the brain, which inhibits the encoding of memories and slows recall. Our goal should be to do all we can to maintain the neurochemicals needed for the transmission of messages from one cell to another.

"But," you may be asking at this point, "How can we develop healthy neurons and neurotransmitters?"

Neurons and neurotransmitters are damaged or destroyed by free radicals. Free radicals may be thought of as "killer" molecules that destroy both neurons and neurotransmitters.

If the oxygen supply to the brain is reduced, free radicals are produced. The main inhibitor of oxygen to the brain is smoking. Oxygen flow to the brain can also be hindered if the blood vessels that carry oxygen to the brain are significantly narrowed (by causes such as atherosclerosis or "hardening of the arteries"). Good blood flow to the brain is also important for the removal of the waste products left over after neuron activity. If these waste products remain in the brain cells, they inhibit the general activity of brain cells and eventually cause the cells to die.

All of the factors below can produce high levels of free radicals:
- Viruses
- Alcohol consumption
- Some drugs
- Stress
- Food allergies
- Toxic metals (such as lead, mercury, and cadmium)
- Trauma or injury
- Liver disease
- Toxic chemicals (benzene, toluene)
- Certain amino acids (MSG)

Excessive minerals can also lead to free radicals—most notably, excesses in iron, manganese, and copper.

In addition, intestinal imbalances, white blood cell activity, and insufficient nutrients of various types can cause free radicals.

Neurons are also damaged if they are "poisoned." The three main poisons that seem to target brain tissue are heavy metal poisoning (especially lead and mercury), aspartame poisoning (sugar-free substitute), and alcohol. We will discuss the poisoning of the brain and what action to take in Chapters 7, 8, and 9.

Please note this simple fact: The vast majority of the most potent sources of free radicals are *subject to our own behavioral control.* We can *choose* not to smoke, drink alcohol, take drugs, or drink diet soda. We can *choose* to reduce stress levels in our lives. We can *choose* to avoid toxic metal, chemical and excessive mineral consumption.

It isn't enough, however, simply to *avoid* or reduce those things that cause free radicals. The body will produce some free radicals in normal cell metabolism. We also must provide the body and brain with sufficient nutrients to fight free radicals and to promote the healthy functioning of neurons and neurotransmitters. We will discuss various categories of helpful nutrients in Chapters 3, 4, 5, and 6.

In summary, we need to

- build up the health of the neurons and neurotransmitters by taking sufficient brain-cell-building nutrients, avoiding harmful brain poisons, and taking sufficient antioxidants and essential fatty acids.
- keep oxygen flowing fully to the brain by maintaining a strong vascular system. To do this, we must not smoke, and we must do all we can to reduce arterial wall plaques.
- keep cellular by-products sufficiently transported away from the brain.

These basics involved in the development and maintenance of healthy brain tissue are where we will turn first.

1. Pesonen, E., Hirvonen, J., Karkola, K. et al. Dimensions of the coronary arteries in children. *Ann Med* 1991 (23): 95–88.

   Moilanen, T., et al. Tracking of serum fatty acid composition: a 6-year follow-up study in Finnish youths. *Am J. Epidem* 1992 (136;12): 1487–92.

2. Morrison, J.H., Hof, P.R. Life and death of neurons in the aging brain. *Science* 1997 (278): 412–419.

TAKING ACTION FOR HEALTHY BRAIN FUNCTION

1. Make a commitment today to developing the best general physical health possible.

2. Make a commitment today to do all you can to build up and maintain healthy brain cells and neurotransmitters.

CHAPTER 6

FIGHTING FREE RADICALS
USING AN
"A TO E" ARSENAL

Most people I know have an aversion to the word "radical." For those who remember the sixties, radicals were the ones who tore against the "establishment" with a vengeance, often destroying public property even as they did great damage to themselves with drugs and so-called "free" sex. For those who watch the news today, it is often the "radical" fringes that are the instigators of terrorist acts that destroy lives and property.

"Free radical" is the word used to describe rogue oxygen cells that have become "oxidized." It's an appropriate phrase. What these free radicals do in the body is to destroy tissue and devastate health. They are "free" to do their damage in much the same way a "loose cannon" is loose.

By the way, the term "loose cannon" comes from Navy history. If a wooden war ship had a loose cannon on deck and the ship hit a big wave, the cannon could become airborn and then crash through the deck, creating an "exciting moment" for those in the bottom of the ship!

Think for a moment about an apple that you might cut and leave standing on the kitchen countertop. Within a matter of minutes, it will turn brown. That's the effect of oxidation. Cells in the body suffer a fate that is not all that dissimilar when they are oxidized by these cells that have "gone bad."

A General Deterioration of the Nervous System

The scientific research consistently shows that a general degeneration of the entire nervous system, including brain tissue, is associated with"free radicals." Free radicals also directly impact the immune system and specifically, the body's ability to destroy invading bacteria, malignant cells, and chemical pollutants.

Where do free radicals come from? In very simple terms, free radicals are generated during the normal processes of cellular metabolism. They are produced in *greater amounts*, however, when any of these factors occur:

- the body's blood supply is decreased for some reason, (such as smoking or as a consequence of insufficient cardiovascular exercise),
- stress hormones are increased owing to either emotional factors or physical trauma, (such as a hard day at work),
- the body is fighting bacterial or viral infection, (such as catching a cold)
- toxins are present in the blood stream, (such as those created by drinking diet sodas or eating junk food), or
- the body has undergone radiation, (such as that used in traditional cancer therapy).

The body is generally protected against free radicals by "antioxidants." If, however, we don't have enough antioxidants in the bloodstream to counteract the free radicals, damage is inflicted at the cellular level.

Free radicals seem to target "mitochondria," which are the microscopic particles in every living cell that produce the energy required for the cell to function fully. When mitochondria are damaged, the cell as a whole not only suffers damage but it produces even more free radicals, which means that the entire process of damage escalates and becomes cyclical.

Several well-known degenerative diseases have been linked to this process:

Alzheimer's disease research has been linked to four processes: *a defect in mitochondrial energy production,* an inflammatory response to one or more brain proteins, an increased amount of brain iron or exposure to aluminum, and *ineffective antioxidant activity.*

Parkinson's disease has been linked to a *flaw in mitochonodrial energy production,* and *increased free radical enhancing brain iron.* The most important of all the nervous system antioxidants, glutathione, seems to be particularly impacted. (Inflammation is less of a factor than in Alzheimer's disease but there is evidence that in Parkinson's disease, the liver fails to detoxify various environmental toxins.)

ALS, also known as Lou Gehrig's Disease, is also being linked increasingly to *damaged mitochondria and excessive free radical production.*

One hallmark of **multiple sclerosis** is related to excessive free radical activity and its impact on myelin, the protective insulation surrounding brain neurons. A lack of antioxidants has also been linked to this disease.

What are the two central themes to these serious debilitating diseases related to the brain and nervous system?

- reduced mitochondrial energy production (caused by high levels of free radicals)
- defective antioxidant protection (in other words, antioxidants are not present in sufficient amount to counteract dangerous free radicals)

What can we do?

One, we must reduce the amount of free radicals in our body. That means reducing the amount of toxins and carcinogenic substances we take into our bodies. That, in turn, means reducing our stress level, fighting any infection that may be at work in the body, and making sure our blood cells are in proper quantity and proportion (red and white).

Two, we must introduce more antioxidants to our body. The use of antioxidants to limit the activity of free radicals has been studied extensively over the past decade. The reports are overwhelmingly positive. Antioxidants do *work* to destroy free radicals if they are taken in high enough dosages.

The Power of Vitamins to Restore Tissues

The word "vitamin" literally is short-hand for the phrase "vital mineral." We all need vitamins in adequate supply for health.

Folklore wisdom about the power of vitamins to improve brain function has abounded for decades. The latest scientific research is bearing out that folklore wisdom. Mom knew what she was doing when she said, "Eat your fruits and veggies." Grandma knew what she was saying when she advised, "An apple a day keeps the doctor away." Certain key vitamins have been shown repeatedly in countless research studies to improve memory, thinking, learning, and other cognitive functions of the brain.

Let me give you a very simply "short course" on vitamins. Vitamins are organic substances that help regulate the chemical reactions in the body to protect cells and convert food into energy and living tissues. Vitamins are divided into two groups: water-soluble and fat-soluble. The body can store fat-soluble vitamins, but water-soluble vitamins must be constantly replenished.

Many people believe that we automatically get all the vitamins and minerals they need from the food they eat, especially if we eat a "balanced" diet. That may have been true at one time, but no longer. Many minerals have been depleted from our soil. Other minerals are stripped from our foods as they are processed. Still other vitamins and minerals are destroyed in cooking. The vast majority of people do *not* get all the nutrients they need from food.

Another common misconception is that people need only the recommended daily allowances of vitamins and minerals (and electrolytes) to avoid disease and to maintain normal behavioral and brain function. Any more than the published RDA minimum and a person is thought to have taken unnecessary amounts and wasted money in the process. The scientific facts, however, say otherwise.

More than 160 diseases are directly linked to a deficiency in vitamins and minerals. Some of these diseases are major, life-threatening, highly dreaded ones, including several forms of cancer.

Not only does a deficiency in nutrients lead to physical disease, but it can lead to a "lessening" of mental function. A study published in the prestigious British medical journal, *Lancet*, reported on the *benefits of vitamin supplementation on the IQ of school children*. Ninety children aged twelve and thirteen were given either a multivitamin/mineral supplement or a placebo for six months. The supplement group showed a significant increase in nonverbal intelligence in just that short time! [1]

There are several dozen human disorders or diseases that respond to doses of vitamins that are anyplace from ten to one hundred times greater than the recommended normal dietary amounts. Genetic defects sometimes produce disorders that result in virtually *no* absorption of a specific vitamin or mineral. In some cases, megavitamin therapy to treat these disorders may be very effective. [2]

Many of the studies on vitamin and mineral supplementation have been done on people who already had schizophrenia, Alzheimer's, or some other nervous system or brain disorder. A few major studies, however, have also been done on *normal* adult subjects. In one study conducted by researchers from the National Institutes of Health, a dietary addition of only ten grams of choline a day was shown to have an obvious effect on some components of memory in *normal* subjects who had an average age of twenty-four.[3] Another study—this one with elderly patients—showed marked memory improvement in sixty percent of the people studied. (Note: Choline is classified as a metabolite rather than a vitamin because it is partially synthesized within the body.)

Key Antioxidants: Vitamins A, B, C, D, E

The vitamins that have been given the first five letters of the alphabet are among the most potent antioxidants a person can take, especially for brain function. If you're going to fight free radicals, stock up on this ammunition!

Vitamin A from Beta-Carotene

Beta-carotene is found in some fruits and dark-green and orange vegetables. Beta-carotene is not itself a vitamin—rather, it is what is converted into vitamin A in the body. After its transformation, it functions as an antioxidant, neutralizing free radicals that damage brain cells.

Many of the studies on beta-carotene have been concerned with its protective effect on the heart, skin, hair, nails, and vision. Beta-carotene has been shown to help reduce the frequency of heart attacks, stroke, lower rates of lung cancer and tumors of the throat and mouth, and to improve the function of the immune system. It promotes healing and reduces incidences of infection.

When it comes to the mind, Vitamin A protects brain-cell membranes and acts as an antioxidant against free radicals, especially free radicals from polyunsaturated fatty-acids and oxygen.

Vitamin A from beta-carotene is sometimes called pro-vitamin A—it comes primarily from plant food sources. Vitamin A in "retinal" form comes from animal foods, especially fish liver and fish-liver oils. Cod liver oil is a great source—again, I use it daily. If you have an aversion to the smell or taste of cod liver oil, you can take it in the form of an oil-based gelatin capsule.

Vegetables high in beta-carotene are spinach, broccoli, Swiss chard, collard greens, kale, carrots, sweet potatoes, winter squash, pumpkins, apricots, cantaloupes, mangoes, and papaya.

Five Servings a Day? Surely we've all heard the advice in recent years to eat five servings a day of vegetables and fruits. That's a good rule! The problem is...people don't do it. One of the reasons is that they don't like vegetables, or don't *think* they like vegetables. We all know that former president George Bush didn't like broccoli. Actually, I've met George Bush on several occasions. The next time I see him I think I'll ask him why.

One of the reasons people don't like vegetables is probably because they've only encountered vegetables that were over-cooked, undercooked, or flat out prepared badly. Many vegetables in our supermarkets have lost virtually all of their taste given the chemical washes they undergo and the fact that they are picked long before they are ripe. If you are going to eat raw vegetables, make sure you purchase top-quality, organically grown, *ripe* vegetables.

Don't overcook the vegetables you do buy. Cooking destroys most nutrients. Some vegetables may be lightly steamed, but whenever possible, eat your vegetables raw. (Processed and packaged foods have the added problem of preservatives.)

Juicing as an Alternative to Eating Your Vegetables. One way to get vegetables into the average diet is to juice them. Juicing has a number of advantages—it can be a fast and easy alternative to eating a plateful of vegetables. Juicing also helps a person get vitamins, minerals, and enzymes in the right balance—natural foods tend to work together synergistically.

The key to juicing is to buy a juicer you will actually use. And then, be willing to experiment and try new combinations. Those who regularly juice find they enjoy experimenting with unusual vegetable combinations.

A Good Veggie Drink to Boost Memory

Handful of wheatgrass
Handful of watercress
3 stalks celery
½ apple, seeded
½ handful of parsley
4 carrots, green removed
½ cup chopped fennel
1 tablespoon flax seed oil
⅓ scoop powdered multiple vitamin
and mineral mix

Bunch up the wheatgrass, parsley, and watercress. Push it through the juice hopper with carrots, celery, fennel, and apple.

"B" Stands for Brain Power

At least thirteen vitamins have been shown to have positive effects on brain function, including memory. Six of these thirteen vitamins are B vitamins—each of which plays a different role. The B vitamins are best taken as a complex, where they are formulated in balance to one another. These vitamins are water soluble, which means that for the most part they are not stored in the body for long and consequently, they need to be replenished frequently.

Vitamin B1 (Thiamine) for Energy Metabolism. The B1 vitamin, or thiamine, is a strong antioxidant that assists in energy metabolism and general nervous-system function, as well as cell repair. It seems especially effective in helping counteract the negative effects of alcohol oxidation on nerve cells. It has been used to treat organic brain dysfunctions and has been shown to contribute to better brain functioning in the healthy person.

A deficiency in B1 produces, in mild cases, the disease beriberi, which is associated with degeneration of the peripheral nerves. It is also directly related in more extreme cases to a brain disease called Wernicke's Korsakoff syndrome, which is marked by disabling memory loss. Depending on how early the B1 deficiency is discovered, the symptoms *may* be reversed by giving vitamin B1, but not in all cases.

Thiamine is found in wheat germ, rice bran, Brewers yeast, asparagus, broccoli, cauliflower, corn, brown rice and other whole-grain cereals, soybeans, split peas, lima beans, cashews, eggs, dried prunes and raisins, and sunflower seeds.

Most people need between 25 and 100 mg daily. Doses up to 1,000 mg have been taken by people to give an energy lift, but prolonged use of high doses can disrupt the B balance and cause deficiencies in other B vitamins.

Vitamin B3 (Niacin). Vitamin B3, or niacin, helps improve memory and protect against stress. It improves the oxygen-carrying ability of red blood cells and it also has been shown to reduce blood clotting, which can cause strokes and heart attacks and interfere with brain functioning.

A deficiency in B3, which may be taken in the form of niacin, produces the mental symptoms of dementia in a disease called pellagra. In times past, pellagra was one of the two most common diseases that caused people to be admitted to mental hospitals (the other was syphilis of the brain). B3 is chemically very closely related to tryptophan, an amino acid essential for normal brain function. Tryptophan, in turn, is related to the production of serotonin, an important neurotransmitter in the brain.

Niacin can cause flushing, itching, and skin tingling when it is taken in doses larger than 50 mg—this is not dangerous, but can be annoying and even "alarming" if a person is not aware of the cause of these symptoms. The niacin effect can be reduced by taking an aspirin one hour before taking niacin. People with diabetes and high blood pressure should consult a physician before using niacin in large doses.

Niacin is found in high-protein foods such as meat, eggs, and protein-enriched cereals. Normal dosage is 18 mg a day for men and 3 mg a day for women.

Vitamin B5. Vitamin B5, or pantothenic acid, is a powerful antioxidant known for helping reduce stress and increase stamina. Vitamin B5 is essential for converting choline to acetylcholine, a neurotransmitter.

When taking vitamin B5 apart from a complex formula, it is best to start with very small doses and work up to larger ones, taking the vitamin three or four times a day. Staring with large doses can cause short-term diarrhea.

Vitamin B5, by the way, is the substance in royal jelly that extends the life of the queen bee beyond that of the worker bees—royal jelly in the diet has significantly extended the life of certain lab animals. (There's more about this amazing substance in a later chapter.)

Vitamin B6. Vitamin B6, or pyridoxine, is often called the "antistress" vitamin. It is essential for the production of the neurotransmitters serotonin, dopamine, and norepinephrine. Vitamin B6 is a key substance in protein metabolism. A deficiency can lead to depression and increased risk of cardiovascular disease. A severe deficiency can also lead to seizures.

This vitamin is found in meat, fish, nuts, bananas, potatoes, bran, and dairy products. The recommended dosage is 2 mg for men and 1 to 6 mg for women. High doses should never be taken without a physician's supervision—a high dosage can cause central-nervous-system symptoms. (People with Parkinson's disease taking L-Dopa should always consult a physician before using B6.)

Vitamin B12. Vitamin B12, or cyanocobalamin, helps release energy in foods and is often used by athletes to boost their performance. It is an essential growth factor for maintenance of the brain and nerves. B12 plays an important role in the formation of the myelin sheath around nerve fibers in the brain.

Rats given B12 were shown to learn faster. Deficiencies in this vitamin have been linked to both senile dementia and schizophrenia.

When the brain is deficient in B12, confusion, depression, mental slowness, memory difficulties, and abnormalities of nerve function all appear in greater frequency. Several studies have also demonstrated that Alzheimer's patients have significantly lower blood levels of B12. [4]

A lack of folate and this vitamin produces pernicious anemia, which results in an increase in the size of the red blood cells. This condition affects the brain indirectly by reducing the number of red blood cells that transport oxygen. It affects the brain directly by causing a degenerative disease of the spinal cord. This disease, in turn, causes a person to lose the sensation of where his or her limbs are in space. It can cause profound muscle weakness even to the point of spastic muscles.

Vitamin B 12 is also considered to be an antistress agent and is effective in combating fatigue. Vitamin B12—along with B6, B5, and folic acid—has also been shown to prevent the accumulation of damaging homocysteine in the brain.

Vegetarians may fail to get enough B12 because it is not found in plants—only in beef, fish, chicken, and dairy products. B12 is available in sublingual form, as a nasal spray, and by injection. The typical dose is 1 mg a day.

The drug Dilantin depletes B12 so people using it should consult a physician about taking B12 supplements.

Folic Acid. Folic acid is technically Vitamin B9 although it is rarely called that. Folic acid levels are often greatly decreased in patients suffering from dementia or "confusion." Deficiency of folic acid has also been associated with apathy, disorientation, memory deficits, and difficulties with concentration.

Like B12, folic acid seems to help lower the blood vessel damaging effects of the amino acid homocysteine. [5]

The Amazing Vitamin C

Vitamin C, or ascorbic acid, is a strong antioxidant and a substance used in manufacturing both neurotransmitters and nerve cells.

A great deal of research has been done on this vitamin and its protective qualities are numerous. It stimulates the immune system, promotes faster wound healing, reduces cholesterol, is a powerful detoxifier for many pollutants, protects against heart and blood diseases, reduces anxiety, is a natural antihistamine, and promotes sleep. Wow!

In the brain, vitamin C increases mental alertness and functioning in a variety of ways. Not only is it a powerful antioxidant, but it has a "cleaning action" in the cerebrospinal fluids surrounding the brain and spinal cord.

Vitamin C also contributes to the proper production and release of several important neurotransmitters, especially dopamine and norepinephrine. Studies have linked it to increased mental thinking ability and intelligence. Double wow!

In one study, patients in a British hospital who were experiencing mental confusion were given vitamin C supplements to great advantage. In another study, students' scores were five points higher on IQ tests after receiving higher doses of vitamin C.

The body is dependent on outside sources for vitamin C. A dose of 1,000 to 5,000 mg a day is recommended. I personally take 5,000 mg a day.

Foods rich in vitamin C include broccoli, spinach, kale, Brussels sprouts, cabbage, mustard greens, and collard greens, citrus fruits (such as oranges and grapefruit), kiwifruit, pineapples, mangoes, and papaya.

Supplements are available in a number of forms, including powder, regular and time-release tablets, and chewable tablets. An advantage of using the bulk powder is the inexpensive price—on the flip side, the powder is difficult to store because ascorbic acid oxidizes when exposed to air. Powdered vitamin C is usually a good alternative for those with sensitive stomachs. A liquid of vitamin C can be used as a lemon or vinegar substitute—try it on fish, vegetables, or salads.

Supplements usually are prepared with ascorbic acid, but less acidic preparations are also available using calcium ascorbate or sodium ascorbate. I use an ascorbate product.

Researchers have found that a group of compounds called rutins and bioflavonoids (vitamin P) are produced along with vitamin C in nature and increase the effectiveness of vitamin C. I recommend you look for a vitamin C product that has "with bioflavonoids" on the label.

It is highly unlikely that any person will ever "overdose" on vitamin C. You can find your body's optimum dosage of vitamin C by starting with 1,000 mg a day and adding 500 mg every few days until you experience mild gastritis, gas, or diarrhea. At that dosage, drop back 500 mg and you are likely to be at your optimum level for your body. Keep in mind that *your* body needs extra vitamin C when it is fighting a bacterial infection or virus.

Vitamin D JoinsThe Antioxidants

Vitamin D was once thought to be beneficial primarily in preserving bone density. Now, however, it is being shown to be a profound antioxidant. Vitamin D is fat soluble, making it an ideal candidate to help protect the brain from free radical scavengers. In one Japanese study, eighty percent of the Alzheimer's patients studied were found to have severe vitamin D deficiencies. [6]

Vitamin E Is the Antioxidant Star

The most widely studied and perhaps the most potent of all antioxidant vitamins is vitamin E. It is a very important substance for good brain function. A deficiency in this vitamin can lead to a number of brain and nervous system symptoms, including abnormal reflexes, a loss of pain and touch sensation, muscle weakness, movement and balance problems, vision problems, and impotency.

Vitamin E is a *fat-soluble* vitamin. The brain is more than sixty percent fat, and it is the fat component of the brain that is at highest risk for free radical damage. Vitamin E becomes part of the cell layers of the neuron membrane and there, it does its vital work against free radicals. [6]

The simple fat-soluble antioxidant vitamin E has been reported in The New England Journal of Medicine to be more effective in Alzheimer's disease than *any* pharmaceutical agent! [7] In this study patients were given vitamin E, selegeline (a so-called "Alzheimer's drug"), or a placebo for two years. The data was compiled into three categories: loss of ability to perform activities of self-care, severe dementia, and death. The group taking vitamin E did best in all areas of longevity and cognitive function—*better than the prescription medication.*

Vitamin E also seems to protect essential fatty acids from being rendered less effective by oxidation. [8]

Foods rich in vitamin E are oils of nuts, seeds, and soybeans, fresh wheat germ and what germ oil, whole grains, and eggs. It is also

> ## An Antioxidant-Rich Brain Boosting Snack
>
> Blend until smooth a cup of cashew nuts and a freshly juiced apple. Chill the mixture until it thickens. Spread on whole-wheat crackers and serve.

concentrated in dark leafy vegetables such as broccoli, Brussels sprouts, asparagus, and cabbage.

Vitamin E supplements come in both natural and synthetic forms. Always look for the natural form—the vast majority of studies showing benefits from vitamin E used the natural form. Look for the letter D, as in d-alpha-tocopherol. This type of vitamin E is made from plants. Avoid vitamin E that has the letter L in it—as in dl-alpha-tocopherol. Let that L to stand for"lousy." Dl-alpha-tocopherol is usually a derivative of petroleum products.

Vitamin E is usually taken in capsule form. I recommend 400–1600 IU a day. Some concern has been shown with doses higher than 1,600 IU. People with high blood pressure, overactive thyroid, heart damage from rheumatic fever should consult a physician before taking high doses of vitamin E. I personally have taken 1600 IU daily for about twenty years.

The Synergistic Effect with Selenium. Vitamin E works with other vitamins and substances to increase mental power. Its effectiveness seems to be increased especially by the mineral selenium, a trace element. In fact, taking selenium with vitamin E can increase antibodies thirty-fold!

Selenium is a powerful antioxidant in its own right and it has been shown to be very effective in deactivating free radicals. It is also a great substance for helping the body resist disease. Selenium detoxifies heavy metals, especially lead, mercury, arsenic, and cadmium.

Foods rich in selenium include Brewer's yeast, whole-grain breads and cereals (especially oats), wheat germ, bran, and barley—this is especially true if these foods are grown in a selenium-rich soil. Herring, organ meats such as liver and kidney, butter, cheddar cheese, molasses, garlic, and eggs are also rich in selenium.

Selenium supplements are also available. The suggested dose is 100 to 300 micrograms (mcg) a day. There is some debate over higher dosages so I recommend that you stay within this limit. Seek out chelated or colodial selenium, which is higher in nutritional value and more easily absorbed by the body.

The Synergistic Effect with Alpha Lipoic Acid. Alpha lipoic acid, one of the new breed of antioxidants, has a powerful effect against free radicals and it also increases the effectiveness (of vitamins C and E in the brain.) Many people, including me, take alpha lipoic acid in the form of flax seed oil. It is very important to take vitamin E any time you are supplementing the diet with essential fatty acids (whether flax oil or fish oil capsules) to get maximum benefit from both the vitamin E and the fatty acid. [9]

Foods Rich
in Antioxidants

Below is a list of twenty-five foods that are especially rich in antioxidants E, C, and beta-carotene. My advice to you: Eat them! Choose them and consume them regularly and in generous quantities.

Apricots (dried)
Broccoli
Brussels sprouts
Cantaloupe
Carrots (cooked or raw)
Cauliflower
Cereal grass*
Chlorella*
Currents (fresh)
Grapefruit
Kale (raw)
Kiwifruit

Mango
Olive Oil
Oranges (fresh or juiced)
Papaya
Peppers (green and hot)
Pumpkin Seeds
Spinach (cooked or raw)
Sunflower Seeds
Sweet potatoes
Tomato
Wheat germ
Yellow squash

*You will probably only find this in a nutrition store. Most of the other products are likely to be found in supermarkets.

1. Benton, D., and Roberts, G. Effects of vitamin and mineral supplements on intelligence of a sample of school children. *Lancet* 1998 (8578;1): 140–143.

2. Potter, V.A., Orfali, S., Scott, G.G. *Brain Boosters.* Berkeley, CA: Ronin Publishing, 1993: 141–147.

3. Sitaram, N., Weingartner, H., and Gillin, J.C. "Choline Chloride and Acetylcholine: Effects on Memory and Sleep in Man," found in Wurtman, R., and Wurtman, J., eds. *Nutrition and the Brain,* New York: Raven Press, 1977, vol. 5: 367 ff.

4. Clarke, R., Smith, A.d., Jobst, K.A., et al. Folate, vitamin B, and serum total homocysteine levels in confirmed Alzheimer's disease. *Arch Neurol* 1998 (55): 1449–55.

5. Stao, Y., Asoh, T., Oizumi, K. High prevalence of vitamin D deficiency and reduced bone mass in elderly women with Alzheimer's disease. *Bone* 1998 (23;6): 555–557.

6. Sokol, R.J. Vitamin E deficiency and neurologic disease. *Ann Rev Nutr* 1988(8): 351–73.

7. Sano, M., Ernesto, C., Thomas, R.G., et al. A controlled trial of selegeline, alpha-tocopherol, or both as treatment for Alzheimer's disease. *N. England Journal of Medicine* 1997 (336): 1216–22.

8. Sano, M., Ernesto, C., Thomas, R.G., et al. A controlled trial of selegeline, alpha-tocopherol, or both as treatment for Alzheimer's disease. *N England J Med* 1997 (336): 1216–22.

9. Laganiere, S., Fernandes, G. High peroxidizability of subcellular membrane induced by high fish oil diet is reversed by vitamin E. *Clin Res* 1987(35;3): 565A.

For more information about all of these vitamins, call my office at 1-800-726-1834.

TAKING ACTION FOR HEALTHY BRAIN FUNCTION

1. Regularly eat foods rich in antioxidants.

2. Take antioxidant vitamin supplementation, especially vitamins A, B complex, C, and E. Here are my recommendations:

   - A   10,000 IU (cod liver oil)
   - D   400 IU (mallyce)
   - E   400-800 IU for women; 1600 IU for men
   - C   5,000 mg
   - Two capsules of a high-potency "Homocysteine Balanced" B vitamin complex.

   We have a special "memory pack" of high-quality vitamins and minerals.
   Call **1-800-726-1834**.

CHAPTER 7

IT'S TRUE!
YOUR BRAIN IS
MOSTLY FAT

Most people are surprised to learn that the brain is composed of millions of fibers woven into a tapestry that is sixty percent *fat*.

Having a balance in the brain of the "right" fats and oils is vital to good brain health and to keeping all brain functions at peak performance, including memory. To a great extent, the fat you put in your mouth has a profound influence on how well you think and remember. Perhaps more than any other nutrient, dietary fat has the power to influence who we *are*, not only physically, but intellectually and psychologically. Dietary fats and oils impact learning, intelligence, memory, mood, behavior, sensation, movement, and coordination.

Two Great Errors
about Dietary Fat

Two great errors are made when it comes to fat. Both of these statements below are important:

- Too much fat, in whatever form, can lead to disease.

- Too little fat, in whatever form, can lead to disease.

The kind of fats we eat, and the balance of fats, are critical to health of the overall body, and especially to the brain. The real question is not, "Fat or no fat?" but, "what kinds of fat in what amounts?"

The brain is very particular about the kinds of fat it chooses to use in constructing its own elaborate system of neural fibers. Stated very simply, if the right fats are not supplied to the brain, brain structure is altered, and if brain structure is changed, function changes.

It is ironic that Americans today are consuming more fat than ever—in fact, over the last one hundred years, the percentage of fat we consume in the average diet has more than doubled. Not only has the amount of fat increased, but the type of fat we are consuming has changed. We are consuming vast amounts of hydrogenated and saturated fats in processed foods. At the same time, the amount of necessary "brain fats" we consume has declined by more than eighty percent! [1]

We Need Some Cholesterol. Cholesterol has taken a serious rap in recent years, but cholesterol is used to make certain hormones, without which the body becomes diseased. Cholesterol, in fact, is required for nerve cell membranes. It is an important source of fuel for cells. It helps the body combat inflammation, clot the blood, contract and relax blood vessels, and build the immune system.

Good Fats and Bad Fats

Many people are confused as to which fats are "good" for them and which are bad. Let me provide a very easy overview of fat.

All fats are made of carbon and hydrogen molecules, with one or two molecules of oxygen. Fats that have a carbon atom linked to a hydrogen atom at all possible positions are called **saturated**—the carbon atom is saturated, or filled with hydrogen.

If two carbon atoms are double-bonded to each other, each has one less hydrogen and the fat is called **unsaturated**.

Saturated fats are solid at room temperature. They include the fats from animal products: beef, lamb, and some dairy products. Unsaturated fats are mostly from plant sources and are liquid at room temperature—they are more commonly called oils. Some fish and other sea creatures have high amounts of unsaturated fatty acids in them.

The two main categories of unsaturated fatty acids that we are concerned about are referred to as omega-6 and omega-3 fatty acids. The "omega" factor refers to where the fatty acid has its first double bond—at either the sixth carbon from the end of the chain or the third carbon molecule from the end of the chain. Linoleic acid (LA), gamma-linolenic acid (GLA), and arachidonic acid (AA) are all omega-6 fatty acids. Alpha-linolenic acid (ALA), eicosapentaenoic acid (EPA), and docosahexaenoic acid (DHA) are all omega-3 fatty acids.

What is important is that we have about a one-to-one (1:1) ratio of omega-6 to omega-3 fatty acids in our bodies. This appears to be the ideal ratio for brain function. The average ratio today, however, appears to be from 20:1 to 30:1. We have far more omega-6 fatty acids...or stated another way, we have a deficit of omega-3 fatty acids.

There are several reasons behind this imbalance in our Western diet:

- an increased consumption of oils that are deficient in omega-3 (more corn, sunflower, and sesame oil)
- a loss of cereal germ in the diet owing to modern refining processes for grain (it's the germ that contains the fatty acids in grains)
- a great increase in the amount of sugar in our diet (which interferes with enzymes of fatty acid synthesis

(some estimate as much as a 250 percent increase in sugar in the last seventy-five years)

- hydrogenation of oils in commercial processing
- decreased consumption of fish
- a great increase in the percentage of trans fatty acids we eat (which interferes with fatty acid synthesis—some estimate that we've increased these harmful fats by 2500 percent!)

Avoiding the Worst of All Fats—"Trans fats"

Trans fatty acids are "altered fats." They are formed when any unsaturated oil is heated for a long period (such as in deep frying). They are also formed as a result of the hydrogenation process used in making margarine, shortening, and other products. [2]

Anything that contains "partially hydrogenated fat" contains trans fatty acids. Deep-fried foods as well as many packaged and prepared foods have trans fats.

One of the best things you can do for your general health *and* your brain health is to check the labels on the food products you purchase. If you read "partially hydrogenated," don't put that item in your grocery cart. In my book, *Maximum Energy*, I list with detailed explanations the top ten foods never to eat. Hydrogenated fats are #4 on the list!

Parents, it is helpful to know enough about fats so you can tell your child *why* you are refusing to purchase certain items for them, such as packages of cookies, cereals, and chips. You don't need to be a chemistry expert. Letting your child know that saturated fats and especially hydrogenated "trans fats" are bad for them is sufficient.

Not only do these fats have *NO* nutritional value, but they pose a special threat to the brain. Trans fats tend to become "lodged" within cell membranes of various organs, and in the brain, this is particularly dangerous because trans fatty acid tend to reside where the beneficial omega-3 fatty acid DHA normally resides in brain membranes. [3] Not only that, but trans fatty acids can block the enzymes needed to manufacture DHA. Brain metabolism can be seriously effected.

When high trans fatty acids are found and the omega-3 fatty acids are low, the trans fats seem to be *double* in the brain. [4]

No person should ever eat foods containing trans fats, but especially pregnant and nursing mothers, those with brain and nervous system diseases, those with heart and blood vessel disorders, those with learning, mood, and behavioral disorders, toddlers and small children, the elderly, and any person who requires peak mental performance in his or her job. Actually, as far as I'm concerned, that pretty much says EVERYBODY!

What foods are high in trans fatty acids? Below is a "short list:"

French fries	Deep fried chicken nuggets
Puffed cheese snacks	Margarine
Corn chips	Salad dressing (other than olive
Tortilla chips	oil and vinegar)
Peanut butter (major	Deep fried mushrooms, and
brands)	other deep-fried vegetables
Potato chips	and "cheese" bits
Mayonnaise	Cake
Cookies	Candy
Deep fried fish burgers	Shortening
Doughnuts	

I realize this may sound like "basics" in the America diet. Well...yes. Sad, but true. We are consuming vast amounts of the very fats that not only destroy our bodies but destroy our brain power!

The simple fact is that your body and brain do not NEED any of these foods.

"But what can I use," you may be asking, "for salad dressing?" Use olive oil and apple cider vinegar. Olive oil is high in omega-9 fatty acid oleic acid, which only has one double bond—it is a very stable oil and does not easily form trans fatty acids. Hazelnut oil is also good for salads.

What's the Best Alternative to Margarine? Butter is rich in saturated fat and contains no omega-3 fatty acids. In my opinion, however, butter is better to use than margarine because of the trans fatty acids in margarine. Keep butter intake to a minimum and choose organic butter whenever possible to avoid the antibiotics and growth hormones often used in commercial animal husbandry. If you are using butter, make sure you have a daily dose of essential fatty acids rich in omega-3.

Some people enjoy mixing equal parts of softened butter with olive oil. This cuts down on the amount of butter needed. Flax oil can also be used with butter. Mix only the amount you need since flax oil quickly becomes rancid if it is not refrigerated.

What Can Be Done? If you have had a diet rich in trans fats, there's still hope. Cells are replaced on a regular basis in the body. Over time, if you stop eating foods high in trans fats and supply your body with ample amounts of essential fatty acids, you will gradually replace the membranes of the brain where trans fats have become lodged.

In summary, if you want a brain that functions to its full potential and a memory that lasts a lifetime, you are going to have to pay close attention to dietary fat.

Oil Do's and Don'ts

Let me give you some very quick and easy do's and don't when it comes to buying oils.

The major DO regarding oil is that it be FRESH. Most of us know that fats can go rancid over time, generally because they are exposed to oxygen. Can the brain, which is sixty percent fat and also the most oxygen-hungry tissue in the body, go rancid? It's a valid question! The answer may very well be "yes."

The first oils to go rancid are those that are polyunsaturated. DHA is the most unsaturated fatty acid in the body.

In order to keep your oils from going rancid, I advise:

- DO buy oil in small quantities—avoid the "giant size" containers. Make sure the oil is in a dark container.

- DO refrigerate oils.

- DO smell an oil before using it—discard it if there is any hint of rancidity. If in doubt, put a bit of the oil on the tip of your finger and taste it. If the oil has a bitter taste, discard it.

- DO make sure oils are kept tightly capped.

DON'T heat an oil to the point of smoking. Smoke from overheated oils is highly carcinogenic—it is dangerous to breathe the vapors. Rather than "fry" foods, place a small amount of water in the pan or skillet and heat it until just below boiling. Add the food you desire and sauté it. As the food becomes cooked, add a very small amount of oil. This method shortens the time the oil is in contact with the heat, yet it preserves the flavor of the food.

DON'T reuse an oil that has been heated to high temperatures. Throw it out.

DON'T eat anything deep-fried in fast-food restaurants.

I also recommend that whenever possible, get your oils from whole foods. This means eating fish, walnuts, flax seed meal, sesame seeds, and other products rich in essential fatty acids.

I recommend that you choose organic, cold-pressed, extra virgin, "unrefined" oils. Organic products do not contain the chemicals applied in the growing process, which commonly concentrate in the oil portion of plants and animals. Unrefined oils are cold-processed, expeller pressed oils. Check the label on the oil. It should indicate the temperature at which the oil was processed—ideally this should be no higher than 100 degrees Fahrenheit. Refined oils, in contrast, are commonly gained from toxic solvents and are processed at temperatures above 400 degrees Fahrenheit.

Oils and Body Fat

One of the things I've noticed as I have traveled is that the types of fats used by various cultures tend to be reflected in the rate of obesity in that culture. During a research trip to Greece, Egypt, and Israel, I noticed that I saw very few overweight people. I believe that's directly related to the Mediterranean diet these people eat—and especially so in Egypt and Israel where, primarily for religious reasons, the people do not eat a lot of red meat and no pork products, and they eat very little bread that is not whole-grain. They eat cous-cous and other whole grains, as well as a great many vegetables, and they use olive oil almost exclusively.

On the other hand...

The Danes have a relatively high percentage of cancer, heart disease, and dementia. We went to Copenhagen to get first-hand information about the diet of the Danish people. My wife, who is an avid horsewoman, said she would like to ride while we were in Denmark. We were able to arrange for a ride at the queen's

A Quick Guide to Fats and Oils

Here is a very quick guide to the fats and oils
you are likely to find in your marketplace:

OIL	OPINION
Avocado	No flavor; expensive
Beef fat	Avoid entirely
Butter	Mix with olive oil
Canola	Do not use
Chicken fat	Avoid entirely
Cocoa butter	Avoid eating; apply to skin to soften dry areas
Coconut	Avoid completely; (may also be called palm oil)
Cottonseed	May also contain pesticide residue; avoid
Corn oil	Use very rarely and do not heat
Hazelnut oil	Expensive; flavorful; use moderately in salads, marinades, and cold dishes
Lard	Avoid entirely
Margarine	Avoid its use
Milkfats	Whole milk products (butter, cream, ice cream, milk, cheese) are very high in butterfat
Olive oil	Buy cold-pressed extra virgin; use in both hot and cold dishes but avoid heating too hot (not for frying)...this is the BEST oil to use
Peanut	Use moderately
Safflower	Avoid it
Sesame	Highly flavored seasoning for Oriental and Middle Eastern dishes; small amounts for soups and stir fry and marinades; use sparingly in marinades and sauces; do not heat to smoking point; choose dark roasted form
Shortening	Oils have been deformed by chemical processing; (such as Crisco) avoid it completely!
Soy	Cheap, similar to corn oil in composition; use moderately if at all and do not heat
Sunflower	Use moderately if at all and do not heat
Walnut oil	Expensive, flavorful; use moderately in marinades, salads, and cold dishes

estate, which was by a beach. We took the train out to the stables of this estate early in the day. Arriving almost an hour before our ride was scheduled, we decided to sit for awhile on the beach. It was only about 8 A.M. and fairly cool so we were not surprised that we were the only people on the beach as far as we could see in both directions. That wasn't to last long, however.

We had been sitting on the beach for just a few minutes when an obese woman came out and plopped a beach chair about ten feet away from us—why she decided to position herself so close was a mystery to us but that wasn't the end of our surprise. No sooner had she put down her beach chair than this woman proceeded to strip completely naked and sit her nude body down to soak up the sun—all three hundred plus pounds of her. Believe me, my wife and I were *really* surprised at that point! I said to Sharon,"Well, we came here to study the dietary practices of these people, but I hadn't counted on such an up-close and personal case study!"

The Danes eat a great deal of cheese and butter, which I believe contributes greatly not only to their obesity but to their rates of serious disease.

I encourage you to reflect upon your own eating habits and weight. Could there be a correlation between your weight and the types of fat you eat? Could it be possible that if you change the types of fat you consume—as well as cut out other harmful foods and add exercise—that you will lose weight more readily? I encourage you to get my book, *Maximum Fat Loss*.

Be Wary of Low-Fat Diets

From our discussion about fat thus far, you may have concluded that I am in favor of cutting ALL fat from the diet, or that I am a strong advocate for low-fat diets. Not so!

The typical low-fat diet does *not* provide sufficient fatty acids to support good brain and body function. If you are pursuing a low-fat diet, be sure to eat foods rich in the essential fatty acids and to take fatty acid supplements. Any time protein intake from animal products is substantially increased—which is often the case in low-fat diets—arachidonic acid intake is also increased. This particular type of acid in high percentage in the body can have very negative effects. An excess of arachidonic acid has been linked to rheumatoid arthritis, atherosclerosis, certain cancers, psoriasis, and Alzheimer's disease. [5]

Children under the age of two, especially, need to have diets that are higher in fat content than adults. As much as fifty percent of their calories each day should be from fat (as compared to twenty to thirty percent for adults). Cutting unsaturated fatty acids from your child's diet can be especially harmful.

As much as we need to avoid eating the wrong fats, we need to eat the right fats. That's where we turn next.

1. Simopoulos, A.P. Omega-3 fatty acids. In Spiller, G.A., ed., *Handbook of Lipids in Human Nutrition.* Boca Raton, FL: CRC Press, Inc., 1996: 51–73.

2. Booyens, J., and Van Der Merwe, C.F. Margarines and coronary artery disease. *Med Hypothesis* 1992 (37): 241–244.

3. Dopeshwarkar, G.A. *Nutrition and Brain Development.* New York: Plenum Press, 1981: 70–73.

4. Grandgirard, A., Bourri, J.M., Julliard, F., et al. Incorporation of trans long-chain n-3 polyunsaturated fatty acids in rat brain structure and retina. *Lipids* 1994 (20;4): 241–258.

   Petersen, J., Opstvedt, J. Trans fatty acids and the 6- and 9- desaturases in the rat. *Lipids* 1982 (17): 27.

5. Vendemiale, G., Grattaglioano, I., Altomare, E., et al. Effect of acetaminophen on hepatic glutathione compartmentation and mitochondrial energy metabolism in the rat. *Biochem Pharmacol* 1996 (8): 147–54.

   Newman, P.E. Could diet be used to reduce the risk of developing Alzheimer's disease? *Med Hypothesis* 1998 (50): 335–37.

TAKING ACTION FOR HEALTHY BRAIN FUNCTION

I. Cut out all trans fats from your diet, all saturated fats and partially hydrogenated fats, and margarine products.

2. Choose oils that are fresh, unrefined, organic, and mono-unsaturated. Never eat or use rancid oil.

3. Give up all fried foods. When cooking, avoid frying.

4. Use only organic fresh-ground peanut butter, with no hydrogenated oil added. If you have a weight problem, do not use any nut butters.

CHAPTER 8

KEEPING THE BRAIN VOLTAGE STRONG

We've all heard the phrase "he's a dim bulb" to describe people who don't seem to be fully functioning mentally. I like the phrase, "the lights are on but no one is home."

In this chapter, we are going to take a look at the "right" kinds of fats that keep brain voltage HIGH. The essential fatty acids are the foremost way to be a bright light mentally because the fatty acids directly impact the neurotransmitter system of the brain—the strength, speed, and diversity of connections in the brain are all affected.

Note especially that word "essential" in reference to fatty acids. Any product in the nutrition world is called "essential" if the body cannot manufacture it—in other words, if we need to consume it as part of our dietary intake.

The body is capable of making saturated fats and cholesterol. It is the *fatty acids* that we must get from our diet. The primary brain fats we need are these:

- DHA — Docosahexaenoic acid
- AA — Arachidonic acid
- GLA — Gamma-linolenic acid
- ALA — Alpha-linolenic acid

- PC — Phosphatidylcholine
- PS — Phosphatidylserine

Generally speaking, the fatty acids are of two main types: omega-6 and omega-3.

I'm not going to bore you with a lengthy explanation of the transformation process of fatty acids in the diet to fatty acids in the brain, but the chart below may be helpful in giving you an overview of the process as we discuss these various fatty acids. The substances labeled PGE1-3 are prostglandins: leukotrienes, thromboxane, and prostacyclin. Each of these has a great effect on the brain's blood flow. Prostaglandins are also key players in the immune system and the neurotransmitter system.

Essential Fatty Acids in the Diet		
Omega-3	**Omega-6**	
Alpha-Linolenic Acid (good sources are oils of flax, pumpkin, chia, walnut)	**Linoleic Acid** (good sources are oils of corn, safflower, sunflower, sesame)	
EPA (some fish oils)	**Gamma-Linolenic (GLA)** (oils of primrose, borage, and black current oil)	**Arachidonic Acid** (animal meat, eggs, milk)
DHA (some fish oils) **PGE3** (prostacyclin)	**PGE1** (leukotrienes)	**PGE2** (thromboxane)

Let's take these fatty acids one by one.

For DHA, Think Fish

For years, fish was proclaimed to be "good for the brain." This was chalked up by many as one of many old wives' tales about health care...but science is now showing that those old wives may have been wise, indeed! The most abundant sources of DHA (Docosahexaenoic Acid) are salmon, herring, sardines, and anchovies. These fish tend to get their DHA by consuming microscopic marine algae—some forms of algae are also good sources of DHA. Warm water fish has *less* DHA than cold water fish. Salmon that is "farmed" on fresh-water farms has more DHA than wild salmon.

Eggs have variable amounts of DHA but if eggs are overcooked, much of the DHA can be destroyed.

DHA is thought to be the most crucial of the omega-3 fatty acids, but unfortunately, many people get little or no DHA in their diets.

An imbalance of fatty acids, or low levels of key fatty acids have been correlated with multiple sclerosis, moderate to severe depression, hyperactivity, and attention deficit disorders. Studies have also shown:

- individuals with symptoms of hyperactivity and attention deficient had lower levels of the omega-3 fatty acid DHA in their blood. [1]

- learning problems—including memory problems, developmental delays, seizures, autism, and other brain-related disorders have been corrected or improved by adding the appropriate fats and oils to the diet

- violent and aggressive behavior, as well as general school performance, may be linked to dietary fatty acids [2]

- fatty acids absorbed from a mother's diet may be related to the size of a baby's brain at birth.[3] Sadly, no supplementation of fatty acids after birth can increase brain size.

- animals who consumed low amounts of essential fatty acids over three generations experienced an actual drop in the number of brain cells by the third generation.[4]

- animals that consumed low amounts of omega-3 fatty acids prior to conception and during pregnancy had offspring with poor visual acuity. [5]

- animals consuming inadequate amounts of omega-3 fatty acids had a much lower "learning scores" in an exercise aimed at training them to avoid a threatening situation [6]

DHA has been shown to reduce elevated triglycerides, inhibit the clumping together of platelets that are related to atherosclerosis, reduce clotting, and reduce hypertension. [7] DHA also has been shown to help maintain immune function and resistance to bacterial infection. [8]

As an alternative to taking anti-inflammatory drugs, such as ibuprofen, a person may receive benefit from an increased supplementation of DHA/EPA. DHA has been shown to reduce both atherogenic and inflammatory proteins. [9]

One of the most convenient and effective means of getting DHA in sufficient quantities is to take capsules of fish oil. Many people who supplement their diets with DHA take cod liver oil capsules (no smell, no fuss). [10] Individuals who have allergic reactions to fish can supplement their diets with algae-sourced DHA.

Mother's milk is high in DHA and is a great source of DHA for infants. One of the best reasons I know for breast-feeding is that breast milk contains the fatty acids critical to brain development. Formulas contained none of these fatty acids prior to 1997. Cow's milk provides adults with a great deal of saturated fat but no DHA for the brain.

You may find it interesting that DHA is especially concentrated in the eye—in fact, the retina has the highest concentration of this fatty acid of any tissue in the body! [11] Many elderly people fear losing their sight. DHA supplementation may be one way to help maintain healthy eyesight.

You may also find it interesting that in Japan, DHA is considered to be so important to human health that it is used to "enrich" more than twenty different foods. [12]

DHA is made in the human body if enough ALA is provided—as much as one hundred molecules of ALA is needed to make one molecule of DHA, however, and most people do not consume nearly that much ALA.

DHA supplementation is especially recommended for:

- Vegetarians and those on low-cholesterol programs
- pregnant or lactating mothers
- those who cannot convert LNA into DHA. Many times people with the following conditions have a deficiency in the enzyme (delta-6-desaturase) that converts dietary LNA into DHA: high intake of saturated and trans fats, high stress, diabetes, excessive sugar consumption, obesity, high intake of anti-inflammatory agents including aspiring, ibuprofen and corticosteroids; and certain people who have a genetic predisposition to allergies, eczema, retinitis pigmentosa, and other genetic disorders.

ALA Is a Strong Toxin Fighter

Alpha Lipoic Acid (ALA) is a powerful antioxidant that is rapidly absorbed by the body and readily enters the brain to protect neurons from free radical damage. It helps recycle vitamins C and E, and to regenerate glutathione, one of the brain's most important antioxidants. The brains of Alzheimer's patients have been shown to have significantly elevated levels of iron, a catalyst that enhances free radical production.

Lipoic acid acts as a powerful metal chelator—it binds several potentially toxic metals in the body including free iron and cadmium, and facilitates their excretion. [13]

This fatty acid is found in a small number of foods. It is most abundant in flax seed oil and hemp seed oil. Walnut, pumpkin seed, and green leafy vegetables all contain varying amounts of ALA, though less than flax and hemp. Soybeans were once a rich source for ALA but that is no longer true since hybridization of the soybean. The best source for ALA is supplementation by flax seed oil, which is available in capsule supplements. [14]

When flax seed is rough-ground, the beneficial fatty acids spoil rapidly—within ten to fifteen minutes. If you are seeking to gain flax oil by using ground flax seed as part of a cereal product, be aware that you need to "grind and eat" as quickly as possible to avoid oxidation of the oil in the seeds. (Eating whole flax seed is a waste of money because the body cannot extract the goodness of the flax—the whole seeds cannot be digested fully and are passed through the body to no benefit. Flax seed must be ground first to be of use.)

The Four Lesser Known Fatty Acids

Four of the fatty acids are lesser known. They are important substances, however, for good general health and good brain function.

EPA (Eicosapentaenoic Acid). This fatty acid is not found in the brain in great amounts but is a vital "messenger" that influences the immune system, blood vessel activity, blood clotting, inflammation, and the brain's blood supply. EPA is found in the same foods as DHA, though often in higher amounts than DHA.

If you are taking fish oil supplements to supply DHA to your body, you do not need additional EPA supplements.

AA (Arachidonic Acid). This fatty acid is abundant in most people's brain and body cells. The primary reason is likely to be that this type of fatty acid is derived from the fat of animals (beef, pork, chicken, and turkey) as well as peanuts. The danger is not a deficiency of AA but an over supply. When AA is too high in cell membranes, it can cause pain, swelling, inflammation, platelet stickiness, and irregular blood vessel spasms. As stated in the previous chapter, most people should set a goal to consume *less* fat from animal sources and to increase the omega-3 fatty acids.

GLA (gamma-Linolenic Acid). This is not a fat found in brain cells, but is appears to help in neurological conditions because it is converted into a prostaglandin known as PGE1, which is vital to a number of behavioral and neurological functions. People who suffer from depression and mood swings frequently do not have enough PGE1 in their systems. Common sources for GLA are oils of borage seed, evening primrose, and black current seed.

N-Acetyl-Cystein (NAC). Glutathione, one of the most important brain antioxidants, can be enhanced by the oral administration of NAC. NAC specifically helps in reducing the activity and generation of nitric oxide, which is one of the most notorious free radicals implicated in Alzheimer's disease. [15]

The Phospholipds Related to Choline and Lecithin

Phospholipids are substances that contain both fat molecules and the mineral phosophorous. They are important in forming nerve membranes and protecting nerve membranes from toxic injury and attack by free radicals. The two most common phospholipids are phosphatidyl-choline (PC, or lecithin) and phosphatidylserine (PS).

Phosopholipds are increasingly being used to treat memory disorders, depression, attention deficit disorder, schizophrenia, Alzheimer's disease, and Down syndrome. In one study of 347 patients with neuropsychiatric disorders, half of those treated with choline or lecithin showed improvement that ranged from significant to partial. [16]

More than thirty human studies on phosphatidylserine (PS) are being conducted at present to learn more about the effect of PS on memory and brain-related conditions. [17]

Choline and Lecithin

Choline and lecithin are the two substances necessary to produce acetylcholine, which transmits electrical impulses to the brain and nervous system. Choline is found in foods such as fish and defatted soybean flour. Foods high in lecithin are seed oils, liver, egg yolks, peanuts, peas, beans, Brewer's yeast, green leafy vegetables, cheese, cabbage, and cauliflower.

Acetylcholine is essential for storing memories and for optimal mental functioning. Improved memory is often evident a few days after a person begins to take choline or lecithin supplements!

In one study using MIT students as subjects, those students taking 3 grams of choline a day showed improved ability to recall a list of words. [18]

Lecithin helps to emulsify cholesterol, keeping it liquid so it does not harden into deposits on artery walls. A specific kind of lecithin, phosphatidyl choline, is an important structural component of brain cells. Lecithin also nourishes the fatty sheaths that cover nerve fibers. Researchers have estimated that thirty percent of the dry weight of the brain is lecithin.

Lecithin can be found in liquid, granule, and powder form as a supplement. As a liquid, lecithin can be added to scrambled eggs, soups, and stews. Both lecithin and choline can be mixed into protein drinks. Vitamin B5 should be taken along with choline or lecithin—it is needed to convert choline to acetylcholine.

Whether you add lecithin or choline to your diet is a matter of personal choice. They are equally beneficial in boosting brain function. The advantage of lecithin is its cholesterol-emulsifying effect. Also, some people who take choline develop a fish body odor—this can be eliminated by eating yogurt and drinking acidophilus milk. There is no odor associated with taking lecithin.

If you are taking choline, aim at about 2.5 to 3 grams taken four times a day. Lecithin amounts should be somewhat higher since only part of the lecithin is choline. Lecithin acts as something of a time-release form of choline so it only needs to be taken twice a day.

Egg Lecithin. A specific form of lecithin developed by Israeli researchers is made from egg yolk. This substance was developed to treat senility and viral diseases, including AIDS. It has been shown to improve memory and mental functioning. The researchers who developed it believe it makes the cell membranes in the brain more fluid—the greater the fluidity, the more stable the cell's metabolism. Other researchers believe the substance improves intelligence by providing cells with the basic nutrients needed for creating and repairing brain cell membranes. Still others think it provides additional support for the manufacturing of acetylcholine by the brain. Whatever the reasons, this type of lecithin has been shown to improve thinking and intelligence!

This type of egg lecithin is often called AL721, or you may look for the commercial name EggsACT. Dosage is from 2 to 10 mg a day. Like choline and lecithin, it should be taken with vitamin B5. This type of lecithin is available through my office.

The Amazing Properties of Phosphatidylserine

In the past twenty-five years, medical literature has indicated that lecithin is an important substance in preserving normal brain function. More recent research has shown that the truly beneficial part of lecithin is due to one of its components, phosphatidylserine. This substance is one of the key constituents of neuronal membranes, the site where brain cells receive and transmit chemical messages. It is also a basic requirement of the energy production of mitochondria.

The research linking PS to improved attention, memory, learning ability, and general cognitive functioning is growing, and it is impressive. [19]

PS has been shown to be helpful to Alzheimer's patients, as well as to those diagnosed with other forms of dementia. [20]

In one study with PS, a group of people with memory impairment showed dramatic improvement after only twelve weeks of PS supplementation. On the scale that was used in this study, the improvement was likened to "rolling back the clock" on memory by nearly twelve years. In other words, a person who was seventy years old, seemed to have a memory comparable to that of a fifty-eight-year-old. The improvement seemed greatest in those whose memories were more severely impaired. [21]

In another study, subjects with mild memory impairment were studied for the ability of PS to help them concentrate, remember, and perform other brain functions. PS supplementation provided benefit in four of the five functions tested, including memory. [22]

Branch On! In recent years, scientists have found that *some* brain cells send out new "branches" after the cells reach old age or are damaged. These new branches, called dendrites, grow longer and sprout even more branches as a person passes his or her ninetieth birthday. While this phenomenon remains largely a mystery, scientists are discovering that dendritic branching can be stimulated by powerful brain chemicals known as nerve growth factors. These chemicals—there may be several dozen of them—are very much at the cutting edge of brain research.

With age, the brain has a gradual decline in receptors for a substance called nerve growth factor (NGF) in the hippocampus, which is the area of the brain most strongly related to memory. This loss of NGF seems to result in a decline in the number of connections made within the hippocampus. While experiments have not yet been done with humans, PS seems to stimulate NGF production in animals, resulting in an increase in receptors. [23]

PS and PC Supplements

PS (phosphatidylserine) can be taken in supplement form—either in a soy-based product or as "bovine" PS, which is derived from using purified cow cerebral cortex and spinal cord. The bovine product is higher in unsaturated fatty acids such as DHA. I recommend the soy-based product.

PC (phosphatidylcholine) supplements are usually derived from soy or egg. Its common name is lecithin. A number of products are available, from granules to capsules. Compare labels and choose a lecithin product that has over thirty percent PC.

Combination supplements containing both PC and PS are also available.

The general recommendation is to take 300 mg a day at the start, and then 100 mg a day to sustain brain function. Since PS is often sold in a "complex" that includes other active ingredients, make sure that you are getting enough PS. (Example: If a PS complex has 100 mg tablets and there's only twenty percent PS in the complex, you are going to need fifteen tablets a day to start and five tablets a day to maintain.)

BE AWARE that phosphorylated serine—which is also sold as a dietary supplement—does not work like PS. A phospholipid, phosophorylated serine has been linked to some adverse reactions. Buyer beware! Make sure you get phosphatidylserine.

Keeping the Essential Fats in Proper Balance

As we noted in the previous chapter, it is not only important that a person have sufficient omega-6 and omega-3 fatty acids, but that these fats be in balance.

How can you tell if you have a proper balance of fatty acids? An imbalance manifests in many ways and may affect almost any body system. Pay attention, however, to these symptoms—and especially if you have a significant number of these symptoms:

PHYSICAL SYMPTOMS:

Dry skin	Cracked skin on heels
Eczema	or fingertips
Dry, unmanageable hair	Dry eyes
Dry, flaky eyelids	Dandruff
Brittle, frayed nails	Excessive thirst
Psoriasis	Frequent urination
Soft nails	Poor wound healing
Seborrhea	Allergies
"Chicken skin" on backs	Frequent infections
of arms	Lowered immunity
"Alligator" skin	Weakness
Patches of pale skin	Fatigue
on cheeks	

BEHAVIORAL SYMPTOMS:

Irritability	Attention deficit
Hyperactivity	Learning problems

These external symptoms are helpful in determining if a person has an imbalance, but the most reliable test is a blood test, and

KEEPING THE BRAIN VOLTAGE STRONG

specifically, a test of red blood cells. There are a few laboratories in the country that perform fatty acid analysis.

Fatty acid supplements are also available that contain GLA, ALA, and other fatty acids in an approximate 1:1 ratio of omega-6 to omega-3. These are good for general use, especially if they contain DHA.

The Importance of Good Digestion and Absorption

Many people have heard and believe the phrase, "You are what you eat." The greater reality is this: You are what you absorb. Unless you have a healthy digestive tract, capable of *absorbing* the nutrients you take into your body, you will not receive the benefit of those nutrients. They will pass through your system unused.

For essential fatty acids to enter your blood stream and become effective, you first must have adequate digestion and absorption of these substances. There are several things that can impair absorption of dietary fats and oils:

- Antacids
- Inadequate chewing
- Antibiotics
- Bacteria
- Fungi
- Viruses
- Parasites
- Yeast
- Alcohol
- Anti-inflammatory drugs (such as aspirin)

General poor nutrition and food intolerances can also play havoc with digestion and absorption. (The most common food intolerances are dairy products, wheat, soy, peanuts, eggs, and corn.) You will note from this list, however, that much of what impairs proper absorption of dietary fats and oils are practices we can control. We can choose NOT to use antacids, take antibiotics, or drink alcohol.

It is something of a paradox that the intestinal tract, which determines our absorption of dietary fats and oils, is made of billions of cells, each of which has a membrane made of essential fatty acids! Not only do fatty acids help form the structure of the intestinal cells, but they form the "messengers" that convey fatty acids to other areas of the body. A balance of fats and oils helps maintain the integrity of the digestive tract, which is a necessary precondition for maintaining the integrity of brain cells.

Cut Down on the Sugar. A factor that can disrupt your body's ability to use and make fatty acids is too much sugar, too much complex carbohydrate, or the wrong kind of complex carbohydrates. Sugar triggers the release of insulin, and too much insulin causes an increase in AA (arachidonic acid) that can result in too much prostaglandin, priming the body for inflammation at the cellular level.

In general, limit your carbohydrate consumption to no more than forty percent of your calorie intake. Choose foods that a low glycemic index number, such as dried legumes (beans, lentils, peas), nonfat yogurt, and nonfat milk. (If you want to know more about this, order my book, *Maximum Fat Loss.*)

Many foods include food molds and fungi in small amounts. This is especially true in sugary foods where the sugar itself becomes microscopically moldy.

As far as I am concerned, there is *no* good reason to eat sugar. Actually, I can't caution you enough about limiting your consumption of sugar. As a nation, we are experiencing an alarming increase in diabetes—a fact directly related to our high sugar intake.

Recently my eighty-five-year-old mother decided to move to a nursing home. I pulled up in the drive to deliver some things to her. When I came back, I found a small group of people gathered around my car, a Corvette convertible. One man, in particular, asked me a number of questions—the kind that car enthusiasts ask, "What model is it? How many miles do you have on it? How fast have you driven it? Have you made any engine modifications?"

This man was in a wheelchair. He had no legs and only one arm. He seemed relatively young. I asked him in the course of our conversation about the car if he had been in an accident. He replied, "No, I had gangrene."

"Gangrene?" I asked.

"Yes," he replied without hesitation. "I am a type-II diabetic. About three years ago, I went on insulin. I immediately had problems with my circulation."

"How long are you anticipating being here at the nursing home?" I asked.

"Well," he replied, "I don't expect to spend the rest of my life here. I'm only forty-two. I'll probably be here for a couple of more months, at least, while I undergo more rehab and try to learn to walk and use some prosthetic devices that are being made for me."

I told him that next time I visited my mother I would bring him a copy of my book, Maximum Energy, as well as an audio tape I made about "The Top 10 Foods Never to Eat." I also recommended to him that he begin to take vitamin E since it is known to help greatly with circulation. I said, "I hope this information will help you with your circulation so that you do not need any further surgery." He seemed grateful.

I felt great sadness for this young man as I drove away. Most people who become type-II diabetics acquire this disease through bad food choices they make or which are made for them, often beginning in childhood.

Every one of us certainly has the "right" to choose what we eat. At the same time, we do *not* have "rights" when it comes to the consequences of those choices. For example, you can choose to eat junk food any time and in whatever quantities you desire. But if you eat junk food, you do *not* have the right to determine that you will be healthy in body and mind for the rest of your life. The choices you make bear consequences of their own. You have the *right* to choose to smoke and drink alcohol. But once you make that choice, you do *not* have the right to choose to have no health consequences. Those consequences will occur regardless of whether you *want* them to occur.

The Yeast Connection. Essential fatty acids have also been shown to inhibit the growth of yeast organisms. This, in turn, helps oxygen flow more freely to cells. (Yeast is anaerobic and cannot thrive in the presence of oxygen.) Yeast overgrowth can cause a multitude of negative symptoms in the body—these range from allergies and infections to joint swelling and memory loss.

It's Difficult to Remember...
If You're Depressed

Depression is one of the "emotional" factors often linked to memory loss and dementia. Most people know as a rule of thumb that its difficult to "think"—to reason, to make quality decisions, and "order" one's life—if one is depressed.

Many factors impact our mood and emotions. Much has been written about depression through the centuries, although different terms have been used, such as sadness, melancholy, and lingering despair. What is interesting to me is that the number of cases of depression has increased in every generation since 1900!

Are we more depressed than we used to be or is the depression just diagnosed more quickly? I believe we generally *are* more depressed now than in past centuries.

Can increased depression be linked to an increased imbalance in fatty acids in the diet? There's good reason to suggest this.

Remember first that fish is an important source of fatty acids. It should come as no surprise, therefore, that cultures that consume large amounts of fish have *low* rates of depression. [24] For centuries, fish in China has been considered an important food for a "balanced, happy mood and better mental performance." North American and European people, who eat much less fish than Oriental people, have nearly tenfold higher rates of depression than people in fish-consuming societies. [25]

In fact, depression in North America is nearly seven times higher than in Hong Kong. One Japanese study found that the rate of depression in Japan is less than one percent. In a rural fishing village in Japan, psychiatrists could find NO ONE with major depression. [26]

A book titled *The Anatomy of Melancholy* was published three hundred and fifty years ago. In it, the author recommended a low-fat diet, the consumption of borage oil, and the consumption of fish. For severe cases, the author recommended adding cow brains [27] Fish, of course, has DHA. Borage oil is very high in GLA. Biochemically and neurologically, the advice makes good sense.

"But cow brains?" you may ask. Well, cow brains would likely be high in DHA, AA, phosphatidylcholine (PC), and phosphatidylserine (PS). Many ancient cultures, by the way have advocated consuming animal brains to improve mental function, balance mood, and heal "nerve" problems. While I don't advocate adding cow brains to your diet, the proposed therapy in 1652 may have been right on target in improving the fatty acid environment of the brain.

Scientists today are finding that people with depression have higher omega-6 to omega-3 ratios in their blood. An increasingly prescribed therapy for severe depression includes the addition of omega-3 supplementation in the form of fish oils, as well as other co-factor nutrients such as zinc, magnesium, niacin, and vitamin C.

Other researchers are finding that depression along with other problems that I've already mentioned are linked to blood that is too thick. Blood "sludge" has been linked to elevated cholesterol and triglyceride levels. A proper intake of omega-3 fatty acids can help reduce triglycerides and prevent blood sludging. [28]

In an attempt to break the cycle of depression in a patient, physicians sometimes prescribe antidepressants. A number of antidepressants, however, interfere with the neurotransmitter acetylcholine. Sleeping pills and tranquilizers such as Valium(r) and Ativan(r) are quite capable of producing memory loss and general mental deterioration. A number of psychiatric drugs can interrupt or disturb normal brain function—they are prescribed primarily to control behavior and "mood," but in truth, they alter a person's reasoning ability and memory. (These drugs include Melaril, lithium, Thorazine, and Haldol.)

In many cases, a person who is depressed will see more than one physician or counselor. The person can end up with a handful of prescriptions to take, often with negative chemical interactions. Toxic interactions can also build up over time, resulting in some patients developing something of a general "stupor." Not only does memory suffer, but all mental faculties.

Not only are psychiatric drugs "poison" in most cases, but also many over-the-counter medications. Eye drops for treating glaucoma, painkillers such as Darvon, heart and blood pressure medications such as digitalis and Inderal; anti-asthma agents such as aminophylline; anti-Parkinson's disease drugs such as L-dopa; and some gastric drugs can cause mental changes and impair memory. Even anti-seasickness medications containing scopolamine can result in brain poisoning.

Perhaps the best way to prevent depression is to maintain good brain nutrition. First, avoid brain poisons such as alcohol and other drugs. Second, make sure the brain cells are being provided all of the essential vitamins, nutrients, and oxygen level necessary for health. Third, take a close look at the person's environment. It may be low in stimuli, resulting in boredom. It may be filled with confusing stimuli, resulting in frustration. See what might be done to change the general environment to one that offers sufficient, orderly, and varied mental stimulation.

1. Lucas, A., Morley, R., Cole, T.J., et al. Breast milk and subsequent intelligence quotient in children born preterm. *Lancet* 1992 (339): 261–264.

2. Virkkunen, M.E., Horrobin, D.F., Douglas, K., Jenkins, K., Manku, M.S. Plasma phospholipid essential fatty acids and prostaglandin in alcohol, habitually violent, and impulsive offenders. *Biol Psych* 1987 (22): 1087–96.

3. Dobbing, J. Vulnerable periods of brain development. In Elliott, K., Knight, E., eds. *Lipids Malnutrition and the Developing Brain.* Amsterdam: Associated Scientific Publishers, A Ciba Foundation Symposium, Elsevier, 1972: 9–22.

4. Sinclair, A.J., Crawford, M.A. The effect of low fat maternal diet on neonatal rats. *Br J Nutr* 1973 (29): 127–137.

5. Connor, W.E., Neuringer, M. The effects of n-3 fatty acid deficiency and repletion upon the fatty acid composition and function of the brain and retina. In *Biological Membranes: Alterations in Membrane Structure and Function.* Alan R. Liss Inc., 1988: 275–294.

6. Yokota, A. Relationship of polyunsaturated fatty acid composition and learning ability in rats. *Nippon Saniujinka Clakkadji* (in Japanese) 1993 (45): 15–22.

7. Agren, J.J., Vaisanen, S. Hanninen, O, Muller A.D., Hornstra, G. Hemostatic factors and platelet aggregation after a fish-enriched diet or fish oil or docosahexaenoic acid supplementation. *Prostaglandins Leukot Essential Fatty Acids* 1997 (57;4-5): 419–421.

Nelson, G.J., Schmidt, P.C. Bartolini, G.L., Kelley, D.S., Kyle, D. The effect of dietary docosahexaenoic acid on plasma lipoproteins and tissue fatty acid composition in humans. *Lipids* 1997 (32;11): 1137–46.

8. Halvorsen, D.S., Hansen, J.B., Grimsgaard, S., et al. The effect of highly purified eicosapentaenoic and docosahexaenoic acids on monocyte phagocytosis in man. *Lipids* 1997 (32;9): 935–42.

9. Lau, C.S., Morley, K.D., Belch, J.J. Effects of fish oil supplementation on non-steroidal anti-inflammatory drug requirement in patients with mild rheumatoid arthritis-a double-blind placebo controlled study. *Br J Rheumatol* 1 (32;11): 982–89.

   De Caterina, R, Libby, P., Gimbrone, M.A. Jr., Clinton, S.K., Cybulsky, M.A. Omega-3 fatty acids and endothelial leukocyte adhesion molecules. Prostaglandins Leukot Essential Fatty Acids 1994 (52;2-3):191-95.

10. Ley-Jacobs, B.M. DHA: *The Magnificent Marine Oil.* Temecula, CA: BL Publications, 1999.

    Cooper, R. DHA: *The Essential Omega-3 Fatty Acid.* Pleasant Grove, UT: Woodland Publishing, 1998.

11. Bazan, N.G., Gordon, W.C., Rodriguez de Turco, E.B. The uptake, metabolism and conservation of docosahexaenoic acid (22:6n-3) in brain and retina alterations in liver and retinal 22:6 metabolism during inherited progressive retinal degeneration. In Sinclair, A., Gibson, R. eds., *Essential Fatty Acids and Eicosanoids.* Champaign, IL: American Oil Chemists Society, 1992: 107–115.

12. Kinko, Y.Y., Hayakawa, K. Docosahexaenoic acid: A valuable nutraceutical? *Trends Food Sci Tech* 1996(Feb): 59–63.

13. Janetzky, B., Reichmann, H., Youdim, M.B.H. "Iron and Oxidative Damage in Neurodegenerative Diseases," in *Mitochondria and Free Radicals in Neurodegenerative Diseases.* Beal, M.F. (ed), New York: Wiley-Liss Pub. 1997.

14. Bierenbaum, M.L., et al. Reducing atherogenic risk in hyperlipemic humans with flax seed supplementation: A preliminary report. *J Am Coll Nutr* 1993 (12): 501–504.

    Budwig, J. *Flax Oil as a True Aid Against Arthritis, Heart Infarction, Cancer, and Other Diseases.* Vancouver: Apple Publishing Co., 1994 (translated from German).

15. Pahan, J., Sheikh, F.G., Namboodiri, A.M.S. N-acetyl cysteine inhibits induction of NO production by endotoxin or cytokine stimujlated rat periotoneal macrophages, C6 glial cells and astrocytes. *Free Radical Biology and Medicine* 1997 (24;1): 39–48.

16. Woodbury, M.M., Woodbury, M.A. Neuropsychiatric development: Two case reports about the use of dietary fish oils and/or choline supplementation in children. *J Am Col Nutr* 1993 (12;3): 239–45.

17. Kidd, P. *Phosphatidylserine: A Remarkable Brain Cell Nutrient.* Decatur, IL: Lucas Meyes, 1995: 2.

18. Pearson, D., and Shaw, S. *Life Extension: A Practical Scientific Approach,* New York: Warner Books, 1982.

19. Caffara, P., and Santamaria, V. The effects of phosphatidylserine in patients with mild cognitive decline. *Clin Trials Journ* 1987 (24;1): 109–114.

    Granata, Q, and DiMichele, J. Phosphatidylserine in elderly patients: An open trial. *Clin Trials Journ* 1987 (24;1): 99–103.

    Sinforiani, E., Agostinis, C., Merlo, P., Gualtieri, S., Mauri, M., and Mancuso, A. Cognitive decline in aging brain: Therapeutic approach with phosphatidylserine. *Clin Trials Journ* 1987 (24;1): 114–124.

    Puca, F.,M., Savarese, M.A., and Minervini, M.G. Exploratory trial of phosphatidylserine efficacy in mildly demented patients. *Clin Trials Journ* 1987 (24;1): 94–98.

20. Palmieri, G., Palmieri, R., Inzoli, M.R., Lombardi, G., Sottini, C., Tavolato, B., and Giometto, B. Double-blind controlled trial of phosphatidylserine in patients with senile mental deterioration. *Clin Trials Journ* 19987 (24;1): 73–83.

Nerozzi, D. Fosfatidilserina e disturbi della memoria nell-anziano. *La Clinica Terapeutica* 1987 (120): 399–404.

Amaducci, L. and the Smid Group. Phophatidylserine in the treatment of Alzheimer's disease: Results of multicenter study. *Psycholpharmacology Bull* 1988 (24;1): 130–134.

Crook, T.H., Tinklenberg, J., Yesavage, J., Petrie, W., Nunzi, M.G., and Massari, D.C. Effects of phosphatidylserine in age-associated memory impairment. *Neur* 1991 (41;5): 644–649.

Crook, T.W., Petrie, W., Wells, C., and Massari, D.C. Effects of phosphatidylserine in Alzheimer's disease. *Psychopharmacology Bull* 1992 (28;1): 61–66.

Cenacchi, T., Bertoldin, T., Farina, C., Fiori, M.G., Cvrepaldi, G., and participating investigators. Cognitive decline in the elderly: A double-blind, placebo-controlled multicenter study on efficacy of phosphatidylserine administration. *Aging: Clinical and Exper Res* 1993 (5): 123–133.

Gindin, J., Novokov, M., Kedar, D., Walter-Ginzberg, A., Nacr, S., Karta, O., Zur, E., and Levi, S. The effect of plant phosphatidylserine on age-associated memory impairment and mood in the functioning elderly. Unpublished study conducted by researchers at the Geriatric Institute for Education and Research and the Department of Geriatrics at Kaplan Hospital, Rehovot, Israel.

21. Crook, T.H., et al. Effect of phosphatidylserine in age-associated memory impairment. *Neurol* 1991(41): 644–49.

22. Crook, T.H., et al. Effect of phosphatidylserine in Alzheimer's disease. *Psychopharmacol Bull* 1992(28): 61–66.

22. Nunzi, M.G., et al. Dendritic spine loss in hippocampus of aged rats: Effect of brain phosphatidylserine administration. *Neurobiology Aging* 1987(8): 501–510.

Nunzi, M.G., et al. Therapeutic properties of phosphatidylserine in the aging brain. In Hanin, I., Pepeu, G., eds. *Phospholipds: Biochemical, Pharmaceutical, and Analytical Considerations.* New York: Plenum Press, 1990.

23. Hibbeln, J.R., Salem, N. Dietary polyunsaturated fatty acids and depression: when cholesterol does not satisfy. *Am J. Clin Nutr* 1995(62): 1–9.

24. Cross National Collaborative Group. The changing rate of major depression across national comparisons. *JAMA* 1992(268): 3098–3105.

25. Chen, C., Wong. J., Lee, N., et al. The Shatin community mental health survey in Hong Kong II: Major findings. *Arch Gen Psychiatry* 1993 (50): 125–133.

Hirayasu, A. An epidemiological and sociopsychiatric study on the mental and neurologic disorders in an isolated island in Okinawa. *Psychiatry Neurol Japan* 1969 (71): 466–91

Hasegawa, K. The epidemiological study of depression in later life. *J Affect Disord* 1985 (S1): S3–6.

26. Burton, R. *The Anatomy of Melancholy.* (The Classics of Psychiatry and Behavioral Sciences library.) Birmingham, AL: Division of Gryphon Editions, Inc., 1988.

27. Simopoulos, A.P. Omega-3 fatty acids. In Spiller, G.A., ed. *Handbook of Lipids in Human Nutrition.* Boca Raton, FL: CRC Press, Inc., 1996: 51–73.

TAKING ACTION FOR HEALTHY BRAIN FUNCTION

Make sure you have adequate omega-6 and omega-3 essential fatty acids in your system. Here are my recommendations:

- ALA from flax oil: 1-3 teaspoons daily
- ALA from flax seed meal: 2-4 teaspoons
- DHA from algae oil: 25-100 mg DHA daily
- Alternate source of DHA: cod liver oil—providing up to 200 mg EPA and DHA daily (do not use this with infants)
- GLA from borage or primrose oil
- Phosphaditylcholine (PC): 50-100 mg daily
- Phosphaditylserine (PS): 50 mg daily

All of these products are available through my office. Call **1-800-726-1834**.

CHAPTER 9

GOOD NUTRIENTS
FOR
SHARP THINKING

A number of nutrients other than vitamins and essential fatty acids have been shown to be very effective in improving brain function, including several key minerals, electrolytes, and amino acids.

When it comes to minerals, we should never forget that we share the same basic chemical composition as the earth. This goes along, of course, with what the Bible says about the creation of man—the Creator took the "dust of the earth" to form mankind. The minerals that we need come from the food we eat, grown in the soil of the earth. However, many of the minerals vital to brain function have either been greatly depleted from the soil or have been destroyed by food processing methods. A basic mineral supplement is needed by the vast majority of people.

Balance is the Key When It Comes to Minerals

The key word to keep in mind when it comes to minerals is *balance*. Many minerals work in conjunction with other minerals. Too much of one mineral can upset the overall balance and lead to negative results. In fact, many of the minerals we need *if taken in excess* can have toxic effects in the brain. The flip side is equally true—*if deficiencies exist,* brain function can also suffer.

About two dozen minerals—notably iron, magnesium, manganese, zinc, copper, and iodine—are important to the enzyme systems of the body, and thus, important for maintaining the normal mechanism and metabolism of the body and brain. Trace minerals play an important part in supporting brain function, making sure the correct amounts of oxygen, carbon dioxide, carbohydrates, proteins, ions, and trace elements are absorbed by the cells.

I want to call your attention especially to the minerals manganese, zinc, magnesium, and iron.

Manganese and Brain Cells. If manganese is missing in nerve tissues and cells, including brain cells, the cells become both "stiffer" (less tensile, less elastic, less ductile) and show less activity. The result is a "dullness" in reasoning ability and poor memory.

Cells in the body last only about six weeks. As soon as one cell goes, another cell must take its place. Some have estimated that brain cells can last up to six months, although that is a disputed fact. Whether six weeks or six months, brain cells are dying every day and for the information a cell contains to be "passed on" to another living cell in the brain, something of a "photographic" process must take place. Associations, and information needs to be transferred to more vibrant cells. It is this process of retaining the memory associated with a cell that is at the heart of *maintaining* our memory as a whole. Manganese is the chemical element that is vital to keeping this process strong. It is also the manganese in the brain that enables brain cells to act synergistically or in harmony.

Manganese is present in only a few foods, and even then, in small quantities. The highest foods in manganese are California walnuts and almonds. Supplements of manganese usually include sulfur and phosphorus. The three work in balance. [1]

One of the foremost ways of telling if manganese supplementation should be taken is to look at the handwriting of a person. The person who lacks manganese is likely to have shaky handwriting because he or she does not have complete control of the fingers. The person deficient in manganese also tends to suffer from Angina pectoris, tremors, and sudden, strong cravings for food. The deficient person can usually handle cold weather, but not hot weather. The person may have a valvular insufficiency, which is really a problem with the cardiac nerves.

Zinc. A deficiency in zinc has been associated with depression, lower sperm count, lower sexual drive, dementia, retardation, and memory impairment. This mineral needs to be taken in balance with manganese.

Foods high in zinc are herring, sunflower seeds, pumpkin seeds, ground round steak, lamb chops, pecans, Brazil nuts, beef liver, egg yolk whole-wheat bread, oats, almonds, sardines, and chicken.

Magnesium. This mineral has been linked to a number of mental ailments, including anxiety, depression, personality changes, irritability, restlessness, and nervousness. [2] Magnesium must be balanced with calcium in the body—most supplements will come as a calcium-magnesium combination.

Iron. Iron is generally associated with healthy blood cells but it has also been linked to healthy brain function. In fact, a recent study at the University of Rochester showed that teenage girls deficient in iron had a significantly more difficult time in learning.

Too much iron, on the other hand, has been correlated to an increase in heart attacks. If you are feeling weak, fatigued, with achy joints, decreased stamina, and decreased sexual desire, you may want to have your physician run a blood test to see if you actually need more iron. Don't over-medicate yourself when it comes to iron. [3]

I recommend that you use only unsulfured black strap molasses as an iron supplement. Never take "iron pills" or use a multiple vitamin that contains iron.

How Can You Tell If You Are Deficient? A simple hair analysis test can determine if a person has a mineral deficiency or if mineral "proportions" in the body are out of whack. Hair analysis is available through my office, 1-800-727-1834.

Electrolytes "Charge Up" the Brain

An electrolyte is a substance that works in the blood stream to conduct a small electric charge. These particles, called ions, are found inside and outside the membranes of nerve cells and fibers, and they help control the excitability of nerve elements. The concentration of ions in and around the nerve cells of the brain is related to the concentration of ions in the blood serum that circulates to and from the brain. There is a very narrow range of acceptable ion level for sodium, potassium, chloride, calcium, magnesium, and carbonate if brain function is to remain normal. This is especially true for calcium. Too much calcium can even lead to stupor or coma.

Sodium ions in the blood are related to the body's hydration (amount of water). Low sodium levels are often the result of drinking too much water in hot weather, with sodium being lost to excessive perspiration. Overhydration is also more common to heavy beer drinkers—the condition results to the swelling of tissues and even the swelling of the brain. People with this condition become drowsy but giggly. The swelling may cause headache or nausea. If the condition is not reversed, a person may experience confusion, and perhaps even convulsions and coma.

Many of the so-called "sports" drinks on the market have been developed to compensate for this condition and to maintain the body's electrolytes in balance. Small amounts of these drinks may actually be helpful in helping elderly people regulate their body systems, finding a balance between dehydration and overhydration. Most people in nursing homes do *not* drink sufficient water, especially during hot weather. Within a matter of hours, insufficient hydration (either lack of fluid or excessive fluid and perspiration) can lead to short-term memory loss, disorientation, and an inability to find words.

Amino Acids Can Add "Focus" and "Stamina" to Brain Functions

All neurotransmitters are made from amino acids—in other words, protein. Essential amino acids are those that must be obtained from the diet because the body cannot manufacture them. Nonessential amino acids can be manufactured in the body—but the body needs essential amino acids to create them. Free-form amino acids are amino acids that have been extracted from complex proteins in vegetable products such as soybeans and molasses. They are important especially to vegetarians.

Amino acids come in L and D forms. The L-form amino acids can be used directly by the body as proteins and are easily absorbed and used. The body must convert D-form amino acids before they can be absorbed and used. D-form amino acids supplements are prohibited by the FDA.

The FDA requires that a product identify specific amino acids and give the quantity of each. If a label says only "amino acids," it is probably a cheap protein-powder filler, with very little of any particular amino acid.

Amino acids should always be taken with vitamins, minerals, and other nutrients that help metabolize amino acids. Usually, amino acid products should be taken as a complex, because they work together in a synergistic way.

Tyrosine and Tryptophan. Tyrosine and tryptophan are considered to be the most important amino acids for changing brain function. They are directly linked to a person's ability to concentrate. Tryptophan an important metabolic precursor of serotonin, a very important neurotransmitter.

Tyrosine is part of the chemical pathway in the creation of adrenaline and noradrenaline. It works in conjunction with phenylalanine (described later).

These amino acids are not available in supplement form. They are found in dry skim milk, cheddar cheese, eggs, red meat, and poultry. Lean turkey breast meat is one of the best sources.

Methionine. Methionine is a sulfur-based amino acid. Mineral sulfur protects cells from air-borne pollutants and helps transport selenium and zinc in the body. It also aids in protein production. Like tyrosine, it works in conjunction with phenylalanine.

Methionine is found in dairy products, eggs, wheat germ, yogurt, cottage cheese, turkey, beans, Brussels sprouts, onions, garlic, hot red peppers, horseradish, cabbage, brown rice, sesame seeds, pumpkin seeds, oat flakes, and avocado. Far more methionine is found in *animal* products (dairy, eggs, turkey) than in vegetable sources. Vegetarians may want to consider methionine supplements.

One of the main attributes of methionine is that it is a chelator—in other words, it locates and attaches itself to heavy metals, such as lead, cadmium, and mercury, and transports these harmful metals from the body.

The problem with eating foods high in methionine is that without B6, B12, and folic acid in proper balance, the methionine may bcome homocystein, which can lead to arterial plaquing. Be sure to take those B vitamins!

Glutamine. Glutamine is a free-form amino acid widely used to maintain good brain function. It helps improve mental alertness, mood, and clarity of thinking. It also is used for the production of a neurotransmitter called gamma amino butyric acid (GABA).

Glutamine in the brain helps neutralize ammonia metabolic waste. When ammonia levels are too high in the brain, a person can experience nausea and vomiting, become irritable, and experience tremors and hallucinations. When glutamine is low in the brain, ammonia levels rise. Even a small rise can cause fatigue, confusion, an inability to concentrate, and mood swings.

In one study, students taking glutamine supplements found it easier to concentrate on their homework and to study late into the night without fatigue. In another study, students taking glutamine before tests felt more alert, clearheaded, and confident.[4]

Many consider glutamine to be a better brain stimulant than caffeine—with the added benefit that glutamine fuels metabolism and creates energy.

Glutamine supplements are readily available in nutrition stores.

NOTE: Do NOT take glutamic acid. It is an "excitotoxin" and can cause neural death.

Arginine. Low levels of this amino acid have been associated with memory loss and senility. In the body, arginine is converted to spermine, which is found in semen, blood tissue, and brain cells. The process of converting arginine to spermine is chemically complicated, but it is important to note that the process requires vitamin B6, manganese, and magnesium. As manganese reacts with arginine, it produces ornithine, another amino acid.

Phenylalanine. This amino acid is the one most widely recognized as a brain booster. Phenylalanine, however, should NEVER be taken supplemental form. In high concentrations it can cause brain damage. It is a byproduct of Nutrasweet® or Equal®. The natural sources for this amino acid are foods such as beef, chicken, fish, soybeans, eggs, cottage cheese, and milk.

A Word to Coffee Drinkers. Caffeine in coffee works in part to keep us alert and "up" by activating the noradrenaline system. Noradrenaline is a neurotransmitter and the brain's version of adrenaline. When a person is under stress, noradrenaline is used much faster than the body can manufacture it. Coffee does nothing to replenish the noradrenaline it uses up. By the end of a stressful four or five cup day, the jitteriness and irritability a person feels is a sign the *brain* is running on empty—it is literally empty of noradrenaline.

When the noradrenaline system is fully functioning, you feel aware, alert, and are primed to handle stress, danger, or excitement. The neurons that produce noradrenaline originate primarily in a region of the brain known as the locus coeruleus. Although few in number, these neurons have a profound effect since they branch out to nearly every part of the brain and spinal cord.

If you are a coffee drinker, drink no more than one cup a day, every other day. I encourage you to read my book, *Maximum Energy.* In it, I tell my own experience of being a caffeine addict—I once drank eighteen cups of coffee a day. The results were *not* good. I know it is difficult to break a coffee-drinking habit...but I also know it CAN be done!

Three More Potent Brain Boosters

There are three additional substances that boost brain function:

Coenzyme Q10 (CoQ10). Coenzyme Q10 works in the body to transport electrons in the process of energy production in every living cell. When the body has a deficiency of CoQ10, virtually all cells of the body are effected. CoQ10 supplementation has been shown to enhance production in brain neurons and improve their function [5] CoQ10 also has significant antioxidant properties. Unfortunately, two of the most widely prescribed cholesterol-lowering drugs, pravastatin (Pravachol®) and lovastatin (Mevacor®) can significantly lower serum coenzyme Q10 levels.[6] Unfortunately, the statin drugs also have another negative side effect: cancer. I am strongly opposed to these drugs!

Nicotinamide Adenine Dinucleotide (NADH). NADH is also an essential ingredient for the chemical reactions powering all living cells. It is also a powerful antioxidant. It is little wonder, then, that this substance has been shown to provide significant help for those with Alzheimer's. In a major clinical study published in 1996, NADH was linked to significant improvement on mental performance tests in a group of Alzheimer's patients—those who did not receive the supplement continued to deteriorate. NADH was also shown to enhance the production of two important brain chemicals: dopamine and noradrenaline—deficiencies in these two chemicals has been found in Alzheimer's patients. [7]

Acetyl-L-carnitine. This substance functions primarily as a shuttle, transporting critical fuel sources into the mitochondria, which is the energy producing mechanism in neurons. At the same time, it helps remove the toxic byproducts of brain metabolism. It is a vital substance in the fundamental processes required for healthy brain cell function and survival. It also is readily converted into an important neurotransmitter (brain chemical messenger), acetylcholine. Acetylcholine has been shown to be profoundly deficient in the brains of Alzheimer's patients. In one study conducted at the University of California at San Diego, researchers found a striking reduction in the rate of mental decline in those who had taking acetyl-L-carnitive for a one-year period. [8]

Don't Be Overwhelmed...

At this point, you may be thinking, *Just how many supplements does Ted Broer intend for me to take?* My answer would be, eat in a way that promotes general health, supplement with a powdered multiple vitamin with no iron, a homocysteine-balanced B formula and extra vitamin B5, B6, and B12, vitamin C, vitamin E, zinc, cod liver oil and flaxseed oil, a balanced mineral complex, and then take additional supplements *as needed*. I personally supplement CoQ10 daily because it has many positive effects in the body related to both mental and physical energy. At the same time, as I mentioned earlier, I recommend that you cut way down or eliminate altogether the consumption of coffee (or other high-caffeine drinks).

You may have noted that many of the substances in this chapter can be acquired fairly easily through food sources. Listen to your own body. Pay attention to the signals—often called "symptoms"—that it gives you.

My friend Joe, who died recently at age ninety, once told me about an incident that occurred nearly thirty years ago while he and some friends were hunting in the Everglades. He and his friends were in a pick-up on a loop road and they came to a large log blocking the road. They got out to move the log and as they got closer to it, the log moved. It was a huge snake!

Recognize your symptoms for what they are. Negative symptoms are not just a passive log waiting to be "moved"—they can be a dangerous or deadly snake! Don't wait to discover the full extent of a nutritional deficiency that could very well be life-threatening.

What You Should—
And Should Not—
Expect from Supplementation

Everyone is exposed to metals, other toxic substances, and stress. Modern farming, food manufacturing, and cooking changes raw foods, leading to oxidation and a loss of vitamins and trace elements. Supplementation in today's world is virtually a necessity for a person to have optimal levels of vitamins, minerals, and other important substances for the health of body and brain. Do not, however, begin to take supplements with false expectations. They are not a "quick fix,"

Supplements do not act like medicines, which can rapidly take away symptoms without doing anything to heal or cure an underlying cause. Supplements are intended to correct deficiencies at the cellular level and to enhance a person's resistance to harmful influences.

Many supplements require weeks or even months to build to optimal levels in the tissues of the body. The end result, however, is a genuine healing of the cells and the metabolic processes of the body.

Also, be sure you take high-quality nutritional supplements. For a nutritional supplement to be of use to you it should dissolve in about thirty minutes. You can test the substance by placing the tablet in question in a glass of lukewarm water to which a little vinegar has been added. Without touching the tablet, stir the water at short intervals. The tablet should dissolve in less than one hour. If it does not, there is a great likelihood the substance will travel through your intestinal tract undissolved, and if that occurs, it may remain in the lower intestines where it can putrefy or irritate the digestive tract.

Take your supplements at optimal times. Fat soluble nutrients are best taken after a meal. Acidophilus is best taken on an empty stomach between meals or before bedtime.

Recognize, too, that your body's need for nutrients is greater when you are fighting illness or recovering from injury. You may need *more* supplementation during those times.

As a broad generalization, supplementation is a good form of *preventive* health-care. Adequate supplementation can help keep you from developing nutritional deficiencies that are often linked to major diseases of both body and brain. In most cases, supplementation can reverse damage.

Don't wait, however, until damage occurs before you take the vitamins and minerals your body needs.

Think smart about vitamins and minerals...and vitamins and minerals can help you think smart!

---

1. Jensen, B. *The Chemistry of Man*, Escondido, CA: Bernard Jensen International, 1983: 584–590.

2. Webb, W.L., Gehi, M. Electrolyte and fluid imbalance: Neuropsychiatric manifestations. *Psychosomatics* 1981 (22;3): 199–203.

3. Bruner, A.B., Joffe, A., Duggan, A.K., Casella, J.F., and Brandt, J. Randomized study of cognitive effects of iron supplementation in non-anemic iron-deficient adolescent girls. *Lancet* 1996 (348): 992–996.

4. See Erdmann, R. *The Amino Revolution*, New York: Simon & Schuster, 1987.

5. Shults, C.W., Beal, M.F., Fontaine, K. et al. Absorption, tolerability and effects on mitochondrial activity of oral coenzyme Q10 in Parkinsonian patients. *Neur* 1998 (50): 793–795.

6. Mortensen, S.A., Leth, A., Agner, E. Dose-related decrease of serum coenzyme Q10 during treatment with HMG-CoA reductase inhibitors. *Mol Aspects of Med* 1997 (18;Suppl: S17–44.

7. Birkmayer, J.G.D. Coenzyme nicotinamide adenine dinucleotide-new therapeutic approach for improving dementia of the Alzheimer's type. *Ann Clin and Lab Sci* 1996 (26;1):1–9.

8. Thal, L.J., Carta, A., Clarke, W.R., et al. A one-year multicenter placebo-controlled study of acetyl-L-carnitine in patients with Alzheimer's disease. *Neur* 1996 (7): 705–711.

TAKING ACTION FOR HEALTHY BRAIN FUNCTION

1. Take good-quality mineral supplements daily.

2. Have a hair analysis performed to determine any mineral deficiencies. (Call 1-800-726-1834.)

3. Cut down on caffeine consumption.

CHAPTER 10

SMART FOODS—
DO THEY REALLY EXIST?

A number of products on the market today have been linked to the terms "smart drugs," "smart pills," "smart nutrients," or "brain foods."

As a general rule, nutrients that are food substances, including vitamins and minerals, are naturally occurring substances made by the body or in plants. Drugs, in comparison, are synthesized chemicals. In recent years, however, the Food and Drug Administration (FDA) has also included some powerful and unusual combinations of vitamins, minerals, nutrients, and various extracts, hormones, and enzymes as "drugs." The boundary between foods and drugs has become fuzzy, even though these distinctions are largely for legal and regulatory reasons.

A number of these so-called "smart foods" are herbs and spices that have been linked to brain function for centuries.

"Smart" Herbs and Spices

Whether a plant is called an herb or a spice depends on how it is used, not what it is. Plants we normally call herbs can be considered spices if they are used for flavoring or preserving. On the other hand, some minerals—such as salt—are called spices.

Several spices work as antioxidants in preserving food—they work much like synthetic antioxidants (such as BHT and BHA) only they are natural. These include cloves, oregano, sage, rosemary, and vanilla.

Given the many discussions in recent years about herbs and drugs, it may be helpful to give you a very simple explanation about how herbs work in the body. First and foremost, herbs occur in nature and have a general therapeutic effect on the body as a whole. By contrast, drugs are created by refining or purifying a naturally occurring substance to create a concentration of it for addressing a specific problem. The effects of drugs are usually much stronger than the effects of herbs.

The general philosophy underlying herbal therapies is that herbs energize and stimulate the body and brain, and help the immune system function better to enable the body to heal and stay healthy. The general philosophy underlying drug therapies is that drugs address the causes and symptoms of specific ailments.

More research has been done on vitamins and minerals than herbs. One of the difficulties in studying herbs is that not all of the "active ingredients" in various herbs have been identified. Another difficulty is that soil and climate conditions can produce herbs of different potency. Not only have we not fully studied the therapeutic effects of individual herbs, but we are just now beginning to study the effect of "blends" of herbs.

Another problem with herbs is that the active ingredients in various herbs are often destroyed by exposure to air, light, moisture, or heat. Powdered forms of herbs may oxidize. Tinctures are liquid extracts of dried herbs—a tincture is taken by diluting several drops in a small amount of water and then drinking the mixture of extract and water. Freeze-dried herbal extracts are the most concentrated and stable of herbal preparations.

Does this ambiguity mean that we should avoid using herbs? Not at all. While scientific research needs to continue, most herbs have hundreds, some even thousands, of years of anecdotal research backing up their use.

Ginkgo Biloba—The Herbal Star

The star of herbal brain boosters is Ginkgo biloba, an extract of the leaves of the Ginkgo biloba tree. This herb has been revered for many centuries in traditional Chinese medicine for its ability to improve memory, thinking, reasoning, and general alertness. In France, extracts of this herb have been administered orally and intravenously for many years. Ginkgo is also one of the most commonly prescribed pharmaceutical drugs in Germany, where it has been licensed for a wide variety of brain disorders and memory disorders.

Ginkgo increases blood circulation through the brain, improves cerebral metabolism, functions as an antioxidant against free radicals, and facilities the transmission of nerve signals.

Ginkgo biloba extract has been shown to help delay, although not prevent, the onset of Alzheimer's. In one major study, two hundred Alzheimer's patients were evaluated over a year—half the group received Ginkgo biloba and the other half a placebo. The results were dramatic. The placebo group showed a progressive decline in mental function, while the Ginkgo group, on average, actually *improved*. Similar results were noted in independent evaluations of social skills. The authors wrote, "Ginkgo biloba appears to be "safe" and "capable of stabilizing and, in a substantial number of cases, improving the cognitive performance and social functioning of demented patients for six months to one year."[1]

Ginkgo is also effective in reversing those declines in mental deficiency that are the result of vascular insufficiency or depression.

A person usually needs to take Ginkgo extract for two or three weeks before its benefits are experienced. (The extract is available through my office.) The usual regime involves taking the powdered or tinctured form three times a day.

No side effects from the leaf extract have been reported in the scientific literature. Watch out, however, for the Ginkgo fruit. Some people have an allergic reaction to touching the fruit—the reaction is similar to that of touching poison ivy or poison oak.

Ginseng—the Great "Adaptogen"

Ginseng has been used in Chinese medicine for more than four thousand years as a health tonic. It remains the most widely used medicinal plant in the Orient. It has been used to treat fatigue and stress, mental problems, as well as insomnia, TB, indigestion, high blood pressure, arthritis, and cancer.

Ginseng and its extracts come in many types and grades, depending on the source, age, parts of the root used, and the method of preparation. Old, wild, and well-formed roots are the most highly prized. In fact, a highly prized old root from the Orient can sell for more than $2,000!

Ginseng functions as an "adaptogen." This term was coined by a Russian pharmacologist to refer to substances that help the body "normalize"—no matter what the problem may be in the body, adaptogens help the body return to a state of homeostasis and balance. This may be one way of explaining the *many* beneficial effects associated with ginseng.

A great deal of research has been done on ginseng. One of the areas where the research shows great benefit is in "anti-fatigue" activities. For example, mice fed ginseng were able to endure "exercise" up to 183 percent longer than mice who did not get ginseng. Similar results have been found in double-blind scientific studies using soldiers, nurses who work erratic shifts, and athletes.

Ginseng has also been shown to improve concentration, alertness, and reasoning—to a great degree these effects seem to be the result of ginseng's ability to normalize blood-sugar levels. A drop in blood sugar creates a condition known as hypoglycemia. Its symptoms are usually associated with mental fatigue, confused thinking, and difficulty in concentrating. With ginseng, the process is reversed. On the other hand, if the level of glucose in the blood is too high, ginseng can lower the excess level to normal. It is a great blood-sugar "leveler."

Ginseng improves memory, and also helps improve learning, by stimulating the adrenal cortex. Scientific studies have shown that both short-term and long-term memory are positively impacted by ginseng.

Ginseng is available in a variety of forms in most Chinese groceries and nutrition stores—extracts and teas seem to be the forms most easily absorbed by the body. It has something of a bitter taste, but many people come to enjoy the taste over time. Stevia and honey can be used to sweeten ginseng tea.

Again, the main problem with ginseng is that there is no standardization in the processing or potency of products. For information about the best sources for obtaining high-quality ginseng, call my office: 1-800-726-1834.

Gotu-Kola and Fo-Ti-Tieng

Gotu-kola has been linked to improved attention span and concentration. It is widely used in India to improve memory and to produce mental stamina. Many herbalists make very strong claims for this herb as a brain stimulant, detoxifier, and cell energizer.

Fo-ti-tieng is very close to Gotu-kola—in fact, it may be a geographic variant of gotu-kola. It also is widely recognized in the Orient as an herb that has a rejuvenating effect on nerves and brain.

In China, fo-ti-tieng was popularized by Li Chung Yung who was born in 1677 and lived until 1933—that's 256 years, according to Chinese government records! At the time of his death he was living with his twenty-fourth wife. Although these dates are more than a little incredible, it has been established that Li Chung Yun did live an unusually long life and he was physically vigorous until he died. He raised his own food, followed a stringent vegetarian diet, fasted frequently, and used fo-ti-tieng and ginseng regularly. Something to think about!

In general, both gotu-kola and fo-ti-tieng are taken as teas made from the leaves of these plants.

Vinpocetine And Memory

Vincopetine is derived from vincamine, an extract of the periwinkle plant. It has a powerful stimulating effect on memory. Hundreds of studies have shown its effectiveness and safety. It may take up to a year of supplementation, however, for a person to realize the maximum effectiveness of vinpocetine.

Is There Benefit from Chocolate?

I know many people who would love for chocolate to be labeled one of the most potent brain boosters available—they would feel highly justified, then, in consuming *pounds*, rather than ounces, of chocolate! Sorry to disappoint you. There is very little research to support the rumor that chocolate has any effects on cognition.

Of surprise to many people is the fact that chocolate contains proteins, vitamins, and minerals including calcium, phosphorus, iron, sodium, potassium, vitamin A, thiamin, riboflavin, and niacin. It also has theobromine and caffeine, both of which are alkaloids that stimulate the central nervous system and act on the dopamine chemistry of the brain. We are talking about *pure* chocolate here, not the forms of chocolate most Americans consume—which includes a great deal of sugar, cream, and wax.

The caffeine in chocolate may have the same negative effects in the brain as coffee, although the caffeine in chocolate is much less potent per ounce. Very little research has been done on theobromine.

Eating chocolate may be considered a pleasant or aesthetic experience—however, eating chocolate is *not* good nutrition nor does it provide benefit to the brain's functioning.

The Purity of Herbal Nutrients

My main concern with herbs, as well as with all supplements, is a concern about their *purity*. Make sure you purchase your nutrients and herbs from a reputable source and that you check labels to make sure amounts of various nutrients are clearly identified and purity-related facts related to the origin and the manufacturing of the product are also clearly stated. Don't just take something because a large and colorful display or label touts something a being a "smart pill" or a "smart compound."

As a general rule, I favor natural nutrients any day over drugs. Only one fatality due to poisoning by a vitamin supplement was recorded in the United States between 1983 and 1990. In that same period, there were hundreds of thousands of fatalities from the combined categories of prescription and nonprescription pharmaceutical drugs. [2]

The Amazing Properties of Royal Jelly

Royal jelly is a mysterious and fascinating food manufactured by bees. It is made from pollen and honey and secreted from the pharyngeal glands of young nurse bees. Only the "queen bee" is fed royal jelly throughout her entire life. In fact, those who study bees have found that the only difference between the queen and other females is her diet of royal jelly.

The queen bee is extremely fertile and lays more than 2,000 eggs a day—twice her body weight in eggs! While other bees in the hive live only about three months, the queen lives four to five years.

A study done in Russia of people who were a hundred years old or older revealed that many of them had been beekeepers, and *all* of them, without exception, had consumed honey as one of their principal foods throughout their lives.

Is it any wonder that many who use this product take it as an anti-aging supplement?

Royal jelly is a natural and unprocessed food. It is one of the world's richest natural sources of vitamin B5. It is also rich in B1, B2, B3, B6, B12, biotin, folic acid, and the vitamin-B-like substance inositol. It is a natural source of acetylcholine, and contains vitamins A,C,D, and E. And if that isn't impressive enough, royal jelly also has the minerals phosphorus (which protects from stress and improves mental functioning), calcium, potassium, sulfur, iron, manganese, nickel, cobalt, silicon, chromium, gold, bismuth, and trace minerals. It has eighteen of the amino acids. Fatty acids, enzymes, and the hormone testosterone—which is needed by both men and women—are found in royal jelly. All of this in a natural food! And there's still more—royal jelly has antiviral, antifungicidal, and antibacterial properties.

It is probably not an oversimplification to say that if you could only choose one "smart food" to take regularly to boost brain function and memory, it would be royal jelly.

Most people know that honey is highly resistant to spoiling. One of the reasons for this is propolis, a stick substance made of wax, resin, balsam, oil, and pollen collected by the bees from the buds of trees and tree bark. Crude honey with bits of propolis in it have been used for antiseptic and anti-infection purposes for thousands of years. Even today, it is used widely in some cultures to heal wounds and treat skin diseases.

Royal jelly should not be exposed to room-temperature air or sunlight. It is best acquired in more stable forms—such as in sealed capsules or mixed in honey. If it is purchased in pure form, it should be kept refrigerated. The recommended dose is ⅓ teaspoon or a large drop—most people find the taste more palatable if it is mixed with a teaspoon of honey. It can be eaten directly or spread on whole-grain bread.

Royal jelly should *not* be mixed with hot liquids, since this destroys the many beneficial properties. In other words, don't use it with honey as a hot-tea sweetener!

Another way to take royal jelly is in a phial form in which the royal jelly has been mixed with ginseng. This can be found most often in Chinese markets.

Royal jelly needs to be taken regularly for several weeks before most people notice an improvement in their mental function and concentration. Again, as with any product, know your source!

What's All the Fuss about "Smart Drinks"?

Smart drinks are "nutrient cocktails" often served at parties as an alternative to alcohol. They are sometimes served at the beverage counters connected to gyms and at spas. The drinks are made from fast-dissolving mixtures of vitamins, minerals, and amino acids.

Smart drinks tend to come in two types: "pick-me-ups" designed to increase energy and stamina, and "brain tonics" designed to improve thinking and memory. A number of powders to make these smart drinks are available—sometimes with fairly exotic names, such as Energy Elicksure™, Psuper Psonic Psyber Tonic™, Memory Fuel™, or Get Smart Think Drink™. (The label for the Psuper Snoic Psyber Tonic claims it is "a cosmadelicious think drink.") The formulas differ according to ingredients and their amounts—the formulas usually have a long list of vitamins and minerals.

The key ingredient in many of the energy drinks is phenylalanine and the main ingredient in the brain-food drinks is usually choline. Drinks are made by mixing a well-rounded tablespoon of the powder product in four to eight ounces of ice-cold water or fruit juice and serving it over ice. The drinks tend to have a tangy citrus flavor.

Smart drinks should never be given to children, pregnant or lactating women, and are not advised for people taking MAO inhibitors. I do NOT recommend these drinks because of the toxic side effects possible from the phenylalanine in most of them.

The Emergence of "Nootropics"

You should be aware that a special classification of "smart pharmaceuticals" has been designated. These pharmaceuticals, called "nootropics," are advertised by drug companies to improve learning, memory, and recall without other effects on the central nervous system. The term "nootropic," by the way, has Greek roots meaning "acting on the mind. They were first described by a French pharmacological journal in 1972.

Nootropics work by acting on the chemicals that carry impulses or messages between brain cells. They promote the production of neurotransmitters.

The Pyrrolidone Nootropics. A number of nootropics are derived from pyrrolidone, a substance. They include piracetam, oxiracetam, pramiracetam, aniracetam, and pyroglutamate (PCA). The easiest of these nootropics to find is PCA. The reason for its ready availability is that it is also an amino acid and is found commonly in natural foods, including vegetables, fruits, dairy producs, and meats. PCA is more like a nutrient than a drug and it has been shown to pass through the blood-brain barrier into the brain, where it stimulates thinking, memory, and learning.

Hydergine. Another easy-to-obtain brain booster is hydergine. It has been shown to increase memory, learning, and other mental abilities, prevent brain cells from being damaged by free radicals or too little oxygen, and reverse brain-cell damage. It speeds up metabolism of brain cells and helps increase the amount of blood and oxygen to the brain. In the United States, the FDA has approved its use by prescription only for senility and cerebrovascular insufficiency at a maximum dosage of 3 mg a day.

In Europe, physicians can prescribe hydergine in dosages up to 9 mg a day. Hydergine's use is much more common in Europe in preventively helping patients with mild mental deterioration. It is often given in hospital emergency rooms to victims of strokes, heart attacks, hemorrhage, drug overdoses, drowning, and electrocution. It is also administered routinely before surgery in some European hospitals. [3]

Hydergine has been studied extensively, with more than 3,000 research papers published on it to date.

Vasopressin. Vasopression has been shown to have memory-enhancing effects. The most widely known prescription drug is under the trade name Diapid. Vasopressin is a brain hormone secreted by the pituitary gland; it is vital to the acquisition of new information (learning). Studies on vasopressin have been conducted primarily with elderly patients who had memory loss as well as patients who had memory loss resulting from accidental head injuries. Amnesia patients had good results regaining their memories and felt more cheerful. Patients with memory problems showed improved attention span, concentration, recall, and ability to learn. [4]

Research on vasopressin has actually shown why people who use recreational drugs often have memory problems. Stimulants such as LSD, cocaine, and amphetamines cause the pituitary to release vasopressin. Over time, frequent use of these drugs can lead to sluggish mental performance and depression because the pituitary is depleted of vasopressin. On the other hand, marijuana and alcohol, which are depressants, inhibit the release of vasopressin. This explains why regular users, especially of marijuana, often complain of memory loss. The pituitary gland is not being allowed to do its normal work. Almost all of these recreational-drug problems with memory have been shown to be reversed by the taking of vasopressin.

Vasopressin has also been shown to be helpful to those who desire to improve their memory and recall in order to be able to learn large amounts of new information. The FDA has approved the prescribing of Diapid for healthy people to help with memory and learning enhancement. Diapid is administered as a nasal spray, so those who take it may have side effects of nose irritation and headaches. Some experience abdominal cramps and an increased desire to move the bowels. Pregnant women should avoid this substance, as should people with a history of cardiovascular problems.

Centrophenoxine. This substance, commonly known by its trade name Lucidril, rejuvenates brain cells by getting rid of lipofuscin deposits, the cellular "garbage" that builds up in the wake of cellular metabolism. (In the skin, this "garbage" may appear as brown age spots or liver spots.) When too much lipofuscin builds up in brain cells, neurons die. The amount of lipofuscin in the brain is directly related to learning ability. Lucidril also helps protect the brain against oxygen starvation.

In rare instances, people who take Lucidril may experience headaches, muscle stiffness, and excitability. Centrophenoxine is not currently available in the United States, but it is sold in Europe.

Fipexide. A few studies have been done with this substance involving elderly people with cognition disorders. Fipexide has been shown to improve cognition, short-term memory, and attention. Fipexide seems to help learning, but not long-term recall. It appears to work by increasing slightly the amount of dopamine in the brain.

Other Brain-Cell "Rejuvenators."

Although they are not specifically classified as "nootropics," there are several other drugs on the market that are being touted as brain-cell rejuvenators. Some of these products are widely available in Europe or the Orient, but they seem to be coming our way. [5]

D8imethylaminoethanol (DMAE). Depending on how it is packaged, DMAE may be considered a drug or a nutrient. It is naturally found in small amounts in the human brain and in certain sea foods, including sardines and anchovies. DMAE has many of the same effects as centrophenoxine (Lucidril)—it increases intelligence, memory, and learning abilities, as well as produces better mood and more energy. It is considered a "central-nervous-system stimulant. It can take up to two weeks for a person to experience these effects because the substance needs to build up gradually in the system. When it is discontinued, people do not generally have a feeling of "letdown" or a "crash," however. DMAE stimulates the production of choline, which helps the brain produce acetylcholine, major neurotransmitter that promotes memory and learning. The effects of DMAE in the brain are increased if it is taken with vitamin B5 and calcium panthothenate.

As a nutrient, DMAE is available in many forms, including bulk powder, capsules, and liquid under a variety of trade names.

Phenytoin (Dilantin). Phenytoin is a remarkable multipurpose drug, most commonly used to treat epilepsy. More than 8,000 published papers have documents its effects in the body. In general terms, phenytoin normalizes and improves concentration, learning, and thinking. Thinking, memory, and pain are all electrically generated and phenytoin stabilizes the electrical activity in the brain. (Epilepsy results from a misfiring of electrical impulses in the brain, and hence, the substance's use in treating this malady.)

A number of studies have shown an increase of IQ after taking phenytoin. It has positive effects on long-term memory, comprehension, and learning new material.

Although phenytoin has many positive effects and has been prescribed widely, there are some potential negative side-effects. Some people report tremors, insomnia, headaches, nausea, vomiting, and dizziness. During the first few weeks of use, some may experience liver toxicity. The substance also disturbs the absorption of vitamin D and folic acid so those who are taking phenytoin are advised to increase their supplements of vitamin D, calcium, and folic acid.

Phenytoin is available by prescription only.

Dehydroepiandrosterone (DHEA). By comparison to some substances, dehydroepiandrosterone (DHEA) is a "new kid on the block," even though it is the most common steroid in the blood. What we do know about this steroid hormone produced by the adrenal glands is that it may be one of our major weapons in the future against aging, obesity, tumors, and cancer. Early research has also suggested that it helps protect the brain cells from various conditions associated with aging, such as Alzheimer's disease, mental degeneration, and sterility.

Normal brain tissue contains 6.5 times more DHEA than other body tissue. As people age, the amount of DHEA in the blood drops. Therefore, the reasoning behind DHEA supplementation is this: if DHEA reduction can be halted, or even reversed, general brain function may be kept at high levels.

There's more on DHEA in a later chapter.

Tacrine (THA). This substance has been shown to improve memory in Alzheimer's patients by keeping acetylcholine levels in the brain cells at higher levels. Some researchers conducting animal studies are seeing good results from combining THA with deprenyl and lecithin. The FDA has not approved the use of THA and it is hard to find, but preliminary research findings hold promise of potential good things to come.

Gerovital (GH-3). Gerovital was developed by Dr. Ana Aslan, director of the Institute of Geriatrics in Romania in the early 1950's. Very quickly, GH-3 therapy became one of the most popular rejuvenation treatments used by movie stars, world leaders, and politicians. According to news reports, world figures Mao Tse-Tung, Charles de Gaulle, Ho Chi Minh, Winston Churchill, and John F. Kennedy went for treatment. So did many Hollywood stars, including Charlie Chaplin, Greta Garbo, Lena Horne, Lillian Gish, Marlene Dietrich, and Kirk Douglas. The substance was hailed as a miraculous youth formula that reversed the aging process.

Chemically, GH-3 is made of procaine hydrochloride mixed with potassium metabisulfate, disodium phosphate, and benzoic acid. Procaine breaks down in the body into PABA, a B vitamin, and DAEA, which is chemically similar to DMAE and is converted in the cells into choline. PABA, which we have mentioned elsewhere, aids the body in blood-cell formation and if the body has too little

PABA, constipation, depression, digestive disorders, stress, infertiligy, fatigue, gray hair, headaches, and irritability may result. PABA stimulates the intestinal system to produce the B vitamins folic acid, pantothenic acid, and biotin, as well as vitamin K.

DEAE has an antidepressant effect. Choline, of course, is a major neurotransmitter facilitating brain functioning.

Later research on Dr. Aslan's formula showed that it had an MAO inhibiting effect.

All of these chemical reactions resulted in many people feeling relieved of some of the aging symptoms we all hope to avoid—both physical and emotional.

The Dr. Ana Aslan Institute in Miami, Florida, continues to provide treatments using Aslan's original formula. The treatment involves injections three times a week for four weeks, followed by a ten-day rest period, and then another four-week treatment period. (GH-3 therapy may also be administered in tablet form.)

(Vitacel is essentially GYH-3 in tablet form. However, it is not approved by the FDA and is not available in the United States.)

K.H.3. This is another procaine formulation—this time procaine has been linked to hematoporphyrin. It claims to help alertness, concentration, and recall. It is only sold legally in the United States in Nevada but is available over the counter in Europe. It should not be taken with sulfa drugs or MAO inhibitors, used by pregnant or nursing women, or taken by people allergic to procaine.

Piracetam. The medication Piracetam was originally manufactured as a memory enhancer. It improves the metabolism of brain cells through various mechanisms and has been shown to have the potential to enhance both learning and memory. Some clinicians are now prescribing Piracetam for adults with attention disorders.

When Taking Nootropics...

Nootropics may be helpful for some people. I am not a great advocate for them. As with all "medicines," they may have undesirable side effects. I strongly advise that if you choose to take these or other "combination" substances that are marketed as "smart products," you do the following:

1. Keep good records of all pharmaceuticals you take and keep your personal files updated as to your clinical lab test results. A good set of records can help your physician adjust dosages and avoid conflicts in medication.

2. Be concerned about potential overdose. Some people seem to think that if they take something to stimulate neurological transmittal, that transmittal will only be increased if they take even more of the substance. Not so! Taking too much of a nootropic may be very harmful.

3. Be aware that nootropics may interact with other pharmaceuticals and over-the-counter medications, including herbs and nutrients. The extent of potential harm from these combinations has not been documented fully.

4. Before you begin using any new nutrient or drug, have clinical lab tests run to establish a baseline for body and brain functions. Then have these clinical lab tests rerun at specified intervals, perhaps once every three to six months and at the very least, once a year.

5. Dosages of these substances should be increased *slowly*. To reduce dosages, taper off gradually. Do not change dosages of more than one nutrient, nootropic, or pharmaceutical at a time unless a physician is monitoring you closely.

My general advice is this: Dietary change and supplementation with high-quality nutrients should ALWAYS be undertaken as a

first line of therapy. Give the nutrients and dietary changes time
to work before any drug therapy is considered.

1. Le Bars, P., Katz, M.M., Berman, N., et al. A placebo-controlled, double-blind randomized trial of an extract of Ginkgo biloba for dementia. *JAMA* 1997 (278;16): 1327–32.

2. Loomis, D.C. "Which is safer: Drugs or vitamins?" *Townsend Letter for Doctors*. Found in Potter, V.A., Orfali, S., Scott, G.G., *Brain Boosters*. Berkeley, CA: Ronin Publishing, 1993: 72.

3. Pelton, R. *Mind Foods and Smart Pills: A Sourcebook for the Vitamins, Herbs, and Drugs that Can Increase Intelligence, Improve Memory, and Prevent Brain Aging.* New York: Doubleday, 1989.

4. Potter, V.A., Orfali, S., Scott, G.G. *Brain Boosters*. Berkeley, CA: Ronin Publishing, 1993:106.

5. For more information on these substances, see Potter, V.A., Orfali, S., Scott, G.G., *Brain Boosters*. Berkeley, CA: Ronin Publishing, 1993: 93–130.

TAKING ACTION FOR HEALTHY BRAIN FUNCTION

1. Consider adding Gingko biloba, ginseng, and royal jelly to your diet.

2. Refrain from using "smart drinks." Use nootropics with great caution. Make sure you are closely supervised if you choose to take pharmaceuticals intended to enhance brain functioning.

3. When using herbs, only use high-quality products from reputable sources.

An excellent general resource on this topic is:

Pelton, Ross, *Mind Foods and Smart Pills: A Sourcebook for the Vitamins, Herbs, and Drugs that Can Increase Intelligence, Improve Memory, and Prevent Brain Aging,* New York: Doubleday, 1989.

CHAPTER 11

THE THREE
"A" CLASS BRAIN POISONS
USED BY MILLIONS

Several years ago, I met a woman named Cindy who was working for a friend of mine in a marketing business. Cindy was eighteen, married to a young man who was only nineteen. One day I noticed that Cindy wasn't at work with my friend and I asked about her. My friend said, "Her husband died."

"Died?" I asked. "What happened? Was he in an accident?"

"No," my friend said. "He was mowing his lawn last Saturday and came in and asked Cindy for a glass of water and then went back out outside. She went out a few minutes later and found him curled up on the porch, dead. He had a massive heart attack."

I was stunned. Cindy's husband was one of those people who advocated that a person could eat anything he wanted to eat and live a long life. I meet these people regularly. They invariably call in to the radio programs on which I am a guest, or appear at lectures I give about nutritional practices. They hold to the opinion that they can eat anything that is classified as "safe" to be on the market, and especially so when they are young. I am continually amazed at the number of people who seem to think they only need to be concerned about their dietary habits, weight, and memory as they get older. Friend, the time to be concerned is *now*, no matter what age you may be.

Even if you are just a teenager reading this book, take this information to heart. It is *not* too soon to be concerned about the health of your cardiovascular system or brain tissues. Several years ago I went to a continuing education seminar conducted by Charlie Atwood, M.D. He stated that he had not examined a nineteen-year-old patient in recent years that did not already have *advanced atherosclerotic plaquing* in their arteries. Atwood, by the way, works in Louisiana, a state notorious for its seafood and sausage dishes.

There are three main brain poisons that impact people *regardless of their age*. In fact, in my opinion young people should be especially concerned about these three poisons because young people tend to consume *greater* quantities of these poisons than older people.

"A" Is for Aspartame

Aspartame, in my opinion, should be labeled as a highly potent brain poison with a huge skull and crossbones emblem. Unfortunately, this poison is being consumed by Americans at a rate of *millions* of gallons a year. Aspartame is generally available as NutraSweet® or Equal®. Yes, the stuff in the little blue packets.

Among the 92 documented symptoms from aspartame poisoning are memory loss, headaches, dizziness, seizures, hearing loss, tinnitus, anxiety attacks, vertigo, blurred vision, and loss of taste. Diseases associated with or triggered by aspartame include brain tumors, Alzheimer's, mental retardation, and a number of other serious disorders from multiple sclerosis to lymphoma to lupus to Parkinson's.

The best way to think about NutraSweet® is to think of it as a small dose of nerve gas that eradicates brain and nerve function.

Animals, by the way, are far smarter about this substance that we human beings. Roaches won't eat it, cats and dogs won't touch it, ants avoid it, and flies fly the other way from it. People, however, seem to flock to it. Many have become addicted to it.

Any time you see a product that claims to be "sugar-free," check the label for aspartame. It is found in more than nine thousand products on the market today, including:

- instant breakfast drinks
- tabletop sweeteners
- cereals
- sugar-free chewing gum
- instant teas and coffees
- cocoa mixes
- frozen desserts
- flavored coffee and tea beverages
- protein drink powders
- puddings
- gelatin desserts
- juice beverages
- soft drinks
- laxatives
- some multivitamins
- breath mints
- milk drinks
- sugar-free yogurt
- some pharmaceuticals
- wine coolers
- topping mixes

In the body, aspartame breaks down in the chemicals methanol, aspartic acid, phenylalanine, and diketopiperazine (DKP). Each of these components is, by itself, a known toxin.

Methanol, also known as wood alcohol, breaks down into formaldehyde and formic acid. Just one little blue packet of sweetener (one gram) breaks down into 100 mg of methanol. In the body, the methanol breaks down into formaldehyde—yes, the embalming fluid. Since the body has difficulty eliminating formaldehyde, some of it is stored in fat cells of the body. What is not stored is converted to formic acid, which is used as an activator to strip epoxy and urethane coatings. It's powerful stuff.

Phenylalanine and aspartic acid are amino acids normally used in the synthesis of proteoplasm when they are found naturally in foods. When they are unaccompanied by other amino acids in natural foods, however, they pass through the blood-brain barrier and deteriorate the neurons of the brain. Phenylalanine is what breaks down into diketopiperazine (DKP). The process basically allows too much calcium into the neural cells and the result is the formation of excessive amounts of free radicals that stimulate or "excite" the neural cells to death.

Aspartame especially targets the brain. It negatively effects dopamine, cerebral cholecystokinin (CCK), serotonin, endorphins, and other important neurotransmitters, the permeability of the blood-brain barrier to phenylalanine, and insulin.

Both aspartame and MSG have been shown to be directly linked to "brain holes" in laboratory animals. Aspartame has also been linked to brain cancer in animal studies.

Aspartame is not only highly dangerous to brain cells, but it is highly addictive. Many people find that the more they use aspartame-based sodas to quench their thirst, the more thirst they experience and hence, the more they drink. This addictive power seems especially potent in children.

And that isn't all. When you combine Nutrasweet® and nitrites, you have the potential of forming a nitrosurea. Nitrusoreas are the most effective agents known for producing malignant brain tumors in laboratory animals. So, if you eat luncheon meat, pepperoni, bacon, ham, or anything with nitrites and then drink a diet soda or glass of tea or coffee sweetened with aspartame, you have just given your body all the raw materials needed to form the most potent brain cancer causing agent known to man. How many people do you know who eat pepperoni pizza and chase it down with a diet soda?

I cannot overemphasize my conclusion about aspartame: DO NOT USE IT!!! In my opinion, this is the most dangerous product ever released for general consumption into the population. If you need more information and research to convince you about this substance, please see my books *Maximum Energy* and *Maximum Fat Loss.* [1]

So What Can We Use as a Sweetener? A great natural alternative to sugar exists, although you may have to look for it at a nutrition store. This product has all the benefits of artificial sweeteners and none of the drawbacks. It is an especially good product for diabetes, and those who suffer from hypoglycemia, high blood pressure, obesity, or chronic yeast infections. The product is called stevia.

Not only is stevia *very sweet*, but it actually is *good for you*. Clinical studies have shown that it helps normalize blood sugar, aids digestion, helps prevent tooth decay and gingivitis, and can help lower elevated blood pressure levels.

Stevia can be found in both powder and liquid forms. In most cases, one half to one teaspoon of the liquid achieves the same sweetening effect as a cup of white sugar. A little goes a long way. Those who are accustomed to dishing out white sugar granules often use way too much stevia at first. It is many times sweeter than sugar.

Stevia works especially well on dairy products, fruit dishes, in beverages, and in making fresh desserts.

Stevia has been around for hundreds of years without any recorded side effects. The Japanese have used it in great quantities without any anomalies ever observed in cellular function, enzyme production, chromosomes, blood chemistry, or other physiological parameters.

In summary, stevia is

- safe for diabetics
- calorie-free
- 50 to 400 times sweeter than white sugar
- has no adverse effects on blood sugar levels

- is non-toxic
- contains no artificial ingredients
- can be used in baking and cooking
- inhibits the formation of plaque and cavities
- does not promote growth of microorganisms such as bacteria and yeast. [2]

"A" Is for Alcohol

A second potent brain poison we Americans routinely guzzle by the billion barrel-full is alcohol. Alcohol acts negatively on brain tissue in two very basic ways.

First, it makes a person's blood vessels more susceptible to hemorrhaging. Some people have been told that alcohol increases HDL (high-density lipoproteins, or "good cholesterol") and this helps decrease hardening of blood vessels. While that may be true, the protective effect is very small and it may actually be related to factors other than the alcohol consumption. The research bears out the fact that alcohol—even when consumed in moderate amounts—increases a person's risk of brain hemorrhage.

Second, alcohol acts as an outright poison on brain tissue. Through the years, some physicians have argued this point, claiming that Korsakoff's disease produces memory loss in chronic alcoholics. (Korsakoff's disease is related to a thiamine or vitamin B1 deficiency.) Others claim that the reason alcoholics become demented is because they tend to suffer head injuries. Both of these claims are *partially* true but neither of these "excuses" can explain away the general brain deterioration that is observable in chronic alcoholics.

In the early 1960's, a brain researcher named J.C. Lee demonstrated the effects of alcohol on the blood-brain barrier, another name for the "barrier" around the capillaries of blood vessels that prevents unwanted substances from coming into contact with the delicate and balanced neuroelectric and neurochemical environment in many brain cells. This barrier can be impacted negatively by various diseases—such as brain tumors, strokes, infection—as well as brain injury. It is also destroyed, temporarily, by alcohol.

During the time when the brain is poisoned by alcohol, the effects are just as disabling as the effects caused by tumors, strokes, infections, and injuries. The injury may last for a matter of hours, or perhaps a day, depending on the amount of alcohol consumed. Repeated doses of alcohol produce lasting changes, however. Over time, some of the normal fatty substance around the neurofibers is removed. This causes a shrinkage of the internal structures of the brain and expands the fluid-filled spaces within the brain. If the poisoning continues for a long enough period, these structural changes are irreversible.

My advice, for a variety of health reasons, is not to drink. Any so-called "benefits" of alcohol are far outweighed by negative consequences. Alcohol *never* improves brain performance or mental capacity; it never helps a person's memory. I have a family member who drinks heavily. I find it very sad that he cannot remember some of the memories that I consider to be the "best moments" of his past.

Regular consumption of alcohol, in whatever amount and by whatever "brand name," decreases the *long-term* quality of a person's life.

Related Poisons. In addition to alcohol, cocaine, amphetamines, barbiturates, and many other "drugs" are also poisons to the brain. They produce both temporary and lasting effects. Very simply put, don't use these substances if you want to improve your mind or keep your mental faculties sharp.

Think about More than Taste or Mood Effect. Years ago, while my family and I were once on a vacation cruise in the Caribbean, a tray of petit fours was delivered to our room—they were flowery and pretty, but we knew they were pure sugar. My wife, Sharon, warned our young son Austin not to eat them, telling him, "These are nothing but sugar. They aren't good for you."

Austin, however, decided to check out these lovely confections for himself. Biting down hard, he nearly broke a tooth. The petit fours were *ceramic*!

Just because something looks beautiful, it is not necessarily good for you. For that matter, just because something has a pleasant taste, it is not necessarily good for your body or your brain. Even if it gives you a buzz or mellows you out, giving you a "feel good feeling" for awhile, it is not necessarily good for your body or brain. ALWAYS ask about everything you put into your mouth, "Is this really *good* for my HEALTH?"

"A" Is for Additives

A number of years ago, a great deal was written about the so-called "Chinese restaurant syndrome," which was linked to monosodium glutamate (MSG). MSG has been used widely in the food industry as a flavor enhancer. In fact, after salt and pepper, the most widely used flavor enhancer in the world is MSG. (In Japan, it is known as Aji-no-moto.)

More than a flavor enhancer, MSG is a poison to many people who are sensitive to its effects. Clinical data has shown that nearly one in three people experiences some symptoms from MSG in amounts commonly added to foods consumed routinely in the United States. Even those who do not seem to have an immediate reaction to MSG may develop a low-grade inflammatory response to MSG over time.

Consumption of MSG has doubled in every decade since the 1940s. More than eighty million people a year use MSG—most don't even know they are doing so. The reason is that MSG is *widely* used in many of the food items that fill the average supermarket cart. More and more people are using prepackaged, processed foods—and this seems to be especially true for the elderly who spend considerably less time in meal preparation and are more likely to rely on fast-food, canned, and frozen foods and dinners.

Those who are allergic to this substance often feel a general numbness radiating from the back of the neck into the arms—they tend to feel weak and have heart palpitations. However, the symptoms of those who are sensitive to MSG can be much more varied than that:

Cramps	Weakness
Tightness around eyes, face or in chest	Heaviness of arms and legs
	Dizziness
Diarrhea	Excessive perspiration
Blurred vision; difficulty focusing	Insomnia
	Fast heartbeat
Nausea	Confusion
Rash, hives	Staggering or
Headaches	balance problems
Muscle aches and jaw stiffness	Slurred speech
	Asthma or shortness of breath

Even those without immediate symptoms may develop internal "allergic" reactions over time. These reactions can manifest as inflammation. MSG has been linked to arthritis and tendonitis.

When you are shopping, especially check the labels for MSG. You will frequently find MSG is an ingredient in canned and dried meats; prepared dinners and side dishes; canned soups and dry soup mixes; cured meats; cookies and crackers, freeze-dried and frozen foods, gravy and seasoning mixes, potato chips and prepared snacks; salad dressings; croutons, sauces, spices, and multi-spice seasoning mixes.

Be aware that sometimes you will find monosodium glutamate listed as just that, rather than in the more common form MSG. It may also be listed on a label as accent, ajinomoto, zest, vetsin, gourmet powder, subu, glutavene, glutacyl, Rl-50, Chinese seasoning, hydrolyzed plant protein; hydrolyzed vegetable protein (12-20% MSG—natural flavorings can also be hydrolyzed vegetable protein); flavorings, kombu extract, mei-jin, and wei-jing.

A number of fast-food chains routinely use MSG. It is frequently found in seasoning mixes, salad dressings, breaded and unbreaded chicken and beef products, breaded onion rings, sausage, cheese and barbecue sauces, croutons, gravies, and soups.[3] Since the full effects of MSG are still not known, I recommend that you avoid restaurants that use MSG in the preparation of their foods.

When you are dining out:

1. Request that your food be prepared without any salt or seasoning salts.

2. Avoid foods with gravies or sauces.

3. Avoid foods that are breaded and deep fried.

4. Choose oil and vinegar salad dressing over pre-mixed dressings (preferably with the oil and vinegar presented to your table so you can mix your own dressing).

Shake Them Off

When my wife Sharon and I first moved to Auburndale, Florida, we had a pool that had a Jacuzzi tub adjacent to it. The water of the whirlpool tub was at the same level as the pool.

One night we went out to relax in the whirlpool after putting our son to bed. It was a steamy night, and given the warm water of the whirlpool, I found it refreshing periodically to scoop up the cooler water of the adjacent pool and splash it on my face. One time as I reached back to scoop up some of the cool pool water, a snake wrapped itself around my arm. It apparently had come into the pool and was attracted to the warm water of the Jacuzzi so had swum over to a position very near us. I flung that snake off my arm as fast as I could and both Sharon and I were out of that Jacuzzi in a matter of seconds!

There are some things in our lives that we need to shake off—and shake them off *now*. Aspartame, alcohol, and food additives, especially MSG, are three of those poisons that can easily attach themselves to us with the potential of causing devastating harm. Get rid of them!

1. Blundell, J.E., and Hill, A.H. Paradoxical effects of an intense sweetener (aspartame) on appetite. *Lancet* (1986): 1092–93.

Boehm, M., and Bada, J. Racemization of aspartic acid and phenylalanine in the sweetener aspartame at100 degrees C *Proc Natl Acad Sci* USA 1984 (81).

Garriga, M., and Metcalf, D. Aspartame intolerance. *Annals of Allergy* 1988 (61): 63–66.

Saleman, M. The morbidity and mortality of brain tumors. *Neurol Clin* 1985 (3): 229–57.

Monte, W.C. Aspartame: Methanol and the public health. *Journ of Appl Nutr* 1984 (16;1): abstract.

Olney, J.W., et al. Brain damage in mice from voluntary ingestion of glutamate and aspartame. *Neurobehav Tox* 1980 (2): 125–29.

Partridge, W.M. Potential effects of the dipeptide sweetener aspartame on the brain. *Nut and the Brain* 1986 (7): 199–241.

Ptenza, D., et al. Aspartame: Clinical update. *Connecticut Med Journ* 1989 (53;7): 3997–3400.

Roberts, H.J. Does aspartame cause human brain cancer? *Journ of Adv in Med* 1991 (4;1): 231–40.

Roberts, H. and Roberts, J. Reactions attributed to aspartame-containing products: 551 cases. *Journ of App Nutr* 1988 (49): 85–94.

U.S. Air Force, Aspartame alert. *Flying Safety* 1992 (48;5): 20–21.

U.S. Department of Health and Human Services, National Institutes of Health. National Library of Medicine pamphlet. Current bibliography series. *Adverse Effects of*

Aspartame—January '86 through December '90, 1991. This report lists 167 citations of aspartame studies.

"Most Scientists in Poll Doubt NutraSweet's Safety." *New York Times,* August 17, 1987.

Walton, R.G., et al. Adverse reactions to aspartame: Double-blind challenge in patients with a vulnerable population. *Biological Psych* 1993 (34): 13–17.

Wurtman, R.J. Aspartame: possible effect on seizure susceptibility. Lancet 1985 (2):1060.

2. Bonvie, L., Bonvie, B., and Gates, D. *The Stevia Story.* Atlanta, GA: B.E.D., 1997.

3. For more about MSG, consult Schwartz, G.R. *In Bad Taste: The MSG Syndrome.* New York: Penguin Books, 1988.

TAKING ACTION FOR HEALTHY BRAIN FUNCTION

1. Say NO to aspartame.

2. Say NO to alcohol.

3. Say NO to additives in foods, especially MSG.

CHAPTER 12

A POLLUTED
ENVIRONMENT CAN RESULT
IN A POLLUTED BRAIN

Years ago as I was just starting my health-care business and nutritional counseling practice, Sharon and I lived with my mother for a short while. One day as we were sitting in the house, we heard a horrible screeching sound—not just once, but repeatedly. We could tell the sound was coming from the back yard so I went out to investigate.

Now my mother had hot-wired the fence in her back yard to keep stray dogs in the neighborhood from entering and destroying her garden. I expected to find that an animal had become tangled in the fence. I was *not* prepared to find a cat *willfully* attacking the fence!

This cat had managed to get in the yard, and in attempting to exit the yard, it had come into contact with the fence. That was obvious to all of us—the fur on that cat was sticking straight up from the electric shock. This cat, however, thought it could win a battle against my mother's hot-wired fence and it ran at that fence repeatedly, each time suffering yet another shock.

Although the appearance of this cat was comical—like something straight out of a Saturday morning cartoon—this cat battle was also one of the saddest sights I have ever seen. We tried coaxing the cat in various directions but without any success.

The cat was too intent on fighting its "shocking" enemy. Finally, after several attempts at taking on the fence, the cat sprang to the top of one of the fence poles, jumped down on the other side, and went its way.

So many people today are taking on chemicals and harmful substances—substances that are, in effect, "hot wires" that harm our bodies—*thinking* they will still win the nutritional war. In the case of this cat, the fence won. Sad but true—the harmful chemicals, toxins, additives, and bad fats in our diet will also win if we continue to consume them.

Brain Poisons Are On the Rise... and So Are Brain Diseases

When most people think of brain pollution, they think of media and print materials that are not worthy of a person's time and effort. While those may very well be very potent and damaging "thought" pollutants, the real "brain" pollutants are much more concrete. Our environment is filled today with toxins that destroy both body and brain, many times in insidious ways that cause great suffering and anguish, not only for the person experiencing the ailment but for those who are caregivers and loved ones.

Brain Cancer Is on the Rise

Are you aware that brain cancer rates are rising dramatically? Brain cancer rates have risen particularly among the elderly. Between 1973 and 1991, brain cancers among all Americans rose 25 percent. That's 25 percent in just eighteen years! Those over age sixty-five had a 54 percent rise. This pattern is mirrored in other nations of the industrialized world.

It perhaps should come as no surprise that in a very close parallel fashion, our use of synthetic chemicals has also been on the rise.

In the last several decades, we in the United States and various other industrialized countries of the world have found ourselves facing a rising tide of biologically active, synthetic organic materials. Some of these interfere with our hormones, some attached themselves to our chromosomes, some over-stimulate the activity of enzymes, and others cripple the immune system. Many of these materials are similar enough to naturally occurring chemicals so that our bodies do not immediately seek to reject them, but rather, our bodies seek ways of accommodating them.

A number of these chemicals are soluble in fat, and therefore, they collect in tissues high in fat content. Two examples of this are the synthetic organic solvents perchloroethylene and trichloroethylene. These chemicals are specially designed to dissolve oil- and fat-soluble chemicals. In paint, they carry oil-based pigments. As degreasing agents in factories, they work well to clean lubricated machine parts. In dry cleaning fluid, they dissolve human body oils and greasy stains. On the human body, they can help dissolve human body oils. Unfortunately, they also can be absorbed by the skin and by the membranes in the lungs. Once inside our bodies, they take up residence in fat-containing tissues.

For women, the breasts are notoriously high in fat content. Other organs of the body high in fat are the liver, the bone marrow—which seems to be the target organ for benzene—*and the nerve cells of the brain.*

Many solvents have been used as anesthetic gases because of their ability to affect brain functioning—chloroform is an example. Most of us, however, do not anticipate being mildly anesthetized by the air we breathe daily, the water we drink, or the food we eat.

Chloroform continues to be used as a fumigant, solvent, and as an ingredient in pesticides and synthetic dyes. Trace amounts are also formed when water is chlorinated. Chloroform has been classified as a probable human carcinogen. And the plain fact is—according to the U.S. Agency for Toxic Substances and Disease Registry, we all receive at least low levels of chloroform in our food, water, and air.

Not only do we need to be concerned about synthetic chemicals, but in particular, the use of pesticides, herbicides, and fungicides. The rise in pesticide use in the United States closely parallels the rise of synthetic chemical production. Insecticide use began rising first, then herbicides, then fungicides. Not only are these products used commercially—at the rate of more than two billion pounds a year—but 82 percent of U.S. households use pesticides of some kind. In one survey of Missouri families, nearly 98 percent said they used pesticides at least once a year, and almost two-thirds of those polled said they use them five or more times a year. Yard and garden weed killers are used by half of all U.S. families.

Other widely-used products are the insecticidal flea collars, dusts, shampoos, sprays, and dips commonly used for household pets. A number of these pesticides have been linked to soft-tissue cancers in children, including brain cancer. [1]

The Messages from Gene p53

This is not a book about cancer per se, but since brain cancer is one of the most dreaded of all diseases, I want to give you some insight into *how* the brain can come to be damaged by cancer. As something of a by-product from the current surge in genetic research, we are learning a great deal about how cancer develops.

One specific gene located on chromosome 17 has been isolated as a major player in a number of malignancies, including cancers of the brain. Alterations of this gene, named p53, may be involved in as many as half of all human cancers.

In much the same way that a gunshot wound indicates what kind of firearm was used in an assault, the particular nature of a p53 gene mutation can indicate the type of carcinogen responsible for the damage. Cigarette smoke leaves one kind of lesion, ultraviolet radiation another, and exposure to vinyl chloride a third, and so forth.

How can this be helpful to us down the line?

Well, we know that the formation of a cancer cell involves three overlapping stages: initiation, promotion, and progression. For a full-blown malignancy, a cancer cell must pass through each of these stages.

Initiation. In the first stage, small structural alterations are made to the cell's DNA strands. These can arise spontaneously or result from an encounter with a carcinogen. The changes are swift, permanent, and often very subtle.

Promotion. It is at this point that the immune system plays a vital role. In a healthy immune system, the cancer cells are recognized as abnormal and a reaction is mounted against the cell. In an unhealthy immune system, the cancer cell is allowed to remain in the system. There, it may undergo repeated additional exposures to cancer-stimulating substances. Some substances operate as "cancer promoters." Estrogen, for example, is primarily a cancer promoter, as are many organo-chlorine compounds.

Let me insert another word about estrogen. There are a number of organic compounds that posses estrogenic properties—from pesticides to plastics. The name given to these compounds is "xenoestrogens"—they are far more common that researchers once thought. Not only do these substances cause harm by themselves, but there seems to be a strong synergistic negative outcome when several xenoestrogens are present in significant quantity. Sadly, these xenoestrogens can linger in the body for decades. They tend to turn the natural hormone estrogen into something of a cellular explosive. Among these xenoestrogenic contaminants are the pesticides DDT, atrazine, and endosulfan, as well as benzene and certain PCBs.

A number of synthetic environmental contaminants, such as dioxin, suppress human immunity and that suppression has been directly linked to cancer, notably leukemias and lympohomas. Pesticides have been shown to depress the immune system's T-cells.

The one ray of good news in all this bad news is that these effects wane when the contaminants are flushed from the body and there is no further exposure to them.

Progression. In the progression stage, the DNA molecule experiences injury—mutations pile up, chromosomes fall into disrepair and become unstable. Substances that promote the progression process allow cells to spread and invade neighboring cells, cause cells to be more sensitive to some hormones, and cause cells to attract blood vessels to form a growing mass of tumor cells. Arsenic, asbestos, and benzene are environmental contaminants that function as cancer progressors under certain conditions.

Not all carcinogenic chemicals fall neatly into the categories of initiator, promoter, or progressor. Some, such as radiation, play all three roles. Others initiate at low doses and promote and progress if their concentration in the body rises.

What is the bottom line on all this?

First, there are *no* "safe doses" of carcinogens. All are potentially hazardous to health.

Second, one of the best things we can do for ourselves is to remove as many known carcinogenic materials from our lives as possible. If you are working for a manufacturing entity, find out what chemicals you are being exposed to, and if you don't like the answer you receive, change jobs. Seek out the purest food, purest water, and purest air you can find.

Third, do everything in your power to build up your immune system.

Fourth, specifically seek to eliminate fluoride and heavy metals from your immediate environment. They are two of the most toxic substances to both body and brain.

Putting the Cap Back on Fluoride Toothpaste

Fluoride speeds up the aging process in a number of ways. It has a degenerative effect on bones and cartilage, and in some areas, it has been linked to arthritic symptoms and bone fractures. It causes premature aging of the skin, arteries, and other tissues in the body that have collagen-synthesizing cells (fibroblasts). It damages the immune system and is a known cause of cancer. [2]

Fluoridated toothpaste contains 1000 parts per million fluoride. A family-sized tube of fluoridated toothpaste (seven ounces) has enough fluoride to kill a small child of up to twenty pounds if the child consumed the entire tube. Now most children that size will not consume an entire tube of toothpaste, but this shows you how lethal fluoride can be.

For years, we have been "taught" by advertisers that we need fluoride to prevent tooth decay. That simply isn't so. In fact, research has shown repeatedly that fluoridated toothpaste does *nothing* to reduce tooth decay. As long ago as 1979, *Science News* reported, "In a large study carried out recently in Holland, Dutch scientists found essentially no reduction in cavities when the fluoride users and non-users had been carefully matched." [3] U.S. Public Health Service and the American Dental Association reports have backed up this conclusion. Although tooth decay has declined significantly in the last fifty years, it has declined in both nonfluoridated as well as fluoridated areas. There is nothing to suggest that fluoridation is the primary reason for the decline. A far more potent and prevalent source of fluoride is tap water. Fluoridated water is frequently used to make soft drinks (as well as beers). I recommend that you avoid these products as a general health principle, but if you do drink them, make certain they are not manufactured in an area where the water is routinely fluoridated.

People living in the vicinity of phosphate, aluminum, steel, clay, glass, or frit manufacturers are often exposed to high levels of fluoride in the air. My advice is to move, even if it means seeking a new job.

Foods grown in polluted areas, especially fruits, vegetables, and grains, also become contaminated with fluoride. The same is true for crops grown using cheap, fluorine-containing fertilizer. Make it a point to know where your food comes from—and if your grocer doesn't know, ask him to find out! [4]

Make sure you filter and purify your water thoroughly. Call my office for more information: 1-800-726-1834.

Heavy Metal Is More than a Style of Music

There's no doubt about it. Literally thousands of scientific studies through the decades have revealed that arsenic, lead, mercury, and other heavy metals produce brain dysfunction. A number of heavy metals, as well as a number of organic solvents, are found in industrial waste and insecticides. When these substances contaminate water supplies, they are ingested by edible fish and the symptoms of poisoning can be transferred on to humans who eat that fish—especially over time. Thus, we get heavy metals into our bodies through not only the water we drink, but also the food we eat as well as the air we breathe. An analysis of human hair taken from people living today and from people who died 1,600 years ago has shown that traces of metal in the hair are now up to a thousand times greater.

Heavy metals tend to accumulate in the brain, kidneys, and immune system. Conservative estimates have suggested that nearly twenty-five percent of all people in the United States suffer to some extent from heavy metal poisoning.

Check Your Paint for Lead

One of the most potent brain destroying metals is lead. Even a small amount of lead can cause learning disorders, mental retardation, lower IQ scores in children, and lower brain and memory function. Lead can accumulate in the tissues until it reaches lethal levels. Ceramic glazes often contain lead to create brilliant colors, but this renders the dishes poisonous. Paint in old buildings often has high lead content.

Mercury Is a Major Enemy

One of the most toxic substances you can have in your body and brain is mercury.

Mercury, like lead, can accumulate in tissues, interfere with brain function, and cause premature senility. Some of the first signs of mercury poisoning are fatigue, headaches, and forgetfulness. If the poisoning is not reversed, the person may experience difficulties in speech, hearing, memory, and concentration.

The World Health Organization has published the table below that estimates the average daily intake and retention (ug/day) of total mercury and mercury compounds in the general population not occupationally exposed to mercury.

Mercury Intake of the Average Person

EXPOSURE	ELEMENTAL MERCURY VAPOR	INORGANIC COMPOUNDS	METHYLMERCURY
Air	.030	.002	.008
Fish	0	.6	2.4
Non-fish Foods	0	3.6	0
Water	0	.05	0
Dental Amalgams	3.8–3.21	0	0

Mercury toxicity has been researched with increased interest in recent years. We now know that mercury attacks the body in many ways—it kills cells by interfering with their ability to exchange oxygen, nutrients, and waste products through the cell membrane. Inside a cell, mercury destroys DNA and triggers a mechanism that causes the immune system to destroy the body's own tissues. Diabetes, multiple sclerosis (MS), scleroderma, and lupus—all of which are autoimmune diseases to some degree—have been linked to high mercury levels. Mercury can also interfere with nerve impulse transmission, causing organs to get wrong messages. This can result directly in memory problems, and especially *short-term memory* problems.

Mercury from Dental Amalgams. One of the main ways in which mercury is introduced to the body is through amalgam fillings used in dentistry. Amalgam is a mixture of mercury, silver, copper, tin, and zinc, with about fifty percent of the mixture being mercury. Mercury is the most toxic component in amalgam, but the other metals can contribute to the overall poisoning effects in the body.

About seventy-five percent of all people in the United States have silver/mercury amalgam fillings.

Chemical and electrochemical processes in the mouth can cause mercury to become vaporized in amounts that have been measured. Over time, a filling may leech out nearly half of its mercury into the mouth. As long as you have silver/mercury fillings, you will be inhaling mercury vapor 24 hours a day, 365 days a year.

The release of mercury vapor from amalgam fillings is greater when a person is chewing and brushing. Those who have these fillings should avoid chewing gum.

A special phenomenon occurs when gold and amalgam are present in the same mouth. When these two metals are present at the same time in the oral cavity, an electric current is generated that can cause an increased amount of mercury to be released. Sometimes amalgam cores are used under gold crowns or gold bridges are placed directly on amalgam filled teeth. A dark discoloration of the tooth and adjacent gum tissues is sometimes visible, indicating a migration of the amalgam components.

People who have a large number of amalgam fillings tend to increase their sensitivity to mercury as time goes by. The general symptoms of mercury poisoning are many, but the earliest noted symptoms are these: headache, fatigue, forgetfulness, an inability to concentrate, general apathy, depression, outbursts of anger, and a decline of intellect. [5]

Should Filling Be Removed? A number of tests can be run to determine if the amalgam fillings in your teeth need to be removed, such as the urine porphytrin test, an electrical reading of amalgams, and basic lab tests such as CBC, blood chemistry profile, hair analysis, and urinalysis. [6] We have hair analysis tests available through my office: 1-800-726-1834.

If you elect to have silver/mercury fillings replaced, make certain that you work with a dentist who will take precautions against mercury vapor exposure during the removal procedure. Ask your dentist about the precautions that he or she intends to have in place during the removal process. Only have a couple of fillings removed at a time, with several weeks between removal procedures.

Mercury in Fish. The greatest source of dietary mercury is fish. The most beneficial counter-balancing nutrient to this form of mercury poisoning is selenium. The benefit of selenium has been cited by the National Academy of Sciences, which stated that "the most consistent beneficial influence of selenium has been the reduction of the lethal and neurotoxic effects of methylmercury compounds." [7]

It is interesting that scientists who have studied the levels of methylmercury in fish have also determined that most of the fish contained even higher levels of selenium, and on this basis, they have concluded that the methylmercury ingested in fish is not as dangerous as the inhaled mercury vapor that is related to dental fillings.

Mercury in Foods and Common Personal Products. These foods should be avoided since they often have mercury in them:

- Grains treated with methyl mercury fungicides, especially wheat
- Kelp and other seaweeds
- Shellfish, including shrimp, lobster, crab, oysters, scallops, and prawns

In addition, a person is wise to avoid alcohol, caffeine, cheese, chocolate, refined carbohydrates, "lite" salt, margarine, milk, soft drinks, and sugar.

Some cosmetics are high in mercury, including some hair dyes, waterproof mascara, and skin-lightening creams.

Some of the most potent sources of mercury are "medications," including many common antiseptic and first-aid preparations, psoriasis preparations, fungicides, acne preparations, bleaching creams, eye preparations, ear and nasal preparations, throat lozenges, hemorrhoid ointments and suppositories, vaginal jellies, tablets and douches, hair tonics, and veterinary preparations.

Around the house, a number of paint products have mercury, especially those with yellow, vermilion, and cinnabar pigments and mildew- and corrosion-resistant paints. Also watch out for many latex and oil-based paints as well as anti-fouling paints for boats. These products also often have mercury in them: mildew preventatives, wood preservatives, photographic solutions, gun bluing, tile cement, lead mercury solder.

In the garden, be aware that these products often have mercury: seed fungicides, protectants, and disinfectants; turf fungicides and disinfectants; plant fungicides; herbicides; insecticides.

In addition, mercury is often used in the manufacturing of adhesives, fabric softeners, air conditioner filters, felts, batteries, floor waxes and polishes, sewage disposal products, and even tattoos! Mercury volatizes at room temperature and condenses on skin and the lining of the respiratory tract. In times past, mercury poisoning was so common in workers who made felt hats that a phrase was coined to describe their condition: "mad as a hatter."

If you work as a barber, hairdresser, lab worker, mortician, physician, dentist, dental technician, or nurse—be on the alert for mercury in products that are frequently used by those in your profession.

If you are concerned that you or a family member may have a toxic metal build-up, please contact my office for information on a hair analysis test. This test will give you the answers you are seeking. Call 1-800-726-1834.

It's Time to Clean Your Home of Toxins

Years ago, we lived near an airport and there were hundreds of acres of palmetto trees between our home and the runways. Once a year, the community would have a rattlesnake round-up. The palmetto trees were shaken vigorously so the rattlesnakes hiding in and around them would flee their nests. Literally hundreds of snakes were caught on round-up day, with many of the skins and much of the venom sold. Those of us who lived in the area considered that to be a day when the groves were "de-poisoned."

Many of us need to have a round-up day in our homes to rid our dwelling places of the toxins that are lurking in hidden cabinets and cupboards, and even the refrigerator and freezer. We need to eliminate not only chemical poisons that we use for cleaning and disinfecting, but we also need to eliminate the chemical poisons and harmful substances that are found in many foods.

If I went into most homes in America, I would likely find chlorine in the tap water. Chlorine is a known cause of free-radicals and it has been linked to cancer and heart disease.

If I went into most homes in America, I may find fluoridated toothpaste in the bathroom's medicine chest. I would likely find a vast number of products containing mercury throughout the house, many of them cleaning supplies and gardening chemicals.

Friends, it's time to clean house! Make it a family project to "search and destroy" the toxic chemicals in your home. Teach your children what you have learned in this book as you work *together* to eliminate the poisons that are all around you.

Better safe than sorry later.

(We carry a complete line of "safe" household, personal care, and make-up products in my office. Let us help.)

Removing Heavy Metals from the Brain

Several things can be done to remove heavy metals from the brain. As noted earlier, one of the most potent substances that aids in this process is selenium. Selenium helps remove lead from brain tissues. Selenium also combines with methyl mercury to make it soluble for excretion from the body. The process is something like a vacuum cleaner—the selenium sucks up the toxic metals and then throws them away.

Bulk fiber is a great ally in removing toxins from the body. If you are not taking in sufficient dietary fiber—in the form of "roughage"from raw vegetables and fruits—be sure to take a bulk fiber supplement. (You should be taking into your body at least 25 grams of fiber a day—a whole fresh apple has only 3–4 grams of fiber.) I recommend a variety of fiber supplements. Please see my books, *Maximum Energy* and *Maximum Fat Loss*, for more information about fiber.

Fiber keeps the bowels moving, helps keep blood glucose levels at optimum, and binds with harmful fats to flush them from the system. It also helps with the removal of heavy metals that may be"chelated"and transported to the excretory system.

Other oral chelators (substances that can be taken by mouth that cleanse metals from the body) as well as intravenous chelation are discussed in the next chapter.

One of the most important ways to battle toxicity in the body is to build up the body's immune system. Again, all roads lead to nutritional therapy when it comes to building *up* health.

Chemotherapy—a Brain Poison

Most people who have undergone chemotherapy as part of cancer treatment readily attest to the fact that their memory is "shot" in the aftermath. Chemotherapy—which is designed to kill cells—very often kills more than the cells intended. It is a potent brain poison.

A young woman whose sister recently died of cancer wrote to a friend of mine: "I believe it is barbaric the way we essentially sentence people to death with chemotherapy. Why are we treating cancer by destroying the patient's immune system with poison? I can't help but believe future generations will look back on current cancer treatments with the same horror we feel when we read how two hundred years ago medicine routinely 'bled' people to death in an effort to cure them." I couldn't agree more.

So many people put their faith in chemotherapy as a genuine therapeutic treatment that will extend their lives. The facts, however, tell a different story. Chemotherapy may reduce the *size* of a person's tumor or tumors, but chemotherapy does *not* extend human life. Chemotherapy patients are alive five years after treatment in only twenty percent of the cases where chemotherapy has been administered. In the months that a person receives chemotherapy, many patients truly feel they lose almost all "quality" of life.

In contrast, nutritional therapy patients are alive five years after treatment in *eighty percent of cases*. They experience an *improved* quality of life.

Why this dramatic difference? Because chemotherapy targets specific tumors and cancer masses, not cancer as a systemic disease. It does not address the underlying conditions that initiate and promote the growth of malignant cells in the body, Nutritional therapy addresses the health of the cells and tissues of the body and promotes a general "healing environment"—when negative influences are removed from the body (from toxins to stress) and metabolic systems are put back into balance, the body can begin to heal itself. If the cancer has not reached an advanced stage when nutritional therapy begins, the nutrients supplied to the body can often reverse the process and ultimately, the body will defeat the tumor on its own. Too often, however, people wait to "try" nutritional therapy until they have exhausted all chemotherapy, radiotherapy, and surgical avenues and are pronounced terminal by their health-care provider with only a few weeks to live.

If you are diagnosed with cancer of any type, I recommend that you seek the best of nutritional therapy as a *first* resort. At the very least, you will be building up your immune system should you later choose to pursue other avenues. At the very best, you may find that your cancer can be contained, or even reversed, by supplying your body with the nutrients it needs to heal itself.

1. *Living Downstream* by Sandra Steingraber is one of the best reference books I know about the impact on health of pesticides, synthetic organic compounds, and environmental contaminants. Steingraber has a Ph.D. in biology from the University of Michigan and taught biology for years at Columbia College in Chicago. She is also an active ecologist and researcher in ecological causes of cancer. Her book is very readable but is filled with medical and scientific documentation to support her conclusions. See Steingraber, S. *Living Downstream*, New York: Random House, 1998.

2. Albright, J.A. The effects of fluoride on the mechanical properties of bone, *Transactions of the Annual Meeting of the Orthopedics Research Society*, 1978: 398.

   Robin, J.C. et al. Studies on osteoporosis III: Effect of estrogens and fluoride. *Journ of Med* 1980 (2): 1–14. Saunders, M. Fluoride toothpastes, a cause of acne-like eruptions. Arch Derm 1975 (3): 793.

   Allmann, D.W., and Benac, M. Effect of inorganic fluoride salts on urine and tissue 3'5' cyclic-AMP concentration in vivo. *Jour Dent Res* 1976 (55;suppl. R): 523.

3. Yiamouyiannis, J. *Fluoride: The Aging Factor*, Delaware, OH: Health Action Press, 1983: 107–108.

4. For more on fluoride, including numerous scientific research references about its effects, see Yiamouyiannis, J. *Fluoride: The Aging Factor*. Delaware, OH: Health Action Press, 1983.

5. Hanson, M. *Mercury Bibliography (3rd edition)*: 285 symptoms of mercury toxicity and 12,000 mercury citations. Orlando, FL: Bio-Probe, Inc.

   Oettingen, W.F., *Poisoning: A Guide to Clinical Diagnosis and Treatment*. Philadelphia: W.B. Saunders Co., 1958.

   World Health Organization, "Environmental Health Criteria 1, Mercury." Geneva, 1976.

   Ziff, S., Ziff, M, and Hanson, M, *Dental Mercury Detox*. Orlando, FL: Bio Probe, Inc., 1988.

6. See Hal A. Huggins, *It's All in Your Head-The Link Between Mercury Amalgams and Illness*, Garden City Park, NY: Avery Publishing Group, 1993.

7. National Academy of Sciences, "An Assessment of Mercury in the Environment." Washington, D.C., 1978.

TAKING ACTION FOR HEALTHY BRAIN FUNCTION

1, Avoid the use of synthetic chemicals, both in your personal care and around the house and yard. Especially remove products that contain mercury from your shelves and cupboards.

2. Refuse to use fluoridated toothpaste or drink fluoridated or chlorinated water.

3. Consider having any mercury amalgam fillings removed from your mouth.

4. Avoid eating ALL shellfish, as well as fish from polluted waters.

5, Consider selenium supplementation.

6. Make sure you are consuming enough fiber. If not, take fiber supplements.

7. Drink purified water.

CHAPTER 1 3

Detoxifying Brain Tissues
and
Blood Vessels

In the beginning stage of virtually all healing, a "negative" influence needs to be removed even as "positive" influences are added to the body. A process of detoxification of the cells is vitally important. A number of means of detoxifying the body are available:

- a short period of fasting—no food, but lots of pure water.

- enemas, including colonic enemas—to cleanse the digestive tract so that toxins are removed prior to an infusion of health-promoting nutrients.

- chelation of the blood stream—either through intravenous chelation or oral chelation.

- bulk fiber—both through eating raw, fresh fruits and vegetables, as well as taking fiber supplements to help eliminate toxins and excess fat from your system.

- the administration of high doses of anti-oxidants, which attack the free radicals in the body's tissues and eliminate them through the excretory and urinary systems.

Detoxification does not happen overnight. It can take weeks, even months, for a person's body and brain to be detoxified, depending in part on the type of poisoning the person has experienced.

Chelation—
the Detox Superstar

Chelation therapy is the most sophisticated form of cellular detoxification known to medical science at present.

Chelation treatments have been shown to help reduce the severity of symptoms associated with senility—especially memory retention, increased IQ, and mental alertness. It has also been used to good advantage in those who have mental dysfunction owing to atherosclerosis or toxic poisoning of the brain. It cannot help with problems such as brain scarring, but it seems to be very useful in preventing further completions of brain injury, such as the onset of a stroke. It has also been shown to help the onset of Alzheimer's disease in those who have a high potential for developing this ailment.

More than two thousand clinical journal articles attesting to the benefits of chelation have been published in the world scientific literature. More than twenty physiological and biochemical actions have been studied extensively. Chelation still remains somewhat out of the maintstream of the medical world, however, largely owing to a lack of information among traditionally trained medical personnel.

What Is Chelation Therapy?

Chelation therapy is a process that curbs the flow of metallic minerals through the blood vessels of the body and brain. The result is that the storage of these harmful metals is prevented, and in many cases, reversed.

Chelation therapy has been used to good advantage in ridding the body and brain of aluminum, mercury, lead, cadmium, iron, manganese, and other dangerous metals.

The most potent form of chelation therapy is administered through an intravenous drip. Intravenous chelation therapy consists of injections of a synthetic amino acid—a protein—called EDTA. (Ethylene diamine tetraacetic acid). These injections are given through an intravenous infusion system.

As the blood circulates through the system, the EDTA locks onto minerals or metals floating in the bloodstream and brain fluids. The EDTA "chelates" the toxic minerals and turns them into metastatic calcium so they can be flushed from the body. One researcher has likened this process to the claw of a lobster seizing its prey. The EDTA surrounds the metallic particle and sends it as a waste product to the excretory and urinary systems so it can be passed safely out of the body.

As part of the process, chelation therapy reduces muscle spasms of the arteries and helps remove clogging material from arterial walls. Deposits that cause arterial clogging are generally formed of fats, collagen, fibrin, mucopolyssacharides, cholesterol, foreign proteins, and other substances that are held together by a "glue-like" material with a calcium base. EDTA removes the calcium so that no more binding glue remains to hold the "bloodstream junk" together. In virtually all cases, a widened or unblocked, more flexible blood vessel passage is left behind. Blood can then circulate more freely to bathe both body and brain tissues.

Metals not only play a role in atherosclerotic plaquing, but also in the creation of "neuronal tangles." (These tangles are a characteristic of Alzheimer's disease.)

EDTA-chelation therapy has been used in the United States to relieve hardening of the arteries since 1952. It has been approved by the Food and Drug Administration (FDA) for detoxification in cases of heavy-metal poisoning involving lead, mercury, and cadmium, and even for radioactive-metal toxicity. Its application has also been recommended for removal of all excessively concentrated, toxic, or unnecessary minerals and as a viable treatment for stopping the advance of many forms of dementia.

Not only does chelation therapy remove harmful metals directly, but it also removes the detrimental iron and copper ions from the body so they cannot assist in the creation of trans fatty acids that become incorporated into the cell membranes of the brain.

Is It Safe? Are There Side Effects? The FDA made an extensive search of the medical literature for reports of adverse or poor results from chelation therapy. It could find no evidence of any kind that indicated chelation therapy was detrimental to human beings. No reports of negative or poor results, or patient complaints were found. Rather, the FDA found the published research indicated intravenous infusions with EDTA were safer than most other approved therapies used for *any* purpose in medicine. It is not only the best, but perhaps the only, effective antidote for heavy-metal toxicity.

As of 1995, the American College of Advancement (ACAM) in Medicine estimated that at least 500,000 people had received EDTA chelation therapy—about 10 million intravenous treatments—under ACAM guidelines without a single fatality attributed to EDTA.

Answers to Commonly Asked Questions. Here are some of the most commonly asked questions and answers related to chelation therapy:

- Is a person ever too old to take chelation therapy? Probably not. Some patients in their nineties have responded very well to treatments with EDTA chelation.

- How can I tell if I need chelation therapy? The best way to detect heavy-metal toxicity is to take an EDTA challenge dose and have a physician's lab measure the amount of heavy metals that come out in your urine. If there is a high level of metals or a significant increase in metallic urine content from the baseline level, you likely have too many heavy metals in your body.

- Is chelation therapy covered by insurance? It is possible that health insurance will cover chelation therapy if heavy metals are detected in a patient's urine. You would need to take an EDTA challenge dose and have lab work done to determine the level of heavy metal toxicity.

The Big Question: Does It Work? In a word, yes. I know this not only from the scientific research, but also from numerous instances in which clients of mine have undergone chelation therapy. Here's just one example...

Several years ago one of my neighbors developed the beginning stages of gangrene in his big toe. He and his wife called to ask if I could help. I told him that chelation should help the circulation to his feet. I then recommended that he go to the Robinson Family Clinic in Lakeland, Florida, for treatment. Dr. Robinson and his son have long been known as pioneers in the field of health and prevention.

My neighbor took my advice. He visited Dr. Robinson, had chelation therapy, and the gangrenous condition completely cleared up. In addition he saw significant improvement in his circulation, energy level, and memory. It's always rewarding to me when people listen to me and obtain positive results! By the way, if any of my immediate family members or I have a medical need, we go to Dr. Robinson.

Heavy Metal's Foremost Enemy. EDTA chelation therapy is the only treatment for poisoning by manganese, a heavy metal that produces profound neurological dysfunction if it is found in concentrations that are too high,

Cadmium, a close chemical relative of mercury, is present in the dust, fumes, and mists that are commonly produced in the refining of zinc, copper, and lead. Cadmium toxicity is directly linked to dementia. There is only one treatment for serious cadmium exposure: EDTA chelation therapy.

Lead destroys brain and nerve cells. EDTA chelation therapy is the most effective means of removing lead from the bodies and brains of children, young adults, and the elderly. [1]

Chelation and Cholesterol Plaquing

When toxic metals accumulate in the body, they cause extremely large quantities of free radicals to be produced in the body. It is the free radicals produced from these metals that cause arteries to become hardened and blocked.

Intravenous chelation therapy removes these heavy metals. This cuts out the production of billions and billions of free radicals.

Once the metals are removed from the blood stream and the excessive free radicals are eliminated, the tissues of the arteries begin to recover or heal themselves. Cells pick up calcium as they are weakened by free radicals. Therefore, when there are fewer free radicals, the cells are better able to kick out the errant calcium particles. In this way, the "calcium deposits" from the sides of the arterial walls are slowly reduced and eliminated. There is also some research to indicate that EDTA may block the entry of calcium into the cells once free radicals are no longer a factor.

As we have stated a number of times, a good flow of oxygen to the brain is vital to brain function. Blood flow is compromised if blood vessels become "blocked" or "narrowed" by plaquing on the arterial walls.

Cholesterol, itself, however, may not be the biological ogre that many have thought it to be. Let me explain.

Medical researchers have known the correlation between elevated LDL cholesterol and heart disease for some time, but they have never fully understood *why* this is true. Now, there is research to show that cholesterol may be as much the *effect* as the cause of heart disease. In fact, elevated blood cholesterol may not cause heart disease as much as be associated with the appearance of heart disease.

More than a hundred years ago, a German physiologist Rudolph Virchow theorized that heart disease was an inflammation of the heart and the arteries that brought blood to the heart. He based his theory on detail autopsy studies and pathology studies of individuals who had died of heart disease. He found that their arteries looked as if they had been "wounded," suggesting some type of inflammatory condition.

Then in the early twentieth century, a Russian physiologist named Nikolai Anitschow offered a competing theory—that dietary fat was the cause of heart disease. He fed white rabbits a high-fat, high-cholesterol diet and was able to produce serious heart and artery disease in them. He proposed that dietary fat caused the fatty streaks on the walls of the arteries and heart muscle in the rabbits that were autopsied. By the way, nobody seemed to question at the time that rabbits do not *eat* animal fat—they are pure vegetarians! In feeding the rabbits a high-cholesterol diet, he was feeding them a diet completely foreign to their genetic make-up.

About twenty hears ago, investigators at Harvard Medical School took another look at the Anitschow conclusions. [2] They fed rabbits a cholesterol product that was 99.999999 percent pure and they were unable to produce the same high level of heart disease that Anitschow had found. When they fed the rabbits an impure cholesterol product, suddenly the signs of the heart disease appeared.

The impure cholesterol product was high in "cholesterol oxides"—in other words, the cholesterol had been damaged by oxidation. This form of cholesterol caused white blood cells to infiltrate the artery walls and begin the atherosclerosis process. The higher the level of blood cholesterol, the more cholesterol oxides were found. The more oxidative stress a person is under, including inflammation, the more damage to the cholesterol, leading to the formation of cholesterol oxides. What causes oxidative stress? Four main culprits: cigarette smoking, high serum iron levels, chronic infection, and dietary antioxidant deficiencies. [3]

The process of atheroma (mass of plaque of degenerated, thickened arterial material) formation may reveal why dietary antioxidants such as vitamin E are helpful in preventing heart disease. Vitamin E attacks free radicals that cause the oxidizing process. Vitamin C and the minerals magnesium, zinc, copper, and selenium also protect against heart disease.

Nearly thirty years ago, Kilmer McCully, M.D., suggested that an amino acid called homocysteine triggers heart disease. His book, the *Homocysteine Revolution*, went largely unheralded by the mainstream of medical science until fairly recently. [4] Today, elevated homocystein in the blood is universally accepted as a strong predictor of death from heart disease. [5] Fairly extensive research indicates that *at least* ten percent of the population, carries a genetic risk for producing elevated levels of homocysteine. They are, therefore, those who are at increased risk of heart disease.

The good news is that homocysteine levels can be reduced by taking increased folic acid, vitamin B12, vitamin B6, and betaine. These nutrients are generally found in a"Homocysteine Balanced

B Complex" formula. The levels of vitamins necessary to promote proper metabolism of homocysteine are much higher than the Recommended Dietary Allowances. Depending on the severity of the condition, a person may have to consume from 5 times to 100 times the RDA levels of folate, vitamin B12, or vitamin B6 to lower his homocysteine levels.

The toxic effects of homocystein are also associated with methionine. Animal proteins, particular egg protein, are very high in sulfure amino acids like methionine. Luncheon meats are generally "off the charts" high in methionine. Those who consume a great deal of methionine in the form of luncheon meats have a significantly increased risk of elevating their homocysteine, and if this tendency is coupled with both age and a genetic predisposition to developing homocysteine, a person can be at serious risk.

In some cases, supplementation of folate and vitamins B12 and B6 are not sufficient. Some individuals also seem to need betain, a B-complex nutrient. Remarkable results have been achieved when betain was added to the folate and B-vitamin mix—one man's prematurely gray hair returned to its natural color, in another case a child's learning disorders improved dramatically, and in yet another case, a man in his mid-twenties, was able for the first time in his life to hold a job without eruptions of violent aberrant behavior.

By-Pass Surgery or Chelation Therapy?

Several months ago, a friend phoned me and said, "My father has been diagnosed with clogged coronary arteries and his physicians have told him that he needs quadruple coronary by-pass surgery. Is there anything you can do to help our family?"

I said, "Unless this situation is an immediate life-or-death situation, let's try chelation therapy, the addition of several supplements and modifications to your father's diet, and an exercise program for a few weeks. There is a great deal of research to show that atherosclerosis—the plaquing of the arterial walls that causes the arteries to become blocked—can be reversed."

I met with the man and he said, "My doctor told me that by-pass surgery is routine—they do it all the time."

"Your surgeon may do by-pass surgery all the time," I said, "but it is a very dangerous surgery nonetheless. Forty percent of the people who undergo coronary by-pass surgery are so debilitated by the procedure that they never return to a normal life. Ninety percent of these people experience marked personality changes as well. Depending on the amount of time you are on the heart-lung bypass pump, which circulates blood to the brain and other parts of your body during the hours you will be in surgery, you are going to experience a lesser or greater change in the way your brain functions. Any time the oxygen levels to the brain are interrupted or altered, brain function changes. Encephalograms show that brain waves before and after heart surgery are *different*. Many people experience ongoing dizziness the rest of their lives. And...a large percentage of people have strokes after this surgery. Not only that, but many people who have this surgery suffer from impotency and many have serious problems with their memory."

This man said soberly, "I've never heard this before."

"No," I said, "and your heart doctor or heart surgeon will probably not admit to you what all doctors and surgeons know— they will explore every alternative and do everything they can to avoid having heart surgery performed on *themselves*."

Please remember always that a surgeon doesn't make any money unless he or she performs surgery. Also remember that a physician has fixed overhead. A surgeon *must* perform a certain number of surgeries per month to pay these expenses. Now, I'm not saying that all surgeons perform unnecessary surgeries, but statistical evidence shows that tens of thousands of unnecessary surgeries are done every year. Always get multiple opinions. Don't make a *fatal* mistake.

I told this man about a dear friend of mine, James, had to have heart valve replacement surgery years ago. Prior to the surgery, James was an upbeat, very positive man. His heart valve became diseased with an infection and there was no alternative at the time but surgery. The man who emerged from that surgical experience was not the man who entered the surgical suite. He became depressed, very negative, and very lethargic...and he has remained that way since the surgery.

In spite of all my pleading and preaching—and in spite of all the scientifically verifiable facts and figures I gave him—this man chose to go ahead with the by-pass surgery. He had a stroke the day after the surgery and months later, was still in rehab to regain use of his right arm and leg. Once an avid golfer, he not only *can't* play golf at present but he seems to have no desire to pick up a club. He has become sullen and argumentative, personality traits he never exhibited before. Much of what I had warned him about has come to pass in his life.

In the vast majority of cases, by-pass surgery is *not* necessary. Much can be done to improve a person's circulation and quality of life apart from surgery.

Clogged arteries are symptomatic of other system-wide health problems. We are much wiser to address the *widespread*, generalized health problems than to focus *solely* on a few inches of narrow or blocked arteries in the heart. In fact, if the other system-wide health problems are *not* addressed in the aftermath of by-pass surgery, the newly opened arteries will close again.

I am amazed at the number of people today who are having bypass surgery. The number of multiple bypass surgeries in the United States has risen dramatically in the last three decades. The price tag has also risen—the average multiple bypass surgery now costs about $50,000.

In comparison, chelation therapy costs about $120 per treatment. Usually twenty to thirty treatments are recommended. When you add in costs for physical exams and nutritional supplements, a person may pay between $4,000 and $5,000.

When it comes to death rate, the death rates from bypass surgery varies from one percent to as high as twenty-five percent, depending on which surgeon holds the knife. Overall, the death rate is about five percent.

In comparison, the death rate while undergoing intravenous chelation therapy is *zero*.

Bypass surgery patients are generally relieved from angina pain immediately. (At the same time, it should be noted that they are usually in bed without much activity for several weeks.) Intravenous chelation therapy also relieves angina pain, but it may take four or five treatments. A person normally takes two to four chelation treatments a week, with each treatment taking three hours. This means, that relief from angina pain can take a week or two with chelation treatment. About fifteen hours of intravenous treatment may be necessary to reach this level of relief. Bypass surgery can take several hours, with several hours in recovery rooms, and then months of additional recovery.

Given the choice between an immediate fix and lots of recovery time from bypass surgery, and a slightly slower fix and no recovery time from chelation therapy, I'd choose the chelation therapy every time.

After surgery, bypass patients usually have to take life easy for a while—usually for months and sometimes years. Chelation patients are often playing golf after the first week.

Bypass surgery operations often have to be repeated—usually about every five years or so. Chelation patients often receive "booster" sessions every month or several times a year after the initial series of treatments. Every bypass surgery will cost at least

$50,000. The "booster" chelation treatments will total a few hundred dollars.

What about longevity? Bypass surgery patients who have been studied over long periods of time tend to experience *no* longevity increases when compared to heart patients who had the same symptoms but didn't have the surgery. I realize that fact flies in the face of what many people have been told and believe, but the research is clear—there is virtually *no* net effect in longevity for a bypass surgery patient.

In comparison, chelation patients have a tremendous increase in their expected life although chelation physicians are often reluctant to boast about this. Intravenous chelation therapy not only cuts the risk of further heart disease and atherosclerosis (which can lead to strokes), but it also greatly reduces the risk of cancer. Chelation treatment deals with the basic source of many illnesses—the tiny particles of metal that accumulate over time and increase the production of free radicals in the body. When the interior source of free radical production is reduced by more than one million times, the acceleration of aging stops and people usually feel much younger after chelation therapy.

Insurance companies pay for bypass surgery, depending on a person's coverage. A percentage of the surgery is usually left for the patient to pay since insurance policies rarely pay the *entire* cost of the procedure. Chelation is usually self-pay. Even so, chelation usually comes out to be the cheaper form of therapy.

Several years ago I had a phone call from a woman who ordered *all* of my educational tapes. I asked her, "Are you sure you want to invest in this much material?" She started laughing and said, "My husband has had two by-pass operations. Our share of the bill was more than a $100,000. If he will follow your advice on these tapes, I don't think he'll need a third operation. That makes your educational material a *bargain!*" I agree!

Oral Chelation

Intravenous chelation is not the only means by which the chelating process can be activated in the body. There are a number of other natural products that have a chelating effect. They include garlic, chlorella, alginates (algae products), vitamin C, and sulfhydryl products containing amino acids such as cysteine. We carry a complete line of oral chelating agents in my office. Call for details: 1-800-726-1834.

Apples are a very good chelating food. They bind to metals in the colon and help excrete them from the body.

Microalgae Has Cleansing Properties

Microalgae are single-celled plants grown in fresh water. In large concentrations, this forms the "slime" we see growing on ponds. Don't let that image, however, turn you off. The algae used in the commercial "green" products is usually grown in stainless steel vats with pure water, and then harvested in sterile conditions.

Spirulina and chlorella are the most widely used food algaes. Seaweed is another form of alga that has been used in food dishes in the Orient for thousands of years. A little more than fifty years ago, researchers discovered that microalgae was an excellent source of nutrients.

Chlorella has more protein than beef or other meats, more protein than soybeans, and is a rich source of amino acids. It is high in vitamins A, B, C, and E, high in unsaturated fatty acids, and as the name suggests, high in chlorophyll.

Are Green Foods Elixirs for the Brain?

Juiced barley and wheat grass have become popular in recent years. Wheat grass is a rich source of vitamins A, B, C, and E, all of which are antioxidants. Grasses also contain the minerals calcium, phosphorous, iron, potassium, sulfur, cobalt, and zinc. Many of these minerals are also essential for good brain function.

These grasses also are high in chlorophyll, which is a good antidote in the system against pesticides. It has also been shown to help decrease the effects of radiation. Toxins from radiation form free radicals that attack brain cells.

Why not eat the grass directly? Because the human body does not have the ability to digest raw grass. To get the nutritional benefits of these grasses, the grass must be juiced. A typical serving is one to four ounces. Some people experience nausea when they begin using juiced grass—this is likely owing to the powerful cleansing properties of the grasses and their ability to cause toxins to be released from body and brain tissues. I recommend that you start with just one ounce and work your way up over time.

Once juiced, grass is not stable and it can go bad quickly. Drink juiced grass within ten minutes of juicing it. Cut grass can be stored in plastic containers in a refrigerator without spoiling for about a week.

Chelation and Green Foods Are Not Risky

Some people seem to think that because they have never heard about chelation—either intravenous or oral chelators—and have never thought about taking or drinking "green" foods, that there is something risky about these options for cleansing the blood stream. Not so. These therapies may be *innovative*, but they are definitely not dangerous. Ultimately, they are *successful*.

A friend and I once were stopped at the entrance to St. Peter's Cathedral because we were wearing shorts. My wife and my son went on into the cathedral because they were properly dressed, but we were forced to stay outside. A few minutes later, two nuns came by and asked us if we would like to borrow two pairs of long pants from the homeless shelter they operated. We agreed and made a contribution to their work in exchange for the use of two pairs of pre-worn pants.

Did we look stylish? No. Did we get into the cathedral? Yes.

Sometimes you need to take an innovative approach to get the job done. When it comes to getting rid of the toxins and heavy metals from your bloodstream and brain tissues, do whatever it takes!

1. Walker, M. *The Chelation Way: The Complete Book of Chelation Therapy*, Garden City Park, NY: Avery Publishing Group, 1990.

   Cranton, E.M. and Frackelton, J.P. Free radical pathology in age-associated diseases: Treatment with EDTA chelation, nutrition, and anti-oxidants. *Journ Adv in Med* 1989 (2, 1–2): 9.

   Halstead, B.W. *The Scientific Basis of EDTA Chelation Therapy*, Colton, CA: Golden Quill Publishers, 1979.

   Grumbles, L.A. Radionuclide studies of cerebral and cardiac arteriography before and after chelation therapy. *New Horizons in Holistic Health II* (a symposium), May 27, 1979, Chicago, IL.

   Casdorph, H.R. EDTA Chelation therapy II: Efficacy in brain disorders. *Journ of Holistic Med* 1981 (3; 1–2): 101–117.

   Rudolph, C.J., McDonagh, E.W., Barber, R.K. Effect of EDTA chelation on serum iron. *Journ Adv in Med* 4 (Spring 1991;1): 39.

   Meltzer, L.E. and Kitchell, J.R. The treatment of coronary artery disease with disodium EDTA. Found in *Metal Binding in Medicine*, ed. M.J. Seven. Philadelphia: J.B. Lippincott Co., 1960: 132–136.

   Casdorph, H.R. EDTA chelation therapy, efficacy in arteriosclerotic heart disease. *Journ Hol Med* 1981 (3): 101–117.

   Adams, W.J. and McGee, C.T. Chelation therapy: A survey of treatment outcomes and selected sociomedical factors. *Journ Adv in Med* 992 (5;3): 189–1997.

2. Taylor, C.B., Peng, S.K., Lee, K.T. Spontaneously occurring angiotoxic derivatives of cholesterol. *Amer Journ Clin Nutr* 1979(32):40-57.

   Peng, S.., Taylor, C.B. Cytotoxicity of oxidation derivatives of cholesterol on cultured aortic smooth muscle cells and their effects on cholesterol biosynthesis. *Amer Journ Clin Nutr* 1979 (32): 1033–42.

   Benditt, E. The origin of atherosclerosis. *Scientif Amer* 1977 (236): 74–85.

3. McCully, K. *The Homocysteine Revolution: Medicine for the New Millennium*. New Canaan, CT: Keats, 1997.

   Stacey, M. The fall and rise of Kilmer McCully. *New York Times Magazine* Aug. 10, 1997: 25–29.

4. McCully, K.S. Chemical pathology of homocysteine III. Cellular function and aging. *Annals of Clin and Lab Sci* (1999 (24): 134–52.

McCully, K.S. Importance of homocysteine-induced abnormalities of proteoglycan structure in arteriosclerosis. *Amer Journ of Path* (1970 (59): 181–93.

Graham, I.M., Daly, L.E., Refsum, H.M., et al. Plasma homocysteine as a risk factor for vascular disease. *JAMA* 1997 (277): 1775–81.

TAKING ACTION FOR HEALTHY BRAIN FUNCTION

1. Consider going on a short (three-day) fast of pure water to cleanse your system of impurities. You may also want to consider a colonic.

2. Consider intravenous chelation to rid your body of toxic metal build-up.

3. Consider adding "green foods" to your diet.

4. Consider doing a more advanced seven-day cleansing program. This program is available from my office and I highly recommend it. I have done it more than a dozen times. It's the best! Call 1-800-726-1834 or 863-967-8284.

CHAPTER 14

CONFRONTING THE
DISEASE EVERYONE FEARS:
ALZHEIMER'S

An estimated 4.5 million people in the United States are living with Alzheimer's disease. Their care costs more than $60 billion annually. But this is nothing compared to what is projected for the future. By 2030, more than nine million Alzheimer's patients are anticipated, which will be close to *half* of the population of those 85 years old and older.[1] An effective treatment that would delay the onset of Alzheimer's by just five years would reduce the cost to our nation by as much as $30 billion annually![2] Certainly, the emotional costs borne by families and caregivers are immeasurable.

Alzheimer's, of course, is not the only degenerative disease associated with the nervous system and the brain. The mortality from Parkinson's disease rose more than 400 percent in the thirty years between 1955 and 1986. Deaths from Lou Gehrig's disease (Amyotrophic laterial sclerosis or ALS) increased 328 percent in the period from 1977 to 1986.[3] Alzheimer's disease, however, is perhaps the most feared of all brain disorders because to date, the medical community hold out very little hope for either a slow-down or reversal of the disease once it has been diagnosed.

What is behind this tremendous rise in these diseases related to the nervous system and brain?

Part of the reason is that an increasing number of environmental, nutritional, and even emotional and behavioral factors seem to be having a negative impact on brain tissue.

Aluminum and Alzheimer's Disease

A major risk factor associated with Alzheimer's disease and other types of dementia is exposure to aluminum. Aluminum is the only element found to accumulate in the tangle-bearing neurons characteristic of Alzheimer's disease, and it is also the element found in elevated amounts in four regions of the brain of Alzheimer's patients. [4] Enough study has been done that we know *how* aluminum increases the risk. Like other metals, aluminum directly enhances the formation of free radicals.

Food cooked in aluminum cookware can absorb substantial amounts of aluminum. I recommend that you choose glass or stainless steel cookware. Also, avoid direct contact between aluminum foil and food. In many cases, foods can be baked safely in aluminum foil *if* parchment paper is placed between the foil and the food. This is also my recommendation if you are storing food in aluminum foil.

Aluminum cookware, however, is far from the most common source of aluminum for most people. Municipal drinking water in some cities is very high in aluminum!

One study found an astonishing 250 percent increased risk of Alzheimer's disease in individuals who consumed drinking water high in aluminum for ten or more years. Even water with lower levels of aluminum caused the risk for Alzheimer's to be increased by seventy percent. [5] The effects of aluminum seem especially to impact people who fall into "older age groups." Unfortunately, that's where we all hope to be one day—in an older age group!

Beyond municipal drinking water, other sources for aluminum exposure include nondairy creamers, self-rising flours, cake mixes, and various processed foods, especially individually wrapped cheese slices. Perhaps the most potent form of ingested aluminum, however, is the antacid tablet. The human body seems to be able to excrete about twenty milligrams of ingested aluminum each day, but just one antacid tablet may provide as much as 200 milligrams of aluminum.[6]

Other medications high in aluminum include many buffered analgesic products, including Vanquish Caplets and Cope Tablets. If you need analgesic medication, these are products that do *not* have aluminum: Bayer Select Maximum Strength Headache Caplets, Anacin Caplets and Tablets, and Anacin Maximum Strength Tablets.[7]

I heartily recommend drinking purified, filtered, and distilled water and avoiding any of these medications or products that have aluminum in them. Read ingredient labels of food products closely.

Melatonin has been shown to limit aluminum's damaging effects, but I caution you in the use of melatonin. It has its own set of problems if taken in excess.

Eating a diet that is high in fiber and includes apple pectin may also help. Apple pectin binds with aluminum in the colon and excretes it from the body.

Electromagnetic Fields and Alzheimer's Disease

Do hand-held cellular phones, personal computers, and an abundance of other electronic devices contribute to memory loss or brain disorders?

A possible link between electromagnetic radiation and Alzheimer's disease was noted in a 1995 study reported in the *American Journal of Epidemiology*. These same researchers confirmed a relationship between certain occupations that expose individuals to high levels of electromagnetic radiation and the risk of developing Alzheimer's disease.[8] Specifically, they noted that occupations such as electrician, machinist, machine operator, seamstress, sewing factory worker, sheet metal worker, typist, keypunch operator, welder, machine shop worker, and several other occupations put people into a "high risk" category for Alzheimer's disease, with the disease occurring in these individuals at a rate up to *four times higher* than the general population. This study involved individuals who had experienced electromagnetic exposure long before cellular phones, personal computers, and other such devices were widespread.

There is still considerable research to be done as to how electromagnetic fields may contribute to dementia. It appears that electronic equipment may enhance the formation of beta amyloid, a protein that is prevalent in the brains of Alzheimer's patients. Exactly how beta amyloid is produced, however, is still unclear. I personally believe that environmental contaminants such as aluminum play a great role in its production. At the same time, I recommend that you choose *not* to live under high power lines. Also stay away from your microwave oven when it is in use, and limit your cellular phone use.

The Link Between Inflammation and Alzheimer's

People who have chronic inflammation, such as many people who suffer from arthritis, seem at special risk for Alzheimer's and especially so if they are taking aspirin to help with the pain of their disease. Inflammation has been linked to a greater presence of chemicals known as cytokines in the brains of Alzheimer's patients, and especially those patients who are taking nonsteroidal anti-inflammatory drugs (NSAIDs) or aspirin.

One study found that the relative risk of Alzheimer's disease was significantly increased in those who had been regularly taking aspirin or Tylenol® for two years or more. Acetaminophen, the anti-inflammatory chemical in these medications, has been shown to reduce glutathione production. Glutathione is one of the primary brain antioxidants, so a deficiency in this antioxidant may pave the way for enhanced brain damage by free radicals. [9]

An aspirin a day? No thanks. I suggest you take Vitamin E to reduce the risk of heart disease. It has far more beneficial effects than aspirin and is even more protective.

Inflammation itself has been shown to be caused by an increase of arachidonic acid—in fact, it is the reduction of this type of acid that is the basis for many of the anti-inflammatory drugs on the market. The increase of arachidonic acid, in turn, has been linked to the Western diet that typically is high in meat, meat-products, and eggs. The Western diet typically results in a person consuming between 100 and 100 milligrams a day of arachidonic acid—the normal requirement of arachidonic acid is only about one milligram! Over the years, a person eating a diet high in meat and eggs can build up an excessive pool of arachidonic acid, which is one of the many reasons that older people in Western societies tend to develop rheumatoid arthritis, atherosclerosis, certain neoplasm (cancers), psoriasis, and Alzheimer's disease at rates higher than those in the Orient. [10]

New research has also found that homocysteine is related to Alzheimer's disease. In one study, researchers found a 200 percent increase in risk for the disease in individuals who had elevated blood homocysteine levels. [11]

Elevated homocysteine levels have also been linked to some medications, including L-dopa (Sinemet®) which is often used for treating Parkins's disease, and the antibiotics containing trimethoprim (Bactrim® and Septra®). [12]

Reducing Inflammation. The most powerful way to reduce inflammation in the body is to change the amount of dietary fat a person consumes. The basic formula is this:

Less meat and eggs and
More omega-3 and omega-6 fatty acids

As discussed in a previous chapter, the best sources of omega-3 fatty acids are fish oils. (Flaxseed is also a source for omega-3, but it provides considerably less compared to supplements made from fish oil.) The best source of omega-6 fatty acids are borage seed oil and evening primrose oil.

Zinc, magnesium, and vitamins B3 and B6 enhance the anti-inflammatory effects of both these essential fatty acids.

If you have inflammation or arthritis, I recommend the use of flax seed oil and cod liver oil daily. Call my office for dosage amounts. Also remember to eliminate night-shade vegetables from your diet if you have arthritis—these vegetables include potatoes, tomatoes, eggplant, and bell peppers.

Herpes Simplex and Alzheimer's

A group of researchers have discovered that many Alzheimer's patients have an infection with herpes simplex, the virus that is often associated with cold sores and genital viral infections. Those with the apoE4 geotype characteristics are also more susceptible to other causes of inflammation, including viruses, toxic substances, allergic disorders, trauma, and certain medications that may promote inflammation. [13]

Anti-inflammatory medications appear to be one of the things that helps fight the infections that impact the brain. Anti-inflammatory medication may also help reduce the risk of heart disease. [14]

Again, I recommend Vitamin E to thin the blood and help prevent cardiovascular disease.

What about the So-Called Alzheimer's "Drugs"?

A number of pharmaceutical treatments for dementia have appeared on the market in recent years. None of these so-called "Alzheimer's drugs," however, seems to offer definitive help. In the June 1999 issue of *Archives of Neurology*, Dr. William Pryse-Phillips wrote of the lack of usefulness of two of the major drugs being used: tacrine (Cognex®) and donepezil (Aricept®). Tacrine, according to Dr. Pryse-Phillips has highly adverse effects on the liver and has no clear long-term "evidence of efficacy or effectiveness." Donepezil "may improve certain neuro-psychological test scores, but its clinically meaningful benefits in treatment of Alzheimer's disease seem to be minimal." [15] The tens of thousands of prescriptions written each year for these two drugs seem to be written *not* on the basis of the drugs' effectiveness, but rather, on the basis of the pharmaceutical advertising.

Helping Those with Alzheimer's: Therapies that Work

Effective therapies for Alzheimer's disease focus on three processes:

- limiting the damaging effects of free radicals
- reducing inflammation
- enhancing neuronal function

Here are my top six recommendations that accomplish the above goals:

1. Avoid prolonged use of potential sources of electromagnetic radiation, such as hand-held cellular telephones, microwave ovens, electric blankets, hand-held hair dryers, clock-radios near the head of the bed, and close exposure to desktop computers.

2. Stop cooking with aluminum cookware. Avoid contact between aluminum foil and foods.

3. Avoid using antiperspirant deodorants.

4. Avoid medications containing acetaminophen. Choose Advil® over Tylenol®.

5. Cut back your consumption of meat. A vegetarian diet with added fish is recommended. Supplement with oils rich in omega-3 and omega-6 fatty acids. I especially recommend cod liver oil. I recommend 500 mg of cod liver oil a day and 300 mg of evening primrose oil, borage oil, or black current oil.

5. Take antioxidants and cellular energizers regularly. I recommend a regular supplementation regimen that includes a homocysteine-balanced vitamin-B complex with folic acid. Also, 80 mg a day of Alpha lipoic acid (ALA), 400 mg of N-acetyl cysteine, 60 mg Ginkgo biloba, 400-1600 IU vitamin E (400-800 IU for women, 1600 IU for men), and 400 IU vitamin D. In addition, I recommend 100 mg Coenzyme Q10, 5 mg (twice daily) NADH, 100 mg Phosphatidylserine, and 400 mg Acetyl-L-carnitine. The minerals magnesium (400 mg/daily) and zinc (20 mg/daily) will help these other substances be more effective in the body and brain.

These recommendations, by the way, apply to other forms of dementia as well as Alzheimer's disease.

Also, if you or someone you know is helping care for an Alzheimer's patient, you may want to consult a very helpful book: Nancy L. MacE, Peter V. Rabins, Paul R. McHugh, *The 36-Hour Day: A Family Guide to Caring for Persons with Alzheimer Disease, Related Dementing Illnesses, and Memory Loss in Later Life,* Third Edition, Baltimore: Johns Hopkins University Press, 1999.

1. Cumings J.L. Current perspectives in Alzheimer's disease. *Neuro* 1998 (51;suppl. 1): S1.
2. Cumings, J.L. Current perspectives in Alzheimer's disease. *Neuro* 1998 (51;suppl. 1): S1.
3. Riggs, Jack E. "The Aging Population—Implications for the Burden of Neurologic Disease." In Riggs, J. (ed.) *Neurologic Clinics,* Philadelphia: W.B. Saunders, 1998: 556.
4. Weiner, M.A. Evidence pints to aluminum's link with Alzheimer's disease. *Townsend Letter for Doctors* 1993 (124): 1103.
5. McLachlan, D.R.C., Bergeron, C., Smith, J.E., et al. Risk for neuropathologically confirmed Alzheimer's disease and residual aluminum in municipal drinking water employing weighted residential histories. *Neur* 1996 (46): 401–405.

6. These are antacid products with aluminum: Maalox tablets, extra-strength tablets, Maalox Plus tablets and extra-strength Maalox Plus tablets, Mintox tablets and Mintox Plus tablets, RuLox #1 and #2 tablets and RuLoxPlus tablets, Acid-X, Duracid tablets, Titalac tablets and extra-strength tablets, Marblen Tablets, Alkets tablets, Mi-Acid gelcaps, Mylanta gelcaps, Calgylicine Antacid, Alenic Alka tablets and extra-strength tablets, Foamicon tablets, Genaton tablets and extra-strength tablets, Gaviscon tablets and double-strength-2 tablets, Mylanta tablets and double-strength tablets, Magalox tablets, Gelusil tablets, Tempo tablets. This information provided by Facts and Comparisons®, 111 West Port Plaza, Suite 300, St. Louis, MO 6316-3098.

7. *Drug Facts and Comparisons®* 1999 Edition, published by Facts and Comparisons®, 111 West Port Plaza, Suite 300, St. Louis, MO 63146-3098.

8. Sobel, E., Davanipour, Z., Sulkave, R., et al., Occupations with exposure to electromagnetic fields: a possible risk factor for Alzheimer's disease. *Am J Epidemiol* 1995 (142): 515–535.

   Sobel, E., Dunn, M., Davanipour, Z., et al. Elevated risk of Alzheimer's disease among workers with likely electromagnetic field exposure. *Neur* 1996 (47): 1477–81.

9. Floyd, R.A. Neuroinflammatory processes are important in neurodegenerative diseases: An hypothesis to explain the increased formation of reactive oxygen and nitrogen species as major factors involved in neurodegenerative disease development. *Free Radical Biology and Medicine* 1999 (26;8/10): 1346–55.

   Stewart, W.F., Kawas, C., Corrada, M. Risk of Alzheimer's disease and duration of NSAID use. *Neur* 1997 (48): 626–632.

10. Vendemiale, G., Grattaglioano, I., Altomare, E., et al. Effect of acetaminophen on hepatic glutathione compartimentation and mitochondrial energy metabolism in the rat. *Biochem Pharmacol* 1996 (25;8): 147–54.

    Newman, P.E., Could diet be used to reduce the risk of developing Alzheimer's disease? *Med Hypothesis* 1998 (50): 335–37.

11. Clarke, R., Smith, A.D., Jobst, K.A., et al. Folate, vitamin B12, and serum total homocysteine levels in confirmed Alzheimer's disease. *Arch Neurol* 1988 (55): 1449–55.

12. Muler, T., Werne, B., Fowler, W., et al. Nigral endothelial dysfunction and Parkinson's disease. *Lancet* 1999 (354): 126–127.

    Smulders, Y.M., de Man, A.M.E., Stehouwer, C.D.A. Trimethoprim and fasting homocysteine. *Lancet* 1998 (352): 1827–28.

13. Fitzhaki, R.F., Lin, W.R., Shang, D., et al. Herpes simplex virus type 1 in brain and risk of Alzheimer's disease. *Lancet* 1997 (349): 241–44.

14. MacKenzie, I.R. Antiinflammatory drugs in the treatment of Alzheimer's disease. *Journ Rheum* 1996 (23): 806–08.

    Breitner, J.C. Inflammatory processes and anti-inflammatory drugs in Alzheimer's disease: A current appraisal. *Neurobiol of Aging* 1996 (17): 789–94. McGeer, P.L., Schulzer, M., McGeer, E.G. Arthritis and antiinflammatory agents as possible protective factors for Alzheimer's disease: A review of 17 epidemiologic studies. *Neur* 1996 (47): 425–32. Breitner, J.C. The role of anti-inflammatory drugs in the prevention and treatment of Alzheimer's disease. *Ann Rev of Med* 1996 (47):401-411.

15. Pryse-Philips, W. Do we have drugs for dementia? Arch Neurol 1999 (56): 735–737.

CHAPTER 15

THE MANY FACES OF DEMENTIA

"Are you *really* dealing with Alzheimer's?" It's a good question to ask if the word Alzheimer's comes up.

Let me share a personal experience involving a different area of health care.

About a year ago, my mother fell. She was eighty-four years old at the time. Her physicians quickly concluded that a rather large lesion on her big toe had caused her fall. Not only that, but they theorized that the lesion was the type that indicates cancer is resident someplace else in the body. The primary physician on my mother's case informed my mother that she had cancer.

I asked the physician, "Why did you tell my mother she has cancer?" He answered, "Because she does."

I said, "Have you found cancer in her body?" He said, "No, but we will."

I said, "Don't you think it is premature to tell her she has cancer when you haven't found any cancer?" He said, "No. I'm 99.9 percent certain she does have cancer."

I said, "I do NOT believe she has cancer. I believe she had an osteoporetic fracture of her toe because she doesn't have enough calcium in her system, and that fracture caused both the lesion and the fall." He shrugged his shoulders and went on.

I felt great sorrow for my mother as she waited through the weekend for more tests to be done the following Monday. Even though I wasn't at all convinced that she had cancer and told her so, *she* believed the physician and was extremely frightened and worried at what he had told her.

When they did the MRI and CT scan, they found *no cancer*. The tests revealed precisely what I had predicted.

If someone gives you a medical opinion of a dreaded condition such as Alzheimer's disease, don't panic. Seek out the best information and all the nutritional support you can get. And by all means, get *multiple* opinions!

In many instances, the use of the term "Alzheimer's" is overused. In the late 1970's, neurologists Tom Sabin and Vernon Mark began what later became a landmark study of nursing homes in the greater Boston area. They discovered that ninety percent of all the patients they surveyed had some loss of intellectual function or memory. About forty percent had Alzheimer's disease, and another twenty percent were suffering from strokes.

But what about the remaining forty percent of the nursing home residents?

To their surprise, they also found that twenty percent of the patients had a variety of causes for their dementia but these causes were treatable. These people had been incorrectly diagnosed at some point before they were placed in the nursing home. The final twenty percent had a mixture of treatable and untreatable diseases—the combination of their symptoms made their conditions worse than they might have been if the treatable conditions had been corrected just a few years prior to their being institutionalized.

Sabin and Hughes concluded that tens of thousands of people nationwide were likely being placed into nursing homes prematurely. Their findings, published in the *Journal of the American*

Medical Association in 1982, were widely reported. In the years that followed, Hughes wrote, "I'd like to report that our study and those of others led to more careful diagnosis and treatment of the elderly, but I know they didn't. What I noticed instead was a change in the way elderly patients were labeled. The diagnosis of hardening of the arteries or senility rapidly fell out of favor. Doctors began labeling the same patients with a more modern diagnosis: Alzheimer's disease, a catchall term that quickly became overused."[1]

Other researchers also seem to be coming to the conclusions drawn by Sabin and Mark. Some now believe that only about ten percent of the 75- to 86-year-old population suffers from Alzheimer's, and less than five percent of 65- to 75-year-olds show symptoms of the disease. Other forms of dementia seem to be at work.

A Diagnosis Of Exclusion

Alzheimer's disease is often a diagnosis of "inclusion" when it should be a diagnosis of exclusion—in other words, it should be the diagnosis when everything else has been positively ruled out. Many people are being consigned to this diagnosis who have treatable problems.

A study at the University of Toronto Sunnybrook Medical Centre reviewed postmorten anatomical studies of patients who, while they were alive, were clinically diagnosed by more than one physician as having Alzheimer's disease. They found that even in this group, more than fourteen percent turned out to have had something else!

The Prevalence of Vascular Dementia

One of the most frequent cause of dementia in the elderly is something called "vascular dementia." This is also known as a brain dysfunction that occurs as a consequence of a disease that strikes the small blood vessels of the brain.

A great deal of research has been conducted in this area—we know that the central cause of the disease is a compromised blood supply to the brain. Damage to the small blood vessels in the brain leads to a progressive decline in function.

Vascular dementia is characterized by these factors, which are quite different than those associated with Alzheimer's disease:

- an abrupt onset
- preservation of personality
- evidence of other vascular disease
- difficulty controlling emotions
- a stepwise progression with fairly well defined stages
- nocturnal confusion
- depression
- hypertension
- history of stroke
- elevated homocysteine level

This last factor, homocysteine—as mentioned earlier—refers to an amino acid that is known to be directly linked to an increased risk for various vascular conditions, including myocardial infarction and stroke. One of the main treatments for vascular dementia involves vitamin therapy since elevation of homocysteine is often a consequence of a deficiency of vitamins B6, B12, and folic acid. A simple blood test can evaluate homocysteine level. An overnight fast is required, similar to a cholesterol test. Normal range is 8-14 umol/L, but a level of below 10 should be the goal.

Blood homocysteine levels are directly related to the B vitamins—the less vitamin B, the higher the homocysteine level. Those who have a strong history of dietary supplementation of the B-complex group (specifically vitamins B6, B12, and folic acid) have a reduced risk of this dementia. [2]

Another substance being used to treat vascular dementia is vinpocetine, an extract of the periwinkle plant, Vinca minor. Vinpocetine works to increase brain blood flow, reduce blood viscosity, increase brain metabolism, and it acts as a potent antioxidant. [3]

Other Diseases and Conditions that Can Impair Brain Function

We have noted Alzheimer's and vascular dementia as the leading causes of brain dysfunction in the elderly, but there are a number of other physical conditions and diseases that impact the brain. Huntington's disease, Parkinson's disease, and multiple sclerosis are three critically important diseases related to the nervous system and brain.

Huntington's Disease. This devastating hereditary illness eventually destroys the brain's motor system, which carries a form of procedural memory. The disease typically has an onset between ages 30 and 50.

Parkinson's Disease. This is a slowly progressing disorder that results when nerve cells in the basal ganglia degenerate. The degeneration results in lower production of dopamine and fewer connections among nerve cells and muscles. Memory impairment occurs in most patients. [4]

Multiple Sclerosis. This degenerative disorder impacts the nerves of the eye, brain, and spinal cord. It causes damage to the myelin sheath of neurons so they can't conduct impulses properly. MS patients tend to perform poorly on tests of long-term memory and learning, although the exact causes for these results are still not known. [5]

Other Brain-Function Compromisers

In addition to the above diseases, the following conditions can result in diminished brain function.

Fugue Amnesia. This type of amnesia occurs usually when a person's life has become so stressful that the person "blanks out" for a few weeks or months as a means of mental or emotional escape. The amnesia is not based on a conscious decision, but rather, is an unconscious response to extreme stress. This type of amnesia is also called functional, hysterical, or psychogenic amnesia. It is relatively rare. Dissociation seems to be the main cause of the condition. This is a process where memory systems that normally communicate in some way seem to lose touch with each other.

Hypertension. The relationship between blood pressure and intellectual function has been established in both lab animals and older humans. People with chronic hypertension (high blood pressure) perform more poorly than those with normal blood pressure on tests of memory, attention, and abstract reasoning.[6] For more information on hypertension and how to correct it nutritionally, obtain a copy of my "Eat, Drink, and Be Healthy" program: 1-800-726-1834.

Multi-Infarct Dementia. Those who experience a series of successive small strokes suffer from multi-infarct dementia. These small strokes, also called "cerebrovascular accidents" cause brief periods of "spacing out" that usually last only a minute or less. The condition tends to occur in those with high blood pressure or diabetes. Unlike normal dementia, the symptoms of multi-infarct dementia can occur quite suddenly.

About twenty percent of all cases of severe cognitive dysfunction and dementia in the elderly are the result of this condition.[7]

Obstructive Sleep Apnea. Chronic sleep disruption that results from obstructive sleep apnea can adversely affect memory. The fundamental problem in this condition is the periodic collapse or relaxation of the pharyngeal airway during sleep. Typically a person is awakened after about ten seconds of oxygen deprivation. The condition usually occurs between the ages of 40 and 60, and its prevalence increases with age. It is common among individuals who are overweight because fat in the neck area puts extra pressure on breathing passages. The condition tends to result in poor cognitive functioning owing to daytime sleepiness from a lack of sufficient sleep at night. The condition has been shown to result in cognitive dysfunction, inability to concentrate, memory and judgment impairment, irritability, and depression. [8]

Diabetes and Hypoglycemia. Both of these blood-sugar-related conditions can result in confusion, inability to concentrate, difficulty in organizing memories, dizziness, and nervousness. [9]

Post-Traumatic Stress Disorder. This is an anxiety condition caused by exposure to an overwhelming traumatic event. Symptoms sometimes don't begin for several months or even years after the event. The symptoms include sleep difficulties, depression, and a general declining ability to perform effectively on tasks that require sustained attention, mental manipulation of data, and initial acquisition of information. Those with the condition perform significantly worse on tasks of delayed free recall. [10]

Chronic Fatigue Syndrome. Severe and prolonged fatigue has been linked to impaired concentration and memory, disturbed sleep, depressed mood, and anxiety. [11]

Use of Benzodiazepines (Tranquilizers). Certain medications can result in memory impairment, notable benzodiazepines such as the tranquilizers Librium, Valium, and Halcion. They can impair memory and result in memory loss and diminished attention span. They may even cause a persion to appear to have dementia. The elderly seem particularly susceptible to the memory impairing effects of benzodiazepines. [12]

Pregnancy. Anecdotally, many women have claimed that their memory declined during pregnancy. There is some scientific support for this claim. Pregnant women have beeen shown to do more poorly than nonpregnant women on objective tests of recall, recognition, and priming memory (where some memory of a recent event remains in the brain even when a person is unaware of it. [13]

Fibromyalgia. This rheumatic disorder is characterized by widespread muscular-skeletal pain and tenderness. One of the most prominent complaints of fibromyalgia patients is impaired cognitive ability, including reduced memory.

Anesthesia. Surgeons often hear their patients complain of "fuzzy thinking" after they undergo surgery. There's scientific validation of that complaint. Anesthesia has been shown to result in cognitive dysfunction—confusion, memory loss, and concentration problems for several months after surgery. Those who are older than seventy years of age are more susceptible to long-term mental impairment than those under seventy. [14]

Temporal Lobe Epilepsy. Epilepsy is actually a broad term for a variety of brain disorders. One type of epilepsy, called temporal lobe epilepsy, is caused if the temporal lobes are injured. Right temporal lobe results in an impaired memory of sounds and shapes. Left temporal lobe epilepsy impairs a person's ability to understand language, express themselves, or cluster information appropriately. Memory of facts and events may be impaired as a result. [15]

Benign Brain Tumors. More than 100,000 Americans a year are diagnosed with brain tumors. The incidence of these tumors is rising at an alarming rate. Tumors that originate in the covering around the brain are especially likely to cause memory loss and difficulty thinking. [16] Again, don't drink diet sodas!

Thyroid Dysfunction. In hyperthryoidism, which results from an overactive thyroid gland producing too much thyroid hormone, confusion can result. Spatial learning ability may also be impaired. In hypothyroidism, when too little hormone is produced, a person can experience declining memory. The impact of these conditions on brain function is especially exaggerated in the elderly. Severe hypothyroidism appears to cause significant memory loss in 25 to 55 percent of the people who have this condition. [17]

Chronic Pain. Chronic pain has a very disabling effect on the human body, often generating depression that can interfere with normal brain function.

Food Allergies. Some food allergies seem to be linked to dementia. Medical investigators in Scandinavia recently found a very high correlation between gluten-sensitive individuals who continue to eat wheat products and the early onset of dementia. The dementia appears to be caused by a food allergy that activates the immune system and increases the inflammatory response. Well before dementia sets in, individuals lose cognitive function, mental clarity, and short-term memory. A general "confusion" of thinking sets in. [18]

People who seems to have an allergy to wheat products should stop eating those products immediately. A several day fast—accompanied by drinking lots of pure water—can help eliminate gluten from the body and reduce the effects of inflammation.

Helping Those with Vascular Dementia and Other Brain Diseases and Conditions: Therapies that Work

Perhaps the most important thing I can say to you if you are diagnosed with vascular dementia or another brain-impacting disease is this: Don't give up!

Make sure you get a proper diagnosis. I always recommend a second opinion.

Make sure you are giving your body and brain all the nutritional support you can. This is especially important regarding homocysteine and vascular dementia—make sure you are getting sufficient vitamin B from a homocysteine-balanced vitamin B complex.

Keep yourself informed as to the latest medical research on your disease or condition. There's great support in many cases for those who have been diagnosed with even the most dreaded disease, and new findings are coming out every month to indicate that even greater support is on the horizon.

Finally, don't *accept* a "poor memory" or "limited brain function" as an automatic outcome of any disease or condition. Fight the condition. Fight for your mind.

---

1. Mark, Vernon, *Brain Power*, Boston: Houghton Mifflin Company, 1989: 55.

2. Fabender, K., Mielke, O., Bertsch, T., et al. Homocysteine in cerebral macroangiography and microangiopathy. *Lancet* 1999 (353): 1586–87.

3. Tamaki, N., Kusonoki, T., Matsumoto, S. The effect of vinpocetine on cerebral blood flow in patients with cerebrovascular disease. *Ther Hung*, 1985 (33): 13–21.

   Olah, V.A. Balla, G., Balla, J., et al. An in vitro study of the hydroxyl scavenger effect of caviton. *Acta* Paediatr Hung, 1990 (30): 309–316.

   Balesteri, R., Fontana, L., and Astengo, F. A double-blind placebo controlled evaluation of the safety and efficacy of vinpocetine in the treatment of patients with chronic vascular senile, cerebral dysfunction. *J Am Geriatr Soc* 1987 (35): 425–430.

   Hindmarch, I., Fuchs, H., Erzigkeit, H. Efficacy and tolerance of vinpocetine in ambulant patients suffering from mild to moderate organic psychosyndromes. *Int Clin Psychoparmacol* 1991 (6): 31–43.

4. Gabrieli, J.D. Memory systems analyses of mnemonic disorders in aging and age-related diseases. *Proceedings of Natl Acad Sci, USA* 1996 (931;24): 13534–13540.

5. Beatty, W.W., Goodkin, D.E., Monson, N., Beatty, P.A., and Hertsgaard, D. Anterograde and retrograde amnesia in patients with chronic progressive multiple sclerosis. *Arch of Neur* 1988 (45): 611–619.

Beatty, W.W., Goodkin, D.,E., Monson, N., and Beatty, P.A. Cognitive disturbances in patients with relapsing remitting multiple sclerosis. *Arch of Neur* 1989 (46): 1113–1119.

Rao, S.M., Leo, G.J., Barnardin, L., and Unverzagt, F. Cognitive dysfunction in multiple sclerosis I: Frequency, patterns, and prediction. *Neur* 1991 (41): 685–691.

Paul, R.H., Blanco, C.R., Hames, K.A., and Beatty, W.W. Autobiographical memory in multiple sclerosis. *Journ of Internatl Neuropsych Soc* 1997 (3): 246–251.

6. Waldstein, S.R., Manuck, S.B., Ryan, C.M., and Muldoon, M.F. Neuropsychological correlates of hypertension: Review and methodologic consideration. *Psych Bull* 1991 (110;3): 451–468.

Makamura-Palacios, E.M., Caldas, C.K., Fiorina, A., Chagas, K.D., Chagas, K.N., and Vazquez, E.C. Deficits of spatial learning and working memory in spontaneously hypertensive rats. *Beh Brain Res* 1996 (74;1-2): 217–227.

Wyss, J.M., Gisk, G., and Van Groen, T. Impaired learning and memory in mature spontaneously hypertensive rats. *Brain Res* 1992 (59;1-2): 135–140.

Launer, L.J., Masaki, K., Petrovitch, H., Foley, D., and Havlik, R.J. The association between midlife blood pressure levels and late-life cognitive function: The Honolulu-Asia aging study. *JAMA* 1995 (274): 1846–1851.

Starr, J.M., Whalley, L.J., and Dreary, I.J. The effects of antihypertensive treatment on cognitive function: Results from the HOPE Study. *Journ of Amer Geriatric Soc* 1996 (44;4): 411–415.

Kuusisto, J., Koivisto, K., Mykkanenm, L., Helkala, E.L., Vanhanen, M., Hanninen, T., Pyorala, K., Riekkinen, P., and Laakso, M. Essential hypertension and cognitive function: The role of hyperinsulinemia. *Hypertension* 1994 (22;5): 771–779.

Strassburger, T.L., Lee, H.C., Daly, E.M., Szczepanik, J., Krasuki, J.S., Mentis, M.J., Salerno, J.A., DeCarli, C., Schapiro, B., and Alexander, G.E. Interactive effects of age and hypertension on volumes of brain structures. *Stroke* 1997 (28;7): 1410–1417.

Elias, P.K., D'Agostino, R.B., Elias, M.F., and Wolf, P.A. Blood pressure, hypertension, and age as risk factors for poor cognitive performance. *Experimental Aging Res* 1995 (21;4): 393–417.

Thyrum, E.T., Blumenthal, J.A., Madden, D.J., and Wiegel, W. Family history of hypertensive patients. *Psychosomatic Med* 1995 (57;5): 496–500.

7. Gray, G.E. Nutrition and dementia. *Journ of the Amer Dietetic Assoc* 1989 (89;12): 1795–1802.

8. Wiegand, L., and Swillich, C.W. Obstructive sleep apnea. *Disease-A-Month* 1994 (49;4): 1997–252.

9. Berkow, R., Beers, M.H., and Fletcher, A.J., eds. *The Merck Manual of Medical Information.* (Home edition) Whitehouse Station, NJ: Merck Research Laboratories, 1997.

10. Jenkins, M.A., Langlais, P.J., Delis, D., and Cohen, R. Learning and memory in rape victims with posttraumatic stress disorder. *Am Journ of Psych* 1998 (155;2): 278–279.

11. Lawrie, S.A. Is the chronic fatigue syndrome best understood as a primary disturbance of the sense of effort? An editorial. *Psych Med* 1997 (27): 996–999.

12. Berkow, R., Beers, M.H., and Fletcher, A.J., eds. *The Merck Manual of Medical Information.* (Home edition) Whitehouse Station, NJ: Merck Research Laboratories, 1997.

13. Sharp, K., Brindle, P.M., Brown, M.W., and Turner, G.J. Memory loss during pregnancy. *Brit Journ of Ob Gyn* 1993 (100;3): 209–215.

14. Sightings Column: Surgery and memory. *Health News* April 20, 1988(4; 5): 5.

15. Helmstaedter, C., Gleissner, U., Di Perna, M., and Elger, C.E. Relational verbal memory processing in patients with temporal lobe epilepsy, *Cortex* 33;4): 667–678.

16. Berkow, R., Beers, M.H., and Fletcher, A.J., eds. *The Merck Manual of Medical Information.* (Home edition) Whitehouse Station, NJ: Merck Research Laboratories, 1997.

17. Gould, E., Woolley, C.S., and McEwen, B.S. The hippocampal formation: Morphological changes induced by thyroid. Gonadal and adrenal hormones. *Psychoneuroendocrinology* 1991 (16;1-3):67-84.

Pavlides, C., Westlind-Danielsoson, A.I., Nyborg, H., and McEwen, B.S. Neonatal hyperthyroidism disrupts hippocampal LTP and spatial learning. *Exper Brain Res* 1991 (85;3): 559–574.

Berkow, R., Beers, M.H., and Fletcher, A.J., eds. *The Merck Manual of Medical Information.* (Home edition) Whitehouse Station, NJ: Merck Research Laboratories, 1997.

Kudrjavcev, T. Neurologic complication of thyroid dysfunction. *Adv in Neur* 1978 (19): 619–636.

18. Hadjivassiliou, M., Gibson, A., Davies-Jones, G.A., et al. Does cryptic gluten sensitivity play a part in neurological illness? *Lancet* 1996 (347): 369–71.

CHAPTER 16

STROKE PREVENTION
AND
RECOVERY

A stroke typically refers to a blockage of the blood supply to a particular part of the brain. It is one of the most serious vascular conditions impacting brain tissue and memory function, and it is the third most frequent cause of death in the United States. Approximately a third of stroke victims do not survive the initial attack. Of those who do, only about ten percent are able to return to work without disability, another forty percent have a mild disability, forty percent are severely disabled, and about ten percent spend the rest of their lives in institutions because of their inability to care for themselves—eating, bathing, and so forth.

Sadly, we have about 1.7 million stroke survivors in the United States today, about three quarters of them between the ages of 55 and 84 years. Their care costs more than $30 billion annually. The emotional impact on them, as well as their families and caregivers, is incalculable. [1]

In the last three decades, we have made *some* but not very much progress in reducing the number of stroke incidences in the United States. Some of this progress has been related to greater publicity being given to several risk factors: high blood pressure, cigarette smoking, diabetes, and elevated cholesterol. Much remains to be done.

Two Types of Strokes

Strokes come in two main varieties. The most common involves a partial or complete plugging up of a blood vessel that brings blood to the brain. This results in the death of the brain tissue that is normally fed with nutrients and oxygen from that blood vessel. Technically, the death of brain tissue is called a "cerebral infarct."

The second type of stroke occurs when a blood vessel hemorrhages, causing bleeding into or around the brain. This is generally the result of blood vessel disease, such as atherosclerosis (hardening of the arteries). These types of bleeds can occur deep in the brain and they generally occur where blood vessels divide. Paralysis in one arm and less, loss of speech, and even unconsciousness are usually the result. At times, a person may experience a sudden severe headache. The type and extent of damage is related to *where* in the brain the hemorrhage occurs.

For decades, physicians have been aware that people who have high blood pressure are more susceptible to strokes than those with normal blood pressure. The common form of treatment is to prescribe drugs to help with the hypertension. Now, physicians are starting to see a different type of problem. It is often marked by a failing memory, difficulty walking, and perhaps fainting spells. The problem is one related to *low* blood pressure coupled with clogged arteries. People who experience this have often taken blood pressure medications for years, even decades, and often in increasing amounts. The medication is increased as their blood pressure rises, but the rise of the blood pressure is actually caused by a narrowing of the blood vessels. In the end, these people do not have enough "pressure" to ensure adequate flow of blood through all the vessels of the brain.

In *all* instances of blood pressure problems and narrowing of the vessels, the main goal must be to *maintain an adequate flow of blood to the brain, without plaque forming on the vessel walls.* This is the level of vascular health we each should strive to achieve.

Again . . . and Again, the Homocysteine Factor

One of the less publicized factors related to stroke is actually one of the easiest factors to change. An elevated homocysteine level has been identified as a major factor in strokes as well as coronary artery disease. The elevation of homocysteine increases the production of atheromatous plaque, which is a mixture of fat and calcified inflammatory tissue that builds up on arterial walls and consequently causes the arteries to progressively "narrow." When the arteries to the brain are effected, the stage is set for a stroke.

The role of homocysteine in causing strokes was identified in the late 1960's by Dr. Kilmer McCully—in fact, his research earned him the Linus Pauling Award. Researchers confirmed Dr. McCully's landmark study in a number of studies that well documented the link between elevated homocysteine and stroke risk. Then, for no clear reason, the studies and interest seemed to decline until the mid 1990's. (Dr. McCully believes this was owing to pressure from pharmaceutical companies marketing cholesterol medications.)

One of the most recent studies correlating homocysteine and stroke risk was done at Tufts University. Researchers there measured blood homocysteine levels and the degree of narrowing of the carotid arteries (one of the main arteries to the brain) in 1,041 elderly men and women. The carotid arteries were measured using ultrasound, a noninvasive technique commonly employed in assessing stroke risk. Nearly sixty percent of the men and forty percent of the women with high homocysteine were found to have extensive arterial narrowing. [2]

The cause of elevated homocysteine is much clearer than the cause of cholesterol, hypertension, and diabetes. Very simply, homocysteine levels reflect the amount of three important vitamins in the blood stream: B6, B12, and folic acid. When one or more of these nutrients are inadequately supplied to the blood stream, homocysteine production increases, which in turn increases the risk for stroke.

Vitamin therapy has been the most effective means for reversing this trend. The Tufts University researchers noted in their study, "A strong case can be made for prevention of the marginal or manifest vitamin deficiency states that may contribute substantially to this potentially important risk factor for vascular disease, the largest cause of mortality in elderly individuals. Efforts to prevent deficiencies of folate, vitamin B12 and vitamin B6 in the increasing number of our population over the age of 65 years now have added impetus."[3]

In a recent study of a hundred men with elevated homocysteine, supplementaion with only .65 mg of folic acid, .4 mg vitamin B12, and 10 mg B6 daily resulted in a reduction of homocysteine by fifty percent! [4]

Healing with Oxygen Therapy

Until fairly recently, most physicians dealing with stroke patients believed that there was little chance for meaningful functional recovery after a stroke or other brain injury after the first few months owing to their belief that the adult brain lacked "plasticity"—the ability of brain tissue to take over the function of a damaged area. New research is dramatically changing this viewpoint.

Researchers now believe the brain has significant potential for recovery following injury well past the sixth-month point.

When a person experiences a stroke, a portion of brain tissue becomes permanently destroyed. It is, in essence, "dead." There is no clear-cut line, however between the dead tissue and tissue that remains fully functional. Between the two areas of tissue are neurons whose function may be diminished by the stroke, but are nevertheless viable. This area of functional but non-functioning tissue has been called the "ischemic penumbra." A more user-friendly term refers to these neurons that are *capable* of function but are not presently functioning as "idling." They are like car engines that are idling, waiting to be put into gear.

The concern for researchers has been how to bring healing to these damaged neurons so they will begin to function again. One of the techniques being used is hyperbaric oxygen therapy (HBOT).

HBOT involves exposing patients to oxygen under conditions that increase the atmospheric pressure around the body. It has been recognized and used for several decades in Europe and Asia as a potent therapy for stroke recovery and other brain-related diseases. It has not been studied or used extensively in the United States, probably and sadly because no one company has been to obtain an exclusive patent on its use or distribution. HBOT, however, has been approved by both the FDA and the AMA for treating a wide variety of medical disorders.

Many people associate this therapy with the treatment of "the bends" and other diving related injuries. In recent years the therapeutic benefits of HBOT have been much more widely explored, and the treatment has been used to treat thermal burns, carbon monoxide poisoning, non-healing skin wounds, diabetic ulcers, and radiation injuries. It is considered the first-line therapy for neurological disorders across Europe and Asia. In West Germany, virtually all stroke patients are eligible to receive a three-week intensive course of hyperbaric oxygen therapy.

In HBOT therapy, oxygen levels are increased in all of the body's fluids: plasma, lymph, intracellular fluids, and cerebrospinal fluid. Healthy tissues receive this added oxygen boost as well as damaged tissues. The treatment results in growth of new blood vessels, increased ability of white blood cells to destroy bacteria and remove toxins, enhanced growth of fibroblasts (cells involved in wound healing), and enhanced metabolic activity of neurons.

This therapy is very simple to receive. Patients enter a chamber in which they breathe one hundred percent oxygen delivered under increased pressure. The treatment typically lasts one to two hours. Patients usually watch television or sleep while they receive the treatment. They are carefully monitored by a highly trained technician with whom they can communicate easily through an intercom system in the see-through chamber in which they are lying.

Since the early 1970's, scientific journals have published more than one thousand cases that have demonstrated a forty percent to one hundred percent rate of improvement for patients treated with hyperbaric oxygen therapy. Dr. Richard Neubauer, a pioneer in the use of HBOT for neurological diseases, has reported outstanding results in stroke patients who received HBOT. In one case, significant functional improvement was noted when hyperbaric oxygen therapy was given as late as 14 years after the initial stroke event! [5]

Typically, HBOT patients report improvements of gait, speech, mental function, motor power, and a reduction of spasticity. The effects of HBOT are enhanced, of course, when the therapy is accompanied by physical, occupational, and speech therapy.

The impact of HBOT can now be measured by a "functional" scanning of the brain using a SPECT (single photon emission computerized tomography) scan. The SPECT scan actually identifies and quantifies brain metabolism, both normal and abnormal.

HBOT for Other Closed Head Injuries. In addition to being helpful in treatment of stroke patients, HBOT has also been shown to be of great help in treating closed head injuries. This should come as no surprise. Brain injuries, regardless of their cause, share common pathophysiologic pathways that result in the destruction of neurons and the creation of "idling" neurons. As with stroke, closed head injury patients benefit most when HBOT is combined with helpful brain-tissue supplements such as Ginkgo biloba, vitamin B12, acetyl-L-carnitine, and phosphatidylserine. [6]

HBOT is a technique that helps what are presently call "marginally functioning neurons"—in other words, the "gray zone" on the spectrum between high brain function and low brain function often caused by brain damage. It may very well be helpful in all conditions where brain function has been reduced, regardless of cause.

Helpful Supplementation
for Stroke Patients

As a corollary treatment to hyperbaric oxygen therapy, several supplements are helpful in energizing reactivated brain cells. Many of these have been discussed previously in greater detail.

Acetyl-L-Carnitine. This element is especially helpful in shuttling fuel to the mitochondria and helping remove toxic by-products of cellular metabolism.

Coenzyme Q10 (CoQ10) and Nicotinamide Adenine Dinucleotide (NADH). Both of these substances help in the process of mitochondrial energy production, increasing the amount of energy available to damaged neurons. An interesting animal study has shown great power for CoQ10 in helping prevent strokes. The carotid artery of rabbits was significantly narrowed, a condition that normally causes severe neurological deficits. Those rabbits that were given a diet enriched with CoQ10 prior to the narrowing procedure showed no neurological deficits and a microscopic evaluation of their brains revealed virtually no evidence of injury. [7]

Unfortunately, most of the popular cholesterol lowering drugs not only reduce cholesterol, but deplete coenzyme Q10 levels as well. [8] (Cholesterol-lowering drugs also have been shown to cause cancer!) If you insist on taking a cholesterol lowering medication, I strongly advise CoQ10 supplementation.

Phosphatidylserine. This substance has a pivotal role in neuron metabolism. It is one of the key components of the nitochondrial membrane, which is where fuel is transformed into energy within the mitochondria. It is not only vital for cellular energy but also in cell-to-cell communication.

Vinpocetine. This extract of the lesser periwinkle plant, *Vinca minor*, has been used in thirty-five nations around the world as a clinically proven treatment for stroke patients. It is widely used in Europe and Japan.

Vinpocetine increases blood flow to the brain and enhances the flow of oxygen and key nutrients to the brain's neurons.

In a 1985 study in Japan, researchers reported "slight to moderate" improvement in two thirds of stroke patients receiving this remarkable natural substance. [9] While it is not a cure for strokes, it is a very helpful substance in restoring mental health to stroke patients. It helps dilate brain arteries, enhances brain blood flow, and improves delivery of life-giving oxygen to damaged areas of the brain. In addition, it is a potent antioxidant that limits the ongoing brain damage caused by free radicals, and it reduces the tendency of red blood cells and platelets to stick together to form tiny clots. [10]

Helping Those with Strokes: Therapies that Work

1. Consider oxygen therapy (HBOT).

2. Make sure you are taking sufficient sufficient Vitamin B in a homocysteine balanced complex.

3. Consider supplementation of acetyl-L-carnitine, CoQ10, NADH, Phosphaditylserine (PS), and Vinpocetine. We have all these products available at my office: 1-800-726-1834 or 1-863-967-8284.

---

1. Birkmayer, J.G.D. Coenzyme nicotinamid adenine dinucleotide-new therapeutic approach for improving dementia of the Alzheimer type. *Ann Clin and Lab Sci* 1996 (26;1): 1–9.

   Birkmayer, J.G.D., et al. Nicotinamide adenine dinucleotide—a new therapeutic approach to Parkinson's disease: Comparison of oral and parenteral application. *Acta neurol Scand* 1993 (87;146): 32–35.

2. Selhub, J., et al. *N Engl J Med* 1995 (32;5): 286–291.

3. Birkmayer, J.G.D. Coenzyme nicotinamide adenine dinucleotide-new therapeutic approach for improving dementia of the Alzheimer type. *Ann Clin and Lab Science* 1996 (26;1): 1–9.

4. Birkmayer, J.G.D., et al. Nicotinamide adenine dinucleotide (NADH)—a new therapeutic approach to Parkinson's disease: Comparison of Oral and Parenteral Application. *Acta Neurol Scand* 1993 (87;146): 32–35.

5. See "Long Term Results of Treatment of Stroke Patients with Combined HBTO and Physical Therapy" found in Jain, K.K., *Textbook of Hyperbaric Medicine*, second edition. Seattle: Hogrefe and Huber, 1996: 269.

6. Neubauer, R.A., Gottlieb, S.F., and Pevsner, N.H. Hyperbaric oxygen for the treatment of closed head injury. *Southern Med Journ* 1994 (878;9): 933–936.

7. Greib, P., Ryba, M.S., Sawicki, J., et al. Oral coenzyme Q10 administration prevents the development of ischemic brain lesions in a rabbit model of symptomatic vasospasm. *Acta Neuropathol* (Berl), 1997 (4): 363–8.

8. Mortensen, S.A., Leth, A., Agner, E. Dose-related decrease of serum coenzyme Q10 during treatment with HMG_CoA reductase inhibitors. *Mol Aspects of Med* 1997 (18;suppl): S137–44.

9. Otomo, E., Atarashi, J., Araki, G., et al. Comparison of Vinpocetine with ifenprodil tartrate and dihydroergotoxine mesylate treatment and results of long-term treatment with vinpocetine. *Curr Ther Res* 1985 (37): 811–821.

10. Tamaki, N., Kusonoki, T., Matsumoto, S. The effect of vinpocetine on cerebral blood flow in patients with crebrovascular disease. *Ther Hung*, 1985 (33): 13–21.

Olah, V.A., Balla, G., Balla, J. et al. An in vitro study of the hydroxyl scavenger effect of caviton. *Acta Paediatr Hung*, 1990 (30): 309–316.

Osawa, M., Maruyama, S. Effects of TCV-3B (Vinpocetine) on blood viscosity in ischemic cerebrovascular disease. *Ther Hung*, 1985 (33): 7–12.

Hayakawa, M. Comparative efficacy of vinpocetine, pentoxifylline and nicergoline on red blood cell deformability. *Arzneimittelforschung* 1992 (42): 108–110.

CHAPTER 17

DON'T STRESS OUT— WORK OUT!

One of the most interesting and entertaining little books I've ever read on stress was written by Dr. Robert Sapolsky, a professor of neuroscience at Stanford university: *Why Zebras Don't Get Ulcers*. This book is highly readable, even though it covers much of the definitive research about the effects of stress on the brain.

Sapolsky notes that zebras actually have a life that is loaded with stress—but much of that stress is perceived by the zebra as a short-term, occasional event (for example, the approaching of a hungry pride of lions). When the zebra senses the approach of a predator, his stress response goes into action. Adrenaline and noradrenaline surge into the bloodstream, glucose comes surging out of the storage tissues into the blood stream for more energy, the heart beats faster and breathing rate increases to better transport oxygen and nutrients, and stress hormones divert blood flow away from the brain and toward the muscles to help the zebra run fast and escape imminent danger. All this happens in a matter of seconds and when the zebra has outrun the lion, he goes back to slow grazing on the grasslands.

Human beings, in contrast, tend to live in a state of stress—not only stress related to work, but stress related to family, financial, and environmental pressures. Dr. Sapolsky asks wryly, "How many hippos worry about whether Social Security is going to last as long as they will, or even what they are going to say on a first date?" [1]

Also, whereas the zebra eats food that is nutritionally appropriate for its body, we human beings tend to eat things that are *not* good for our bodies. Our bad choices in food, beverages, and inhalants (such as cigarette smoking) generate toxins in our systems—these toxins create stress on the body at the cellular level.

Sustained stress causes brain cells to die or be disabled, and over time, our physiological fight-or-flight response becomes a trigger for illness and disease. We become mental and physical casualties of chronic stress.

The Impact of Stress on Memory

Any stress situation tends to lead to strong emotions, and these emotions can interfere with your ability both to learn and to remember. [2]

Biochemically, stress depletes the neurotransmitter norepinephrine, which is important for memory. Stress also lowers blood sugar—the brain uses more than twenty percent of the body's blood sugar supply while at rest, and even more while engaging in mental tasks. In addition, the amount of certain hormones released into the blood stream increase in times of stress—these hormones may shut down the transport of glucose to the brain and thus, deprive the brain of needed fuel for energy.

It's a strange twist of science that the more we worry about losing our memories, the more stress we create for ourselves, and that added stress can negatively impact the brain so that we DO lose memory capability. Stress may be the main factor in self-fulfilling prophecies! In most cases, choose not to worry about a declining memory. Instead, choose to learn more about which supplements can help the memory and get busy with a new nutrition program, exercise plan, and mental exercises.

The Mental Benefits from Exercise

Most people think exercise only effects the body. Not so! Exercise has a direct impact on the mind in these ways:

First, exercise of the right kinds improves blood circulation. The better the blood circulates to the brain, the more oxygen to the brain. At the same time, there is a greater opportunity for toxins in brain tissues to be removed via the blood system. To maximize these benefits, a person must engage in aerobic exercises, such as walking, swimming, cycling, and low-impact dance and movement exercises.

If you have any doubts about this, just ask my good friend Chris Vittito. He owns and operates a successful business in central Florida and he frequently tells me that regular exercise helps him "think clearly" and make better business decisions. I agree with him, of course.

Second, exercise releases endorphins in the brain. These neurotransmitters help "calm" brain tissues and produce a relaxation effect.

Third, exercise keeps us flexible, strong, and gives us greater energy. All of these factors are important to keep us "going" in life. They are part of what it means to be vibrant and active well into old age. The person who exercises tends to be a person who does much more than the sedentary person—goes more places, has more new experiences, is more eager to continue to work or volunteer, and is much more eager to get involved in activities with younger people. All of these factors lead to greater stimulation and less boredom. This, in turn, leads to a more active *mind*. The more active the mind, the longer the mind tends to remain active!

Staying VIGOROUSLY Active. One of the major changes as we grow older tends to be a *decrease* in vigorous activity. Many people have been told that they are too "old" to exercise—or they have been told that they will experience no benefits from exercise. Let me assure you, you are *never* too old to benefit from exercise. Even if you have never exercised regularly in your life, you can *start* exercising now, no matter your age.

Certainly if you have been diagnosed with any major health problems—such as heart disease or lung disease—you will want to see a physician before you begin an exercise program. Most people, however, can readily begin a simple walking program. Buy a good pair of walking shoes, lace them up, and get started. You can begin with just five to ten minutes a day. Work your way up by adding five minutes every few days until you are walking thirty to forty minutes at a time. Then start to walk a little *faster*—pick up your pace! Always take the first five minutes of your walk to "warm up" to your maximum speed and the last five minutes of your total walk time to "cool off" before you stop. This is very important to avoid injury. Over time, you'll find that you are covering more and more territory in your thirty to forty minutes. Try to walk, or engage in another form of aerobic exercise, at least three to four times a week.

In addition to walking, do strength-building exercises—in other words, use weights. You can use simple hand weights—begin with the two-pound dumb bells—or use resistance bands. This type of training is also called "resistance training." The goal is not to bulk up your muscles so you look like a body-builder, but rather, to strengthen your muscles and to build more muscle in the body. The more muscle you have, the less fat you tend to have. Good muscle tone can help give you general feelings of well-being. Plus, the less fat you have in your body, the greater your general heart health is likely to be. Healthier hearts pump blood more efficiently and effectively, and that means more nutrients and oxygen to the brain.

Effects of Physical Exercise on Memory

A number of studies have shown that exercise improves overall health and helps fight both stress and depression. Very specific studies, however, have shown a direct link between exercise and memory. In one study, recall ability was improved for elderly people who participated in a mild range-of-motion exercise class.[3] In another study, significant improvements in reaction time, memory span, and measures of well-being increased for a group of older people who were in a twelve-month group exercise program.[4] In yet another study, significant memory increases were found in a group of cardiac patients who had dementia or brain atrophy after their participation in a walking program.[5]

A recent study reported in the *Journal of Aging and Physical Activity* showed a correlation between regular aerobic exercise and improved memory and other mental abilities. In the study, eighty-four men and women aged 50 to 77 were randomly assigned exercise plans for four months. The researchers concluded that aerobically fit individuals tend to perform better on measures of the mind.[6]

I encourage you to order a copy of both my book, *Maximum Fat Loss* and a copy of my exercise videos and tape series, *Forever Fit*. Call 1-800-726-1834. These materials can really help you!

If you aren't exercising regularly...start *now*.

Getting Enough
Oxygen to the Brain

Exercise is perhaps the foremost means of *increasing* oxygen to the brain. The brain *needs* oxygen—and plenty of it. Let me share an experience I had just recently.

I have been a scuba diver for nearly thirty years. Several years ago, I hopped a cruise ship to get over to the islands of St. Thomas and St. Martin to dive. I was surprised to hear an announcement made on the cruise that those who were over 55 years of age would not be allowed to dive. Only those 54 and younger could participate.

I asked the dock manager why this regulation had been initiated, and I was told that the cruise line had found through years of sponsoring scuba dives that passengers 55 and older were *rarely* in good enough shape to dive. They did not have the physical stamina or the mental acuity necessary for diving. Rather than take the liability risk, the cruise line simply set a cut-off age for the activity.

One of the cruise ship passengers who joined us for the dive was a man about 6 foot 1 inch tall. He seemed to be in pretty good shape even though he was about thirty to forty pounds overweight. We struck up a conversation and I learned that he was a police officer from Canada. I asked him what he thought about the age stipulation. He responded, "I don't like that rule. I'm almost that age and I think I should be able to dive as much as I want to dive."

We dove that day down to a sunken Spanish galleon that was completely encrusted with coral. It was a beautiful and eerie sight. On the surface, the sea was rough and many of the divers, including myself, were nauseous by the time we reached the dive point. We were shown the dive line positioned near the back of the boat to assist us in pulling ourselves toward the boat. Since the sea was so rough, we all knew that getting back into the boat would be no easy feat!

An experienced diver knows that when his air tank gets down to a few hundred pounds of pressure, he needs to go to the surface. So, when I had about three hundred pounds of pressure left, I made my ascent and after much effort, got into the boat, which was riding seven-foot swells. I'm in excellent shape physically, but after the rough ride out to the dive sight, the dive, the exertion of getting back into the boat, and the nausea-producing rolling swells, I was nauseous.

The police officer did not have sufficient air in his tank as he ascended, and apparently he ran out of air just as he broke to the surface. He then proceeded to break a second cardinal rule of scuba diving—he pulled his regulator out of his mouth. I shouted at him, "Put your regulator back in your mouth." The police officer began to aspirate sea water. I turned to the deck hand and said, "He's in trouble. You need to get in the water and help him get to the dive line. He's starting to hyperventilate."

"Nah," the deck hand said, "he's a big strong guy. He's okay." A few minutes later he recognized that the guy was, indeed, in trouble. The deck hand dove into the water and helped the man to the diveline, but he did not have enough strength to pull him to the boat. I jumped down on to the diving platform and helped him back to the boat. By this time, the police officer was so weak he couldn't pull himself up out of the water, plus he was no longer lucid, so with much effort, the deck hand and I got him into the boat, stripped his gear off him, and laid him on the deck. He was disoriented and nearly unconscious. We returned to shore immediately.

Trust me. When your oxygen levels are depleted and you no longer are getting sufficient oxygen to the brain, exhaustion and disorientation are almost immediate. You simply cannot maintain mental composure if you are low on oxygen.

Deep Breathing for More Oxygen

One of the greatest stress relievers—and perhaps the easiest to do—is deep breathing. Any time you are feeling stress, stop and breath deeply and slowly several times.

Close your eyes and concentrate on your breathing. As you inhale, say to your body, "Relax." As you exhale, say, "Release." Do this several times a day. Some relaxation experts suggest inhaling through your nose and exhaling through your mouth. The deep breathing not only helps muscles relax, but it increases oxygen intake.

Diaphragmatic or "belly" breathing is the most beneficial form of breathing. Most of us breath with our shoulders—our shoulders go up and our chests go out as we inhale. In belly breathing, each inhale begins with the expansion of the abdominal muscles (imagine your abdomen is a balloon filling with air). The diaphragm—a large dome-shaped sheet of muscle separating the chest cavity from the abdomen—is the muscle that allows for this. Expand your abdomen as fully as you can, and then exhale slowly, pulling the diaphragm muscles inward to the point where you feel they may be nearing the inside of your back. This contraction of the diaphragm forces air up and out of the lungs.

The body discharges seventy percent of its toxins through breathing. Taking time for deep breathing is purifying for the body, as well as calming for the mind.

Stop Smoking Immediately

Smoking is the foremost inhibitor of oxygen in the blood stream. Not all smokers experience the same level of nerve cell malfunction that results from oxygen starvation, but the fact is also that everyone who has lung problems from smoking experiences oxygen deprivation to brain cells to some extent.

Defining an Oxygen Deficit

How can you tell if you are experiencing oxygen deficit? The body general sends out the warning symptoms of dizziness and lightheadedness. Only a thorough physical exam and analysis of the blood can determine the degree of the deprivation and exact cause of the problem. People who are frequently dizzy or lightheaded should not take these symptoms lightly. They are *not* trivial symptoms. Especially those whose lips and fingernails sometimes take on a blue cast should get a complete physical.

Other Techniques for Relieving Stress

In addition to breathing, there are several other do-anywhere, do-anytime activities you can do to relieve stress and stimulate the mind at the same time:

Daydream. Take time for daydreaming. Let your mind wander to places you might like to travel, experiences you might like to have, people you might like to meet.

Pray. Close your eyes and call the faces of various loved ones and acquaintances to mind as you ask God to help or bless that person. As you think about each person, imagine that person in a wonderful setting, perhaps doing a wonderful deed.

Go for a Stroll. This need not be your aerobics walk, jog, or run. In fact, it should *not* be exercise. Rather, this is a stroll to "take time to smell the roses." Stop periodically just to look around you. Take in all the sensory input you can—not only smell the flowers, but touch the bark on the trees and feel the texture of leaves. Take off our shoes and wiggle your toes in the sand along the shore or the grass of the lawn area outside your corporate headquarters. Listen for birds. Try to isolate the various sounds of the city. Breathe deeply. Sit on a bench and soak up the sun for a few minutes.

Get More Sleep. Many people feel physical and emotional stress because they simply do not get the sleep they need. The more sleep-deprived we are, the more stress we feel, and the more stress we feel, the less likely we are to go to sleep quickly or deeply. It's a vicious cycle. Shakespeare once called sleep the "balm of hurt minds" and "chief nourishers in life's feast." [7] There's much truth in both of those phrases. Readjust your priorities and manage your time—take charge of your schedule to allow for sufficient sleep! In the long run, you'll find that you are healthier both physically, mentally, and emotionally—and your relationships are likely to improve as well!

Three of the things you can do to encourage a good night's sleep are:

- first, do not eat a heavy hard to-digest meal in the evening;
- second, don't take stimulants such as caffeine for several hours before going to bed;
- third, don't exercise within two or three hours of bedtime.

If you awaken in the middle of the night, don't toss and turn—get up and do something quiet and sedentary until you feel sleepy again. You may find reading helpful, but avoid exciting thriller novels—they can stimulate the brain to the point where sleep is impossible. Choose instead something pleasurable or useful. (Many people find that reading certain passages of the Bible has a calming, soothing effect that promotes a return to sleep.)

If you *habitually* awaken in the middle of the night and have difficulty returning to sleep, you may be experiencing low blood sugar. Have a small portion of protein and carbohydrates before going to bed—perhaps a little nonfat milk on a small bowl of whole-grain cereal. Or a half cup of yogurt and half a slice of whole-grain bread.

Develop a New Way of Thinking. A great deal of mental stress comes from playing "what if" games in the mind. Refuse to play them! They are the foundation for worry, anxiety, and unfounded fears of the future. Anytime you find yourself feeling anxious or worried, ask yourself, "What game am I playing here?" If it's a game of trying to analyze all the worst things that *could* happen or *might* happen, you are playing a "what if" game. Choose instead to play a "what would I like to do" game. Focus on alternatives and options. Explore new ideas. Turn your thinking from a *potential* bad situation or environment to an *ideal, wonderful possibility.* It takes times to develop a new way of thinking, but the benefits are well worth the effort.

Lower Stress, Greater DHEA

People who routinely minimize their stress levels through meditation or prayer—or who have strong "faith" systems—have higher levels of DHEA in their bodies.

What's so great about that? Trust me...DHEA is a good thing to have in big quantities.

DHEA (dehydroepiandrosterone) has been called "the mother hormone." DHEA is produced in the adrenal glands and it constitutes the base for the biochemical actions of other hormones such as estrogen, testosterone, progesterone, and corticosterone. These key hormones, along with others, control vital body functions that determine metabolism, energy output, reproductive capabilities, and endocrine mechanisms. Literally thousands of in-depth clinical studies have been done on DHEA, many of them at the most prestigious medical research centers and universities in the United States. Without question, DHEA is becoming known as one of the most important anti-aging substances of the new millennium.

DHEA is available as a non-patented prescription drug and in some over-the-counter forms. Some consider the Mexican wild yam to be a natural source of DHEA. Perhaps the best way to ensure ample DHEA in the body, however, is to do everything possible to provide nutritional support for the adrenal glands.

Various substances deplete DHEA: coffee, nicotine, corticosteroid drugs, beta blockers, alcohol, synthetic hormones (including birth control pills), some hypertensive drugs, calcium channel blockers, and excessive insulin. One of the greatest enemies of DHEA is prolonged stress—including the stress that comes from surgery, physical trauma, prolonged strenuous exercise (beyond normal aerobic and weight-lifting training levels), and psychological stress. DHEA levels are lowered by almost every disease.

On the other hand, certain substances are thought to stimulate DHEA production:

- keeping blood sugar levels low
- serotonin
- niacin
- tyrosine
- arginine
- lysine
- growth hormone
- GABA
- tryptophan
- ornithine
- melatonin

Several major diseases have been linked to low levels of DHEA: arthritis, cardiovascular disease, atherosclerosis, malignant tumors, diabetes, Parkinson's disease, chronic fatigue syndrome, osteoporosis, hypothyroidism, Alzheimer's disease, psychosomatic disorders, disabled immune function (including autoimmune diseases such as lupus), chronic viral infections, hypoglycemia, and chronic bacterial infections. A low level in elderly people creates an even stronger correlation with these diseases.[8]

Do what you can to keep your DHEA levels high. That includes controlling stress.

(We have excellent DHEA supplements available through my office.)

1. Sapolsky, R. *Why Zebras Don't Get Ulcers*, p. 4–5 Kidd, P, Phosphatidylserine, New Canaan, CT: Keats, 1998: 25.

2. Cavanaugh, J.C., Grady, J.G., and Perlmutter, M. Forgetting and use of memory aids in 20- to 70-year olds' everyday life. *Internatl Journ of Aging and Hum Develop* 1983 (17): 113–122.

    Higbee, K.L. *Your Memory: How It Works and How to Improve It.* (2nd edition) New York: Paragon House, 1988.

3. Dawe, D., and Moore-Orr, R. Low-intensity, range-of-motion exercise: Invaluable nursing care for elderly patients. *Journ of Adv Nurs* 1995 (21;4): 675–681.

4. Williams, P., and Lord, S.R. Effects of group exercise on cognitive functioning and mood in older women. *Australian and New Zealand Journ of Public Health* 1997 (21;1): 45–52.

5. Slaven, L., and Lee, C. Mood and symptom reporting among middle-aged women: The relationship between menopausal status, hormone replacement therapy, and exercise participation. *Health Psych* 1997 (16;3): 203–208.

6. See *Journ Aging and Phys Act*, Jan. 9. 2001): 43–47.

7. "Macbeth" 2.2.39.

8. Elkins, R. DHEA: *The Anti-Aging, Anti-Cancer and Anti-Obesity Hormone*, Pleasant Grove, UT: Woodland Publishing, 1996.

TAKING ACTION FOR HEALTHY BRAIN FUNCTION

1. Exercise-regularly, consistently, and vigorously.

2. Control your stress through deep breathing and other stress-reducing methods such as meditation, daydreaming, prayer,

3. If you are low in DHEA, consider supplementation.

CHAPTER 18

AT THE
CUTTING EDGE

Someday we may not need to be worried about brain diseases or deteriorating mental functions. That day, however, is not likely to be in our lifetimes. Even so, you should be encouraged at some of the research that is being done.

Since 1998, an increasing number of "gene therapy" approaches have been undertaken to promote the growth of new blood vessels in the heart to bypass diseased ones. This process is called angiogenesis. This new form of gene therapy may become one way to reduce the failure rate of cardiac bypass surgeries. Essentially, copies of a special gene are inserted into a person's heart muscle at the site of a blocked vessel. The gene then "instructs" the heart cells to make a protein called vascular endothelial growth factor (VEGF). This protein makes new blood vessels grow to bypass the blockage. New blood capillaries have grown and delivered blood to the heart within four days of the treatment! All twenty of the initial patients in the research studies for FGF-1 were alive three years after treatment. Various forms of VEGF and FGF-1 are being studied in a number of institutions in the United States and Europe at present.

What does all this mean for the brain? If growth-factor can create new blood vessels for the heart, it may also be beneficial for creating new blood vessels in the brain, which means a greater flow of oxygen and nutrients to brain tissue. Perhaps.

There's also new research into what causes arterial plaques, a major factor in strokes and dementia.

Scientists used to believe that all plaques in the blood vessels were equal. No longer is that a commonly held opinion. Two general types of plaques have been identified.

The most dangerous plaques are those that appear "soft" and consist largely of a pool of cholesterol covered by a thin fibrous cap. The stress of blood flow can tear away the cap when that happens, the free-floating fibrous cap can function as a blood clot. (Blood flow stress is more common in the large arteries such as the carotid arteries in the neck that transport blood to the brain.) These "soft plaques" are often inflamed. Inflammation further weakens the thin cap.

The harder, more stable, calcium-rich plaques create a different set of problems. These plaques tend to develop pools of blood between the plaque and the arterial wall. Stagnant blood is more likely to clot. If these hard plaques rupture, clots in the stagnant blood break loose.

New magnetic resonance imaging (MRI) techniques are able to show great detail, including the size and *kind* of plaques that are occurring in the large vessels, such as the aorta. As scientists learn more about these types of plaques and what causes them to form clots, we have a much greater likelihood of discovering what can be done to *prevent* both kinds of plaques in the first place.

In addition, gene therapy studies are producing techniques that may help prevent the growth of plaque obstructions in the lining inside of grafted blood vessels. Preliminary studies have already shown the technique to be helpful to people who had bypass surgery for blocked vessels in their legs. This research could have great benefit to the brain if plaque obstructions can be kept from growing in the carotid arteries that carry blood from the heart to the brain.

Gene research is also giving us strong clues as to why some people who eat low-fat diets have success in lowering their blood cholesterol levels, while others do not. It seems that about one in seven people in the United States has a gene that makes a variant of the protein apolioprotein E4 (called apoE4). This variant acts as a "ferry service" for transporting fat through the bloodstream. Individuals with this protein tend to have elevated levels of low-density lipoprotein (LDL, the "bad cholesterol") and they are the ones most likely to develop heart disease. Those with this gene variant respond well to a low-fat diet.

People with two copies of this gene have an increased risk for Alzheimer's, other forms of dementia, and a loss of cognitive function and memory that increases with age. Please note, however, that a genetic predisposition to a cognitive loss does not mean that the loss needs to occur. Many things can be done to prevent cognitive loss!

Remember, as I pointed out in *Maximum Fat Loss*, only twenty percent of our health outcome is based on genetics. The other eighty percent is related to environmental and behavioral factors that allow the genes to express themselves. Most of these environmental and behavioral factors are ones we can control.

By the way, those people who have the "normal" gene variant, called apoE3, show much less reduction in LDL levels when they eat a low-fat diet. This could explain why some diet plans work for some people better than for others.

It seems about one in every three adult men, and one in five to six postmenopausal women, have a trait that is called "LDL subclass pattern B." These people have elevated blood levels of triglycerides in the blood. They have lower levels of the protective cholesterol called high-density lipoprotein (HDL), which helps the body get rid of LDL. People with this subclass pattern B are at a higher risk for developing both diabetes and heart disease. However, patients with this pattern respond much better to low-fat diets than do patients who have the larger, less dense LDL particles (pattern A trait). These studies, by the way, are being conducted at Stanford University School of Medicine.

Yes, there's potential hope on the way. A great deal of research is being done in all areas of blood flow, brain disorders, brain diseases, and cognitive functioning. Tomorrow's health news is worth reading!

Always keep in mind that the "Baby Boomers" are aging and they are fighting it every step of the way. The vast majority of medical research dollars are controlled by the "Boomers!"

In the meantime...do everything you can to support your brain functions nutritionally and through exercise and stress reduction. Do everything you can to develop your mental functions.

I've given you some very practical, real-life things to do throughout this book. It's up to you to choose to do them.

A Personal Story in Closing

In the course of my work, I travel a great deal internationally. My family accompanies me whenever possible. That way, I can introduce my children to the dietary habits of other cultures. My main purpose in traveling overseas is to study other cultures, to determine what the average people eat—not only in their general diet but in specific recipes—and to gain first-hand knowledge regarding the longevity and health problems that the people experience as a result of their dietary choices. I am especially concerned about the relationships between dietary choices and obesity, heart disease, and cancer.

Several years ago, one of these research trips took me to Hawaii, which has a fairly high rate of cancer. After my wife and I had enjoyed a horseback ride through the Valley of the Kings, we returned to our car to find that the man with whom we were traveling had locked the keys inside the vehicle. That was the first time I had to break a vehicle window to get to the keys inside. As we were breaking the window, I couldn't help but think, *It doesn't really matter that I can see the keys. It doesn't really matter that I want the keys to be in my hand rather than dangling in the ignition. I don't have the keys!*

You can wish and hope all day for better health, more energy, improved brain function, and improved mental function. You can even know what it necessary for you to do in order to enjoy greater health, greater energy, and greater "brain power." But unless you *do* something—unless you act on what you know to do—nothing is going to happen. You aren't going to be able to move on down the road to an improved quality of life.

Do you want "maximum memory?"

Then go for it!

CHAPTER 19

PULLING IT
ALL TOGETHER

At this point, I am tempted to say, "So, tell me what you remember from all that you have read in the first eighteen chapters of this book." Tempted, yes, but I won't do that to you. Rather, I am going to give you a summary of the suggestions for maximum brain and mental function that have been put at the end of the various chapters.

Consider these to be...

Ted Broer's Top 12 Recommendations for Maximum Memory!

1. **Make a commitment today to developing the best general physical health and brain health possible.** Do all you can to build up and maintain healthy brain cells and neurotransmitters. As part of developing both a healthy body and a healthy brain:

    * Drink lots of pure water. Make sure that water isn't filled with fluoride or chlorine.
    * Take in sufficient fiber.
    * Exercise regularly. Work for a balanced mix of aerobics, strength-building, and flexibility exercises.

- Don't eat high-fat luncheon meats or pork in any form.
- Don't smoke cigarettes or take drugs.
- Consume about thirty percent of your calories from high—quality protein-lean meat, chicken and turkey (no skin), eggs in moderation, and nonfat dairy products.
- Eat a diet rich in complex carbohydrates—especially raw vegetables and fruits that have been organically grown.
- Don't eat shellfish or fish from polluted waters.
- Don't eat high-sugar junk foods.
- Don't drink alcohol.
- Don't eat products filled with food additives, especially MSG.
- Don't drink sugar-free beverages laced with aspartame (NutraSweet®).
- Cut down on caffeine consumption. Work to stop drinking all coffee and other high-caffeine drinks.
- Cut out all trans fats from your diet—all saturated fats, partially hydrogenated fats, and margarine products. Stop eating fried foods. Choose oils that are fresh, unrefined, organic, and mono-unsaturated. Never eat or use rancid oil. Have your cholesterol checked. Never eat a "fake fat" such as Olestra®. Here are levels to aim for:

  Triglycerides between 40 and 170

  Total cholesterol between 160 and 200

  Raise HDL (good cholesterol) above 35
- If you have a chronic parasitic or bacterial infection, treat it! It may come as a surprise to you that MOST people have bad parasites living in their bodies. Generally these are easy to get rid of—call my office for details. 1-800-726-1834 or 1-863-967-8284.

2. **Take antioxidant vitamin supplementation, especially vitamins A, B complex, C, and E.** Here are my recommendations:

> A . . . . 10,000 IU
>
> D . . . . 400 IU
>
> E (natural) . . . . 400-800 IU women, 1600 IU men
>
> C (ascorbate) . . . . . 5,000 mg
>
> Vitamin B . . . . take a high-potency, homocysteine-balanced vitamin B complex. Plus extra B5, B6, B12, and folic acid

3. **Make sure you have adequate omega-6 and omega-3 essential fatty acids in your system.** Here are my recommendations:

   - ALA from flax oil: 1–3 teaspoons daily
   - ALA from flax seed meal: 2–4 teaspoons
   - DHA from algae oil: 25–100 mg DHA daily
   - Alternate source of DHA: fish oil—providing up to 200 mg EPA and DHA daily (do not use this with infants)
   - GLA from borage or primrose oil
   - Phosphaditylcholine (PC): 50–100 mg daily
   - Phosphaditylserine (PS): 50 mg daily

4. **Take a good-quality mineral supplement daily.** If you suspect that you have deficiencies, have your blood checked for mineral deficiencies as part of your annual physical exam. Consider adding selenium supplementation. This is a good mineral balance:

> Calcium . . . . 1.6 g
>
> Phosphorus . . . . . . 1.6 g
>
> Iodine . . . . 150 mcg

```
Iron  . . . . . . . . . . . . from unsulfured, black strap molasses
              ONLY
Magnesium . . . . . . 400 mg
Copper  . . . . . . . . 3 mg
Zinc . . . . . . . . . . . . 25 mg
```

5. **Consider adding Gingko biloba, ginseng, and royal jelly to your diet.** Use only high-quality products from reputable sources. Avoid"smart drinks."If you choose to take nootropics, which I do NOT recommend, make sure you are closely supervised by medical personnel.

6. **Avoid the use of synthetic chemicals, both in your personal care and around the house and yard.** Especially remove products that contain mercury from your shelves and cupboards. Consider having any mercury amalgam fillings removed from your mouth. Don't use fluoridated toothpaste. Call my office for information on toxic household products and alternatives to them: 1-800-726-1834.

7. **Do everything you can to cleanse your body and brain of toxins.** Consider going on a short (three-day) fast of pure water to cleanse your system of impurities. You may also want to consider a colonic program (call my office). Also consider intravenous chelation to rid your body of toxic metal build-up. Consider adding"green foods"as oral chelators.

8. **Control your stress through regular exercise, deep breathing and other stress-reducing methods such as meditation, daydreaming, prayer,** (If you are low in DHEA, consider supplementation.)

9. **Develop your ability to attend to, focus upon, and concentrate upon stimuli.**

10. **Choose to think about what is good, noble, positive, pleasant, and pure.** Choose to think about the very best concepts, rules, and principles more than transient facts.

11. **Have realistic expectations about your memory.** Don't be overly concerned about minor lapses of memory. But if you are concerned about your ability to remember, test yourself. If you see major warning signs related to memory, seek professional help.

12. **Keep learning, exploring, creating, growing.** Cross-train your mind. Stay creative!

What you do to keep your brain healthy and your mind in high gear *today* could very well determine the *quality* of your tomorrows.

Thank you for giving me the opportunity to help you. If you need more information, please call.

Peace.